KEVIN BROOKS

iBoy

Cornelsen

Kevin Brooks **iBoy**

Herausgegeben von: Dr. Helga Korff
Verlagsredaktion: Ralph Williams
Umschlaggestaltung: Cornelsen Schulverlage Design
Umschlagfoto: © Plainpicture/Rupert Warren
Layout und technische Umsetzung: Buchgestaltung + Berlin

www.cornelsen.de

1. Auflage, 6. Druck 2024

Alle Drucke dieser Auflage sind inhaltlich unverändert
und können im Unterricht nebeneinander verwendet werden.

© 2014 Cornelsen Schulverlage GmbH, Berlin
© 2018 Cornelsen Verlag GmbH, Berlin

Druck: H. Heenemann, Berlin

ISBN 978-3-06-033674-6

PEFC zertifiziert
Dieses Produkt stammt aus nachhaltig
bewirtschafteten Wäldern und kontrollierten
Quellen.

www.pefc.de

PEFC/04-31-1156

Contents

For Dave and Steve,
my most excellent and beloved brothers.

For their invaluable help and technical advice, I'd like to acknowledge
Dave Brooks, Helen Fernandes, Nitin Patel, and Sanj Bassi.
iThank you.

Abbreviations and Annotations

adj	adjective	fml	formal
adv	adverb	infml	informal
AE	American English	Lat.	Latin
ca.	circa; about	n	noun
derog.	derogatory	sb.	somebody
e.g.	exempli gratia; for example	sl	slang
esp.	especially	sth.	something
etc	et cetera; and so on	usu.	usually
fig	figurative	v	verb

The annotations are arranged chronologically; the first time a word is used is where
you will find it explained.

1

The formula[1] for calculating[2] the velocity[3] of a falling object from a given height is: $v = \sqrt{(2ad)}$, where v = velocity, a = acceleration[4] (9.81 m/ s^2) and d = distance.

The mobile phone that shattered[5] my skull[6] was a 32GB iPhone 3GS.
5 It weighed 135 g, measured 115.5 mm x 62.1 mm x 12.3 mm, and at the time of impact[7] it was travelling at approximately[8] 77 mph. Of course, I didn't know any of this at the time. All I knew at the time, the only thing I was vaguely aware of, was a small black object hurtling[9] down through the afternoon sky towards me, and then ...
10 *CRACK!*
A momentary flash[10] of blinding pain ...
And then nothing.

Twenty minutes earlier, everything had been perfectly normal. It was Friday 5 March, and the streets were still mushy[11] with the
15 remains[12] of last week's snow. I'd left school at the usual time, just gone[13] three thirty, and I'd started the walk back home feeling pretty much the same as I always felt. Kind of OK, but not great. Alone, but not lonely. A bit down[14] about things, but not really worried about anything in particular. I was just my perfectly normal ordinary self:
20 I was Tom Harvey, a sixteen-year-old kid from South London. I had no major problems, no secrets, no terrors, no vices[15], no nightmares, no special talents ... I had no story to tell. I was just a kid, that's all. I had my hopes and dreams, of course, just like everyone else. But that's all they were – hopes and dreams.

---

1 formula: *Formel*   **2** calculate sth.: use numbers to find sth. out (e.g. an amount, distance, speed, etc.)   **3** velocity: speed   **4** acceleration: increasing speed
5 shatter sth.: break sth.   **6** skull: bone of the head   **7** impact: collision; crash
8 approximately: about; roughly   **9** hurtle (v): move very fast in one direction
10 flash (n): sudden bright light   **11** mushy: soft and thick   **12** remains: leftover pieces   **13** gone: (here) past   **14** down: (here) sad   **15** vice: (here) bad quality in a person's character

And I suppose one of those hopes, one of those dreams, was the girl I was thinking about as I made my way along the High Street, then down Crow Lane, towards the familiar grey sprawl[1] of Crow Town, the estate[2] where I lived (its official name is the Crow Lane Estate[3], but everyone calls it Crow Town).

The girl's name was Lucy Walker.

I'd known Lucy for years, since we were both little kids and we used to live next door to each other. Her mum used to babysit for my gran[4] sometimes, and my gran would babysit for her, and then later on, when we were both a bit older, me and Lucy used to spend a lot of time playing together – in each other's flats, in the corridors, in the lifts, on the swings and stuff at the kids' playground on the estate. Lucy didn't live next door to me any more, but she was still in the same tower block (Compton House), just a few floors up, and I still knew her quite well. I'd see her at school sometimes, and occasionally we'd walk back home together, and every now and then I'd go round to her place and hang around for a while, or she'd come over to mine ...

But we didn't play on the swings together any more.

And I kind of missed that.

I missed a lot about Lucy Walker.

So it'd been kind of nice when she'd come up to me in the school playground earlier that day and asked if I could come round to her place after school.

'I need to talk to you about something,' she'd said.

'OK,' I'd told her. 'No problem ... what time?'

'About four?'

'OK.'

'Thanks, Tom.'

And I'd been thinking about her ever since.

---

1 sprawl: urban area that spreads outside of the city centre   **2** estate: (here) *Sozialsiedlung*   **3** Crow Lane Estate [krəʊ]: fictitious housing estate   **4** gran: short for grandmother

Right now, as I cut across the stretch of grass between Crow
Lane and Compton House, I was wondering what she wanted to
talk to me about. I was hoping it was something to do with me and
her, but I knew deep down that it probably wasn't. It was probably
5 just something to do with her stupid brother again. Ben was sixteen, a year older than Lucy (but about five years dumber[1]), and he'd
recently started going off the rails[2] a bit – missing school, hanging
around with the wrong kind of people, pretending to be something
he wasn't. I'd never really liked Ben that much, but he wasn't such
10 a bad kid, just a bit of an idiot, and easily led, which isn't the worst
thing in the world ... but Crow Town is the kind of place that preys[3]
on easily led[4] idiots. It eats them up, spits them out, and turns them
into nothing. And I guessed – as I went through the gate[5] in the railings[6] into the square beneath Compton – I guessed that was what
15 Lucy wanted to talk to me about. Did I know what Ben was getting
up to? she'd want to know. Had I heard anything? Could I do anything? Could I talk to him? Could I try to make him see sense[7]? And,
of course, I'd say – *Yes, I'll talk to him, I'll see what I can do.* Knowing
full well[8] that it wouldn't do any good. But hoping that Lucy would
20 *really* appreciate[9] it anyway ...

I looked at my watch. It was ten to four.

(I had thirty-five seconds of normality left.)

I remember realizing, as I headed across the square towards the
front entrance of the tower, that despite the mush of snow on the
25 ground and the icy chill[10] to the air, it was actually a really nice day
– crisp and fresh, bright and clear, birds singing in a sunny spring
sky. The bird songs were almost drowned out[11] by the usual manic[12]
soundtrack of the estate – distant shouts, cars revving[13] up, dogs

---

1 dumber: more stupid   **2** go off the rails (infml.): start behaving badly   **3** prey
on sb.: take advantage of sb.   **4** easily led: easily influenced by others   **5** gate:
door in an outside wall or fence   **6** railings: metal fence   **7** see sense: think
rationally   **8** know sth. full well: understand sth. completely   **9** appreciate sth.:
value sth.   **10** chill (n): coldness   **11** drown sth. out: be louder than sth.
12 manic: overexcited; frantic   **13** rev: turn an engine up, making a lot of noise

barking, music booming from a dozen different high-rise[1] windows
– and although the sun was high and bright, and the sky was bluer
than blue, the square around Compton House was as shadowed and
gloomy as ever.

But it was still a pretty nice day.   5

I paused for a moment, looking at my watch again, wondering if
I was too early. Four o'clock, Lucy had said. And it was still only just
gone ten to. But then, I reminded myself, she hadn't said exactly four
o'clock, had she? She'd said about four.

I took another look at my watch.   10

It was nine and a half minutes to four.

That was *about* four, wasn't it?

(I had five seconds left.)

I took a deep breath.

(Four seconds ...)   15

Told myself not to be so stupid ...

(Three ...)

And I was just about to get going again when I heard a distant
shout from above.

'Hey, HARVEY!'   20

(Two ...)

It was a male voice, and it came from a long way up, somewhere
near the top of the tower, and just for a moment I thought it was
Ben. There was no reason for it to be Ben, it was just that I'd been
thinking about him, and he lived on the thirtieth floor, and he was   25
male ...

I looked up.

(One ...)

And that's when I saw it – that small black object, hurtling down
through the bright blue sky towards me, and then ...   30

CRACK!

A momentary flash of blinding pain ...

And then nothing.

1 high-rise: very tall block of flats; high apartment building

(Zero.)
The end of normality.

10

The binary[1] number system uses only the two digits[2] 0 and 1. Numbers are expressed in powers[3] of two instead of powers of ten, as in the decimal system. In binary notation[4], 2 is written as 10, 3 as 11, 4 as 100, 5 as 101, and so on. Computers calculate in binary notation, the two digits corresponding to two switching[5] positions, e.g. on or off, yes or no. From this on-off, yes-no state, all things flow.

The next thing I knew (or, at least, the next thing I consciously knew), I was opening my eyes and staring up at a dusty[6] fluorescent light-fitting[7] on an unfamiliar white ceiling. My head was throbbing[8] like hell, my throat was bone dry, and I had that not-quite-there feeling you get when you finally wake up from a really long sleep. I didn't feel tired, though. I wasn't sleepy. I wasn't dazed[9]. In fact, apart from the not-quite-thereness, I felt incredibly wide awake.

I didn't move for a while, I didn't make a sound, I just lay there, perfectly still, staring up at the light-fitting on the ceiling, irrationally taking in all the details – it was cracked[10] at one end, the plastic was old and faded[11], there were two dead flies lying on their backs in the dust …

Then I closed my eyes and just listened.

I could hear faint[12] beeps[13] from nearby, something whirring[14], a soft tap-tapping[15]. In the background, I could hear the mutter[16] of quiet voices, a faint swish[17] of cushioned doors, muted[18] phones ringing, the dull clank[19] of trolleys …

1 binary: mathematical system based on two figures   **2** digit: single number
3 power: (here) number of times that a number is multiplied by itself
4 notation: system of symbols representing numbers or amounts   **5** switch:
(here) change   **6** dusty: *staubig*   **7** light-fitting: *Lampenfassung*   **8** throb: feel a
pain that comes and goes regularly   **9** dazed: unable to think clearly
10 cracked: damaged   **11** faded: having lost its original colour   **12** faint: (here)
quiet   **13** beep: short, high sound   **14** whir: make a continuous, low sound like
a machine   **15** tap-tapping (n): soft knocking sound   **16** mutter: speak quietly
17 swish: sound made by moving quickly through the air   **18** muted: *gedämpft*
19 clank: loud metallic sound

I let the sounds flow over me and turned my attention to myself. My body. My position. My place.

I was lying on my back, lying in a bed. My head was resting on a pillow. I could feel things on my skin, in my skin, under my skin.
5 Something up my nose. Something down my throat. There was a faint smell of disinfectant in the air.

I opened my eyes again and – without moving my head – I looked around.

I was in a small white room. There were machines beside the
10 bed. Instruments, canisters[1], drips[2], dials[3], LED[4] displays. Various parts of my body were connected to some of the machines by an ordered tangle[5] of clear plastic tubes – my nose, my mouth, my stomach ... other places – and a number of thin black wires from another machine appeared to be fixed to my head.
15 Hospital room ...

I was in a hospital room.

It's no big deal, I told myself. No problem. You're in a hospital, that's all. There's nothing to worry about.

As I closed my eyes again, trying to relieve the throbbing in
20 my head, I heard a sharp intake of breath[6] to my left – a distinctly human sound – and when I opened my eyes and turned my head, I was hugely relieved to see the familiarly dishevelled[7] figure of my gran. She was sitting on a chair against the wall, her laptop on her knees, her fingers poised[8] over the keyboard. She was staring at me,
25 her eyes a mixture of shock, disbelief, and delight.

I smiled at her.

'Tommy,' she whispered. 'Oh, thank God ...' And then something really strange happened.

---

1 canister: container (usu. for liquids)   **2** drip: *Tropf*   **3** dial: device to select settings on medical equipment   **4** LED: (light emitting diode) light on electronic equipment   **5** tangle: *Gewirr*   **6** intake of breath: *Atemzug*   **7** dishevelled: untidy; messy   **8** poised: placed

How do you describe something indescribable? I mean, how do you describe something that's beyond the limits of human comprehension? How do you even begin to explain it? I suppose it's a bit like trying to describe how a bat[1] senses things. A bat experiences the world through the sense of echolocation[2]: it emits[3] sounds, and it determines[4] the location, size, and manner of objects around it through the echoes they produce. And although as humans we can understand that, and we can try to imagine it, we have no way of actually experiencing it, which makes the actual sensual experience impossible for us to describe.

In my case – as I looked at my gran, and she whispered my name – the phenomenon I experienced inside my head was so alien to anything I'd ever experienced before, I simply couldn't digest[5] it. It happened, it was happening, and it was undoubtedly happening to me, in me … but it couldn't possibly have anything to do with me.

It couldn't be.

But it was.

The best way I think I can describe it is like this. Imagine a billion[6] bees. Imagine the sound of a billion bees, the sight of a billion bees, the *sense* of a billion bees. Imagine their movement, their interactions, their connections, their being. And then try to imagine that these bees are not bees, and these sounds, these images, these feelings are *not* actually sounds, images, or feelings at all. They're something else. Information. Facts. Things. They're data. They're words and voices and pictures and numbers, streams[7] and streams of zeroes and ones, but at the same time they're *not* any of these things … they're somehow just the things that *represent* these things. They're representations of constituent[8] parts, building blocks, frameworks[9], particles, waves … they're symbols of the stuff that things *are*. And then, if you can, try to imagine that you can

---

1 bat: *Fledermaus*   **2** echolocation: finding things by using reflected sound waves   **3** emit sth.: send sth. out   **4** determine: (here) find out   **5** digest sth.: (here) understand sth.   **6** billion: one thousand million   **7** stream: (here) *Reihe*   **8** constituent: essential   **9** framework: structure

not only experience everything about these billion non-bees all at once – their collective non-sound, non-image, non-sense – but you can also experience everything about every individual one of them … all at the same time. And both experiences are instantaneous[1].
5 Continuous. Inseparable[2].

Can you imagine it?

You're lying in a hospital bed, smiling at your gran, and just as she looks at you and whispers your name – 'Tommy. Oh, thank God …' – a billion non-bees explode into life inside your head.

10   Can you imagine that?

There was no *time* to it at all. In one sense, it lasted less than a moment, less than an instant … an unknowable and instantaneous explosion of crazy stuff in my head. But in another sense, a more accurate sense, it didn't even last less than a moment. It didn't *last*
15 at all. It happened without time, beyond time … as if always-there and never-there were one and the same thing.

It didn't hurt, this unknowable experience, but the shock of it made me squeeze[3] my eyes shut and screw up my face[4] as if I was in some kind of terrible pain, and I heard my gran curse[5] under her
20 breath and scramble up[6] out of her chair, knocking her laptop to the floor, and then she was flinging open[7] the door and calling out at the top of her voice …

'Nurse! *NURSE!*'

'It's all right, Gram,' I told her, opening my eyes again. 'I'm OK …
25 it was just –'

'Lie still, Tommy,' she said, scuttling[8] over to me. 'The nurse is coming … just take it easy.'

She sat on the edge of the bed and took hold of my hand.

I smiled at her again. 'I'm all right –'

---

1 instantaneous: sudden   **2** inseparable: unable to be separated   **3** squeeze: press   **4** screw up your face: make an uncomfortable facial expression   **5** curse: swear; use bad language   **6** scramble up: climb   **7** fling sth. open: open sth. with force   **8** scuttle: move quickly

'Shhh ...'

And then a nurse came in, followed shortly by a doctor in a white coat, and everyone started fussing around[1] me, checking the machines, looking into my eyes, listening to my heart ...

I was OK.   5

I wasn't OK, but I was OK.

I'd been in a coma for seventeen days. The iPhone had split my head open, fracturing[2] my skull, and – according to Mr Kirby, the neurosurgeon who'd operated on me – a number of significant complications had arisen[3].   10

'You have what we call a comminuted skull fracture[4],' he explained to me the day after I woke up. 'Basically, this means that the bone just here ...' He indicated the area around the stitched-up[5] wound on the side of my head. 'This area is known as the pterion[6], by the way. Unfortunately, this is the weakest part of the skull, and 15 for some reason yours seems to be particularly weak.'

As he said the word *pterion,* something flashed through my head – a series of symbols, letters and numbers (non-symbols, non-letters, non-numbers), and although I didn't recognize or understand them, they somehow made sense.   20

Pterion, I found myself thinking, pronounced teery-on, the suture[7] where the frontal, squamosal[8], and parietal[9] bones meet the wing of the sphenoid[10].

Very strange.

'Are you all right?' Mr Kirby asked me.   25

'Yeah ... yeah, I'm fine,' I assured him.

---

1 fuss around sb.: do small, annoying things to try and make sb. feel better
2 fracture sth.: break sth. (usu. bone)   **3** arise: happen   **4** comminuted fracture: *Trümmerbruch*   **5** stiched-up: sewn together   **6** pterion: weak area in the front part of the skull where three bones meet   **7** suture: seam holding body tissue together   **8** squamosal: bone in the cheek area of the skull   **9** parietal: *Gehirnlappen*   **10** sphenoid: bone in the middle of the skull

'Well, as I was saying,' he continued, 'the iPhone was apparently thrown from the top floor of the tower block, and when it hit your head, this area here – around the pterion – was shattered, and your brain was lacerated[1] and bruised by a number of broken skull frag-
5 ments and smashed pieces of the phone. There was damage to some of your blood vessels[2] too. We managed to remove all of the bone fragments and most of the phone debris[3], and the bleeding from your ruptured[4] blood vessels doesn't seem to have done any permanent harm. However …'

10 I'd kind of guessed there was a *however* coming.

'I'm afraid we've been unable to remove several pieces of the shattered phone that were driven[5] into your brain at the time of your accident. These fragments, most of which are incredibly small, have lodged[6] themselves into areas of your brain that are simply
15 too delicate to withstand[7] surgery. We have, of course, been closely monitoring these fragments, and, as far as we can tell, they're cur-
rently not moving and they don't seem to be having any injurious[8] effect on your brain.'

I looked at him. 'As far as you can tell?'

20 He smiled. 'Well, the brain's a highly complex organ. To be honest, we're only just beginning to understand how it works. Here, let me show you …'

He spent the next twenty minutes or so showing me X-rays[9], CT and MRI scans[10], showing me where the tiny fragments of iPhone
25 were lodged in my brain, explaining the surgery I'd undergone, and why the fragments couldn't be removed, telling me what to expect over the next few months – headaches, dizziness[11], tiredness …

---

1 lacerate sth.: cut sth.   **2** blood vessel: *Blutgefäß*   **3** debris: remains; fragments
4 ruptured: broken open   **5** drive sth.: (here) push sth.   **6** lodged: stuck
7 withstand sth.: survive sth.   **8** injurious: harmful; damaging   **9** X-ray: photograph of the inner parts of the body   **10** CT and MRI scans: ('computed tomogra-
phy' and 'magnetic resonance imaging') medical processes that produce images
of the inside of the body   **11** dizziness: uncomfortable feeling that you cannot
stand up properly

'Of course,' he added, 'the truth of the matter is we have no way of knowing how *anyone* is going to recuperate[1] after this type of injury, especially someone who's spent a considerable amount of time in a coma ... and I must stress how important it is for you to let us know *immediately* if you start feeling anything ... ah ... unusual.'   5

'What kind of *unusual*?'

He smiled again. 'Any kind.' His smile faded. 'It's very unlikely that the remaining fragments will move any further, but we can't rule it out.' He looked at me. 'We've been monitoring your brain activity continuously since you were admitted, and most of the time every-   10 thing's been fine. But there was a period of a couple of days – this was just over a week ago – when we noticed a series of somewhat unexpected brain patterns, and it's just possible that these may have been caused by an adverse[2] reaction to the fragments. Now, while these slight abnormalities didn't last very long, and there's been no   15 noticeable repetition since, the readings that concerned us were rather ...' He paused, trying to think of the right word.

'Unusual?' I suggested.

He nodded. 'Yes ... unusual.' Another brief smile. 'I'm fairly sure that this isn't anything you need to worry about too much ... but   20 it's always best to be on the safe side. So, as I said, if you do start experiencing any problems, anything at all, you must tell someone immediately. We'll be keeping you in here for another week or so, just to make sure everything's all right, so all you have to do if you do feel anything unusual is let someone know – me, one of the nurses   25 ... anyone really. And when you go home, if anything happens, you can either tell your grandmother or call the hospital yourself.' He paused, looking at me. 'It's just you and your grandmother at home, I believe?'

I nodded. 'My mum died when I was a baby. She was run over   30 by a car.'

'Yes ... your grandmother told me.' He looked at me. 'She said that the driver didn't stop ...'

---

1 recuperate: recover; get better   **2** adverse: negative; unpleasant

'That's right.'

'And the police never found out who it was?'

'No.'

He shook his head sadly. 'And your father ...?'

5 I shrugged. 'I never knew him. He was just some guy my mum slept with one night.'

'So your gran's been looking after you since you were a baby?'

'Yeah, my mum had to go back to work straight after she had me, so Gram was looking after me most of the time anyway. After Mum

10 died, Gram just carried on bringing me up.'

Mr Kirby smiled. 'You call her Gram?'

'Yeah,' I said, slightly embarrassed. 'I don't know why ... it's just what I call her. Always have.'

He nodded again. 'She's a very determined[1] and resolute[2] woman.'

15 'I know.'

'She hasn't left your side for the last seventeen days. She's been here day and night, talking to you, watching you ... encouraging you to wake up.'

I just nodded my head. I was afraid that if I said anything, I might

20 start crying.

Mr Kirby smiled. 'She must mean a lot to you.'

'She means everything to me.'

He smiled again, stood up, and put his hand on my shoulder. 'Right then, Tom ... well, I've given your gran a direct phone number

25 in case you need to contact us urgently when you're at home. So, as I said, any problems, just tell your gran or call us yourself. Have you got a mobile phone?'

I tapped the side of my head.

He grinned.

30 'Yeah,' I told him. 'I've got a mobile phone.'

Later on, in the hospital toilets, I took a good long look at myself in the mirror for the first time. I didn't look very much like myself any

---

1 determined: strong-minded   **2** resolute: stubborn; not giving up quickly

more. For a start, I'd lost a fair bit[1] of weight, and although I'd always
been pretty skinny, my face now had a strangely haunted[2], almost
skeletal[3] look to it. My eyes had sunk into their sockets[4], and my
skin was dull and kind of plasticky[5]-looking, tinged with a yellowish-
grey shadow. My once-longish dirty blond hair had gone, shaved off   5
for the operation, and in its place I had an embarrassingly soft and
babyish No. 1 crop[6]. I looked like Skeletor[7] with a piece of blond felt[8]
on his head.

For some reason, the skin surrounding the wound on my head
was still completely bald[9], which made me look even weirder. The   10
wound itself – a raggedy[10] black track[11] of twenty-five stitches – ran
diagonally from just above my right ear towards the right-hand side
of my forehead, about ten centimetres above my right eye.

I leaned closer to the mirror, gently touching the wound with my
fingertip ... and immediately drew it back, cursing, as a slight elec-   15
tric shock zipped[12] through my finger. It wasn't much – a bit like one
of those static-electric shocks you get sometimes when you touch
the door of a car – but it really took me by surprise. It was just so
unexpected, I suppose.

Unusual.   20

I looked at my fingertip, then gazed[13] at my head wound in the
mirror. Just for a moment, I thought I saw something ... a faint shimmering[14] in the skin around the wound, like ... I don't know. Like
nothing I'd ever seen before. A shimmer of something unknowable.

I leaned in closer to the mirror and looked again. There wasn't   25
anything there any more.

No shimmer.

I was tired, that's all it was.

---

1 fair bit: large amount   **2** haunted: weird; ghostly   **3** skeletal: very thin; like a
skeleton   **4** socket: (here) hole in the skull where your eyes are   **5** plasticky: like
plastic   **6** No. 1 crop: very short haircut   **7** Skeletor: fictional character in the
film series 'Masters of the Universe', enemy of He-Man   **8** felt: *Filz*   **9** bald:
without hair   **10** raggedy: not straight   **11** track: line   **12** zip (v): (here) move
quickly   **13** gaze: stare; look for a long time   **14** shimmer: shine with a soft light

Yeah? I asked myself. And what about the billion non-bees, and that definition of pterion that inexplicably popped[1] into your head earlier on? Was that just tiredness too?

I didn't answer myself. I was too tired.

5   I left the toilets, went back to my room, and got into bed.

---

1 pop: (here) appear suddenly

11

The terms 'Internet' and 'World Wide Web' are often used without any distinction[1]. They are, however, not the same thing. The Internet is a global data communications system, an infrastructure of intercon-nected computer networks, linked by copper[2] wires, fibre-optic[3] cables, wireless connections, and so on. In contrast, the World Wide Web – a 5
collection of interconnected documents and other resources, linked by hyperlinks and URLs[4] – is one of the services communicated via the Internet.

Now that I was no longer in a coma, and seemingly getting back to normal, Gram had taken the opportunity to go home for a few 10
hours so she could change her clothes and take a shower and sort out whatever needed sorting out. As Mr Kirby had said, she'd been sitting with me almost non-stop for the last seventeen days, and now, at last, she could start to relax a little.

So, for the first time since I'd woken up, I was on my own in the 15
hospital room. And now that I was alone, I could finally get round to thinking about things.

Of course, the main thing on my mind was what Mr Kirby had called my 'accident'.

I hadn't forgotten it. 20

Whatever else the head injury had done to me, it hadn't caused any short- or long-term memory loss. I knew who I was, I knew what had happened to me ... and I knew that it *wasn't* an accident.

I could remember quite clearly the distant barked[5] shout from above – *'Hey, HARVEY!'* – and I could remember thinking for a 25
moment that it was Ben, Lucy's brother, shouting down at me from

---

1 distinction: (here) difference   **2** copper: soft metal   **3** fibre-optic: *Glasfaser*
4 URL: (universal resource locator) address of a page on a website   **5** bark (v):
make a sound like a dog

their flat on the thirtieth floor, and I could remember looking up and seeing the iPhone plummeting[1] down towards me ...

But what I couldn't remember very clearly – and what I was trying to remember now – was the figure I'd seen briefly[2] in the window on the thirtieth floor, the figure who'd thrown the phone ... thrown it at me.

It wasn't an accident.

Hey, HARVEY!

It wasn't Ben's voice, I was pretty sure of that.

Hey, HARVEY!

And it definitely wasn't an accident.

I closed my eyes and searched my memory, trying to bring the figure into focus, trying to see his face ... but I couldn't do it. He was too far away. And I got the feeling that he was wearing a hood[3] anyway, a black hooded top. Not that that meant anything. All the kids in Crow Town wear black hooded tops ... at least, all the gang kids do – black hooded tops, black track pants[4]. It's not like it's a uniform or anything, it's just that if they all wear the same kind of clothes it makes it harder for them to be identified individually.

With my eyes still closed, and with a drifty[5] kind of sleepiness beginning to take hold of me, I gave up trying to work out who the figure at the window was and turned my attention to the window he was leaning from. It was definitely on the thirtieth floor. Compton House has thirty floors, so the thirtieth is the top floor, and the picture in my mind clearly showed that the window was on the top floor.

The floor where Lucy lived ...

I pictured her flat, the window of her flat, and I started trying to work out the position of the window in my mind in relation to Lucy's window ... and then I started trying to remember who else lived on the thirtieth floor, and where they lived in relation to Lucy ...

---

1 plummet (v): fall; drop   **2** briefly: only for a moment   **3** hood: *Kapuze*
4 track pants: *Trainingshose*   **5** drifty: slow and comfortable

But my head was getting heavier and heavier now, sleepier and sleepier ...

It was too hard to concentrate.

Too hard to see ...

Too hard to think. I fell asleep.   5

It's not a dream, I know it's not a dream ... it's something real ... something happening inside me. Inside my head. Tingling, racing ... reaching out in electric silence ... reaching out at the speed of light into an infinite invisibility of absolutely everything ... everything ... everything. I see it all, I hear it all, I know it all – pictures and words and voices 10 *and numbers and digits and symbols and zeroes and ones and zeroes and ones and letters and dates and places and times and sounds and faces and music and books and films and worlds and wars and terrible terrible things and everything everything everything all at once ...*

I know it.   15

I know it all.

I know where it is. I am connected.

Wires, waves, networks, webs ... a billion billion humming[1] filaments[2], singing inside my head.

I know it all.   20

I don't know how I know it, I don't know where it is, I don't know how it works. It's just there, inside me, doing what it does ... showing me answers to questions I'm not even aware of asking – your brain is made up of 100 billion nerve cells ... each cell is connected to around 10,000 others ... the total number of connections is about 1,000 trillion 25 *– and letting me hear voices I don't understand – Yeah, yeah, I know ... but Harvey didn't see nothing – and it knows what I'm thinking about, this presence inside my head ... it knows my concerns, my thoughts, my feelings, and it soaks[3] them up and takes them to a place that shows me what I'm scared of, what I unconsciously know, but don't want to* 30

---

1 hum (v): make a low, continuous sound   **2** filament: thin conducting wire
3 soak sth. up: (here) absorb sth. into your mind

face up to[1]. *It shows me the front page of the Southwark Gazette, dated 6 March, sixteen days ago:*

TEEN IN RAPE[2] ORDEAL[3]

5 A 15-year-old girl has been raped by a gang of youths on the Crow Lane Estate. The teenager was attacked in her home on Friday afternoon between 3.45 p.m. and 4.30 p.m. The girl's 16-year-old brother was seriously injured during the assault[4] and another 16-year-old boy suffered a severe head injury when hit by an object thrown from a high- rise win-
10 dow. Detectives believe at least six young men took part in the attack, and are urging[5] anybody with information on the 'heinous[6] assault' to come forward[7]. They have described the suspects[8] as local youths, possibly with gang connections, aged between 13 and 19 years.

15 I woke up suddenly, covered in sweat, with my heart pounding hard and a sleep-strangled scream[9] in my throat.

'Lucy!'

It came out as a petrified[10] whisper.

'It's all right, Tommy,' I heard someone say. 'It's all right ...'

20 It took me a moment to recognize the voice, but then I heard it again – 'It was just a dream, Tommy ... you're OK now,' – and I knew it was Gram. She was sitting on the bed beside me, holding my hand.

I stared at her, breathing hard. 'Lucy ...' I whispered. 'Is she all right? Is she –?'

25 'She's fine,' Gram said, wiping my brow with a tissue[11]. 'She's ... well, no, she's not fine, but she's safe. She's at home with her mum.'

---

1 face up to sth.: accept sth. that is difficult or unpleasant   **2** rape: crime of forced sex (usu. with violence)   **3** ordeal: extremely unpleasant experience
4 assault: attack   **5** urge sb.: encourage sb.   **6** heinous: very bad; evil   **7** come forward: offer your help   **8** suspect (n): person you think has done a crime
9 sleep-strangled scream: scream that is unclear because you are still half asleep
10 petrified: (here) terrified   **11** tissue: paper handkerchief

Gram glanced over her shoulder, and I realized that she wasn't alone. There were two men in suits sitting on chairs behind her.

'Who are they?' I asked Gram.

She turned back to me. 'Police ... they're investigating[1] the attack on Lucy and Ben. I told them you didn't know anything about it –'   5

'Perhaps we could ask Tom himself,' one of the policemen said, getting to his feet. He was tall, fair-haired, with tobacco-stained[2] teeth and bad skin. 'Hi, Tom,' he said, smiling at me. 'I'm DS[3] Johnson, and this ...' He indicated the other man. 'This is my colleague, DC[4] Webster.'   10

Webster nodded at me.

The wound on my head tingled[5], reminding me of the dream that wasn't a dream, the crazy stuff in my head – the electric silence ... an infinite invisibility of absolutely everything ... spoken words, words in a newspaper – *A 15-year-old girl has been raped by a gang of youths*   15
on the Crow Lane Estate ...:

'Who did it?' I asked DS Johnson.

'Who did what, Tom?'

'Lucy was attacked ... Lucy Walker. She's a friend –'

'How do you know she was attacked?'   20

'What?'

'Did you see anything?'

'No ... no, I didn't see anything. I was knocked out[6] ... I was lying on the ground with my head smashed open. I didn't see anything.'

'So how do you know what happened?'   25

'I *don't* know what happened.'

'Sorry, Tom,' Johnson said, 'but you just asked me who did it. You just said that Lucy was attacked ... which seems to suggest that you do know what happened.'

---

1 investigate sth.: examine sth. closely   **2** stained (adj): marked   **3** DS: Detective Sergeant   **4** DC: Detective Constable   **5** tingle (v): *kribbeln*
6 knocked out: unconscious

My mind was struggling now. I was confused, not sure what to say. But I still only hesitated for a second. 'I saw the report in the local paper,' I said. 'The *Southwark Gazette*.'

'Right ...' Johnson said doubtfully. 'And when was this?'

5 'Today ... earlier on. I was in the toilets, down the corridor ... someone had left an old copy of the paper behind.'

Johnson nodded, looking at Webster. Webster shrugged[1]. Johnson looked back at me. 'So you're saying that you don't have any first-hand information[2] about the attack, you only know what hap-
10 pened because you read about it in the newspaper. Is that right?'

'Yeah ...'

And it *was* right, I realized. It *was* the truth. It might not have been the *whole* truth, but I wasn't going to tell him that, was I? I wasn't going to tell him that the newspaper report just appeared in
15 my head out of nowhere.

Gram said to Johnson, 'I think that's enough for now, don't you? Tommy's tired. He's still very weak.'

'Yes, Mrs Harvey, I realize that, but –'

'It's Miss,' Gram said coldly.

20 'I'm sorry?'

'Miss Harvey. Or Ms. Not Mrs.'

'Right ...' Johnson muttered. 'Anyway, if Tom wouldn't mind –'

'He's told you everything he knows.'

'Well –'

25 'No,' Gram said firmly. 'No more. If you need to talk to him again, you'll just have to wait.'

'But –'

'Do you want me to start screaming?' Johnson frowned[3] at her. 'What?'

30 'One more word from you,' Gram told him calmly, 'and I'm going to start screaming and sobbing[4]. And when the nurses and doc-

---

1 shrug: raise and drop your shoulders   **2** first-hand information: sth. you know because you saw it yourself   **3** frown at sb.: give sb. a look of disapproval
4 sob: cry loudly

tors come running in, they'll find a poor old grandmother crying her eyes out because the two nasty policemen have been virtually[1] torturing[2] her gravely[3] ill grandson.' She smiled at DS Johnson. 'Do you understand?'

Johnson nodded. He understood.

'Good,' said Gram. 'Now, if you don't mind, I'd like you both to fuck off[4].'

---

1 virtually: almost   **2** torture sb.: hurt sb. in order to gain information
3 gravely (adv.): seriously   **4** fuck off (infml., derog.): go away

100

'They [gang rapes[1]] happen all the time, man. You hear about them in school ... It's so common. You know that if you talk about it, they can do it again. If they want you to be quiet, that's all you gotta do, just bite your tongue[2] and continue. It's a sad thing, but it's reality. Hard reality.'

http://www.guardian.co.uk/world/2004/jun/05/gender.ukcrime

5 The next seven days were a bewildering[3] mixture of mind-boggling[4] weirdness[5] and mind-numbing[6] boredom[7]. I was kept in my private room for a couple of days so the doctors could keep a close eye on my progress, and then, once they were satisfied that I was doing OK, I was moved to a bed in the general ward[8]. Although Gram wasn't
10 with me all the time now, she still came to see me every day, and she always stayed for at least a couple of hours. I kept asking her about Lucy, but she refused to tell me anything else, insisting that I concentrate on getting better and getting plenty of rest.

   'Lucy's being well looked after for now,' was all she'd tell me. 'And
15 worrying about what happened to her isn't going to do either of you any good. Once we get you settled in back home ... well, we'll talk about things then. All right?'

   It wasn't all right, of course. I wanted to know everything now. But when Gram sets her mind on something, there's no point argu-
20 ing with her. So I just went along with it. I rested. I slept. I ate. I read countless[9] stupid magazines. And I tried not to think about anything.

   Lucy.

   Me.

25 The weirdness inside my head ...

   Electric shocks.

---

1 gang rape: rape committed by more than one person   **2** bite your tongue (infml.): say nothing   **3** bewildering: confusing and scary   **4** mind-boggling: very confusing   **5** weirdness: strangeness   **6** mind-numbing: very boring **7** boredom: state of feeling bored   **8** general ward: *allgemeine Krankenstation* **9** countless: many

Bees, non-bees.

Definitions.

Newspapers.

Billions of humming filaments ...

I really did try my best not to think about any of it, but it was ₅ almost impossible, because whenever anything came into my mind, things started happening. I kept seeing things inside my head – faintly flickering[1] things that I didn't understand, like the vaguest[2] after-images[3] of transparent insects. And I could hear things too – disembodied voices, scraps[4] of conversations. And although ₁₀ these things were too fuzzy[5] and fragmented for me to see or hear them with any real clarity, I sensed that they were related to whatever it was that I was thinking about. It was like that half-dreamy experience you get when you're falling asleep with the TV on, and whatever's on the TV at the time, it all gets mixed up in your half- ₁₅ asleep head with whatever you're thinking or half-dreaming about ... and you know that it's not really coming from inside your head, but that's how it feels.

That's how it felt.

I'd be half-thinking about Lucy, and I'd start seeing bits of news- ₂₀ paper reports about her attack. I'd hear broken voices talking to each other about these newspaper reports, and sometimes those voices would be laughing. I'd see fragments of texts and emails which at first sight didn't seem to have anything to do with Lucy at all, but there was always something in the back of my mind that somehow ₂₅ *knew* that there *was* a connection.

And this kind of stuff didn't just happen when I was thinking about Lucy either, it happened all the time. Whatever I was thinking about, my brain would start tingling, and I'd sense things inside me connecting, searching, reaching out ... ₃₀

It was unbelievable.

---

1 flicker (v): quickly appear and disappear again and again   **2** vague: unclear
3 after-images: optical illusion in which the impression of an image remains after the original image has gone   **4** scrap: small piece   **5** fuzzy: unclear

Incredible.

Bewildering.

Terrifying.

And what's more, whatever it was, it was changing all the time
5 – becoming clearer, but at the same time more complex, as if it was
somehow evolving[1] ... and that was pretty scary too.

But the odd thing was, as the days and nights passed by, I kind of
got used to it, and by the time Mr Kirby decided that it was OK for
me to go home, it felt as if it had always been there. It was still pretty
10 scary, and I still didn't understand it – although the first faint[2] flut-
terings[3] of an impossible explanation were beginning to grow in my
mind – but at least it didn't terrify me any more.

It was just there.

And it was still there when I walked out of the hospital with
15 Gram, on a dull and rainy Tuesday morning, and we got into the
back of a waiting taxi and began the short drive home.

Of course, I knew that I should have mentioned all this weirdness
to someone. I mean, Mr Kirby had told me how important it was to
let someone know immediately if I started experiencing anything
20 unusual, and this was definitely something unusual. But ... well, I
just wanted to go home, I suppose. I'd had enough of hospitals, doctors, nurses ... examinations, questions ... sick people. And I knew
that if I'd told Mr Kirby about all this crazy stuff going on in my head,
he would have wanted to keep me in hospital for more tests, more
25 examinations, more questions. And I didn't want that. I just wanted
to get away from it all and get back to the place I knew.

Not that Crow Town was a particularly nice place to get back
to ... in fact, as the taxi trundled[4] along the familiar South London
streets, and the eight high-rise tower blocks came into view, I began
30 to wonder why I was so pleased to be coming back here. What was
there to be pleased about? The shitty[5] tower blocks, the cramped[6]

---

1 evolve: develop   **2** faint (adj): weak   **3** fluttering: (here) small, excited
movement   **4** trundle: move slowly   **5** shitty (infml., derog.): very bad
6 cramped: small and overcrowded

little flats, the ever-present and overriding[1] sense of emptiness and violence?

Ah, home sweet home …

The gang kids were going to be there too, I realized, and I was pretty sure that whatever had happened to Lucy and Ben – and me – it was bound to have something to do with the local gangs, and that meant that there were going to be repercussions. Because gang stuff always has repercussions[2]. It never goes away – it always just hangs around, staining the air, like the stink of a vast and ever-present fart[3].

I thought about that for a while, wondering which of the gangs was more likely to have been involved in Lucy's assault – the Crows or the FGH – but, in a way, it didn't really make any difference. They were all just Crow Town kids. The Crows were generally from the north-side towers, while the FGH were mainly from the three towers to the south (Fitzroy House, Gladstone House, Heath House – hence the name, FGH), and although the two gangs were supposed to hate each other's guts[4], it didn't always work that way. Sometimes they hated each other, sometimes they didn't. Sometimes they tried to kill each other, sometimes they didn't. Sometimes they got together and tried to kill kids from other gangs …

Sometimes this, sometimes that … It didn't make any difference at all.

Lucy had been raped. Whoever had done it, they'd done it. Everything else was irrelevant.

I stopped thinking about it then and looked at Gram. She was sitting beside me, tapping[5] away at the open laptop resting on her knees.

'How's it going?' I asked her, glancing at the screen.

She shrugged. 'Same as ever.'

---

1 overriding: very clear and obvious   **2** repercussion: consequence; effect
3 fart: *Furz*   **4** hate sb.'s guts (infml.): dislike sb. very much   **5** tap at sth.: hit sth.
lightly

Gram writes romance novels, love stories ... Mills & Boon[1] kind of stuff. Books with titles like *The Lord and the Mistress,* or *Angels in Blue.* She hates them. Hates what they are, hates writing them. She'd much rather write poetry. But poetry doesn't pay the rent, and love
5 stories do ... just about.

'Is this a new one?' I asked her, looking at the screen again.

She smiled. 'It's supposed to be.'

'What's it about?'

'You don't want to know.'

10 'Yeah, I do.'

'Well ...' she said, hitting the save button[2]. 'It's about a woman who falls in love with two brothers. They're twins, these brothers, so they look exactly the same, but their characters are totally different. One of them's a soldier, an all-action kind of guy. The other one's a
15 musician. He's the really sensitive[3] one ... you know, he writes love songs and beautiful poems for her, that sort of thing.'

'And the other one beats up the bad guys?'

Gram smiled. 'Yeah ... which, of course, she finds irresistible.'

'Which one does she end up with?'

20 'I don't know yet.'

'I bet it's the wimp[4].'

'You think so?'

I nodded. 'She'll think she's in love with the tough guy, but eventually she'll realize that her only true love is the wimp. That's always
25 how it happens in books, isn't it?'

Gram smiled. 'But not in real life?'

'No,' I said. 'In real life, the girl always ends up with the tough guy, and the wimp stays at home and writes wimpy poems about how bad he feels.'

---

1 Mills & Boone: British-Canadian publisher of very popular romance novels
2 hit a button: (here) tap a key on the computer   3 sensitive: nice, caring and easily upset   4 wimp (infml.): weak person who isn't brave

The eight tower blocks of Crow Town are spread out in an uneven[1] line along Crow Lane over a distance of about a mile. There are five towers on the north side (Addington, Baldwin, Compton, Disraeli, and Eden), and three towers to the south (Fitzroy, Gladstone, and Heath). In between, about two-thirds of the way along Crow Lane, there's a mini-roundabout[2], a scattering[3] of low-rise[4] flats, and the kids' playground. An industrial estate takes up most of the west side – warehouses, car-repair places, railway tracks and tunnels – and the High Street is about half a mile to the east.

The taxi driver pulled up[5] at the side of the road, near the far end of the High Street.

'Uh, yeah ...' he said, fiddling[6] with his meter[7]. 'That'll be £ 9.50, thanks.'

'Sorry,' said Gram, thinking he'd got the address wrong. 'We wanted Crow Town, please. Compton House.'

'This is as far as I go.'

'What?'

'This is as far I go ... it's £ 9.50.'

'No, you don't understand –'

'I'm not going into Crow Town, OK?'

'Oh, don't be ridiculous,' Gram sighed[8]. 'It's perfectly safe, for Christ's sake.'

'Yeah, well ... whatever. You can either get out here, or I'll take you back to the hospital. It's up to you.'

'But it's raining,' Gram pleaded. 'And my grandson's just got out of hospital ...'

The taxi driver shrugged. 'Sorry, love.'

---

1 uneven: not straight   **2** mini-roundabout: circular traffic junction   **3** scattering of sth.: (here) number of sth. placed randomly   **4** low-rise [ləʊ 'raɪz] (adj.): with only one or two floors   **5** pull up: stop (usu. of a car)   **6** fiddle with sth.: keep touching sth. with your hands   **7** meter: device in a taxi measuring the price of a journey   **8** sigh: breathe out loudly

Gram sighed again, but she knew there was no point arguing. She paid the taxi driver, closed her laptop and put it in her bag, and we got out and started walking.

It didn't take long to walk back, but I hadn't done a lot of walking in
5 the last few weeks – I hadn't done a lot of *any*thing in the last few weeks – and by the time we reached Compton House, I was starting to feel really tired.

'Do you want to stop for a minute?' Gram asked me as we crossed the square towards the entrance. 'You look a bit pale.'
10 'No, I'm all right, thanks,' I told her. 'We're nearly there anyway.'

As we approached the entrance, the glass doors swung open and a bunch of kids came strolling[1] out. There were half a dozen of them, all dressed in the usual black hoodies[2] and tracks. One of them had a brown Staffordshire bull terrier[3] on a thick chain lead. I
15 recognized most of them – Eugene O'Neil, DeWayne Firman, Yusef Hashim, Carl Patrick. They were all gang kids, Crows, and right now they were all nudging[4] each other and pointing at me, grinning and laughing.

'Hey, Harvey,' O'Neil called out. 'How's your head?' The others
20 laughed.

'Yo, look at that scar[5], man,' someone said.

'Yeah, shit, it's Harry fucking Potter ...'

'Just ignore them,' Gram said quietly to me. 'Come on ...'

As we carried on walking towards the doors, the six boys moved
25 aside to let us pass, but they didn't stop making their comments.

'Nice fucking haircut.'

'Lend us your phone.'

'Yeah, I heard you got an iPhone –'

'He bust[6] it.'
30 'Fucking iHead, more like ...'

---

1 stroll: walk confidently   **2** hoodie ['hʊdi] (infml.): sweatshirt with a hood
3 Staffordshire bull terrier ['stæfʊdʃaɪə]: *Kampfhundrasse*   **4** nudge sb.: push
sb. gently   **5** scar: mark left on the skin after a cut   **6** bust sth.: break sth.

'iBrain ...'

We were going through the doors when something hot flicked[1] against the back of my head, and when I turned round I saw a burning cigarette end rolling on the ground. I looked back at the boys. I couldn't tell which one had flicked[2] the cigarette end at me, but it didn't really matter. I mean, I wasn't going to do anything about it, was I? I looked at them all for a moment, then I turned round and carried on into the tower. Just as the glass doors were swinging shut behind me, I heard a couple of parting shouts.

'See you, fuck head.'

'Yeah, see you later, iBoy.'

I couldn't help smiling to myself as I crossed over to the lift with Gram.

'What?' Gram asked me. 'What's so funny?'

'Nothing ...' I looked at her, grinning[3]. 'It's just ... well, iBoy ... I mean, that's actually pretty good, isn't it?'

Gram shrugged. 'It's better than fuck head.'

*

Each of the towers in Crow Town has thirty floors, and each of the floors has six flats. That's 180 flats to a block, 1,440 flats in all. Each of the floors in each of the towers is pretty much the same. There's a central corridor on each floor, with a row of flats on either side, and there's a lift at one end of the corridor and a stairwell[4] at the other.

The lift in Compton is usually OK.

Well, it's not OK – it stinks, it's filthy[5], and it moves really slowly – but at least it usually works. This is because most of the people you'd normally expect to vandalize a lift actually live here, and they don't want to walk up the stairs every day, so they generally leave the lift

---

1 flick sth.: (here) touch sth. quickly   **2** flick sth.: (here) throw sth. without much force   **3** grin: smile   **4** stairwell: space in a building for the stairs   **5** filthy: very dirty

alone. So most of the time it works. Leaving the stairwells free for other purposes – taking drugs, having sex, beating people up … the usual stairwell-based activities.

5   I was so tired by now that if the lift hadn't been working, I would have had to lie down on the floor and wait for it to get fixed. But it was working, and a few minutes after we'd entered the tower, Gram and I were getting out at the twenty-third floor and making our way down the corridor to Flat 4.

Home at last.

10 It was really nice to be back, and I spent a while just wandering[1] slowly around the flat – the front room, the hallway, my room, Gram's room. I wasn't really doing anything, or even looking at anything, I was just enjoying being there, being back with the things I knew.

15 It felt good.

After that, I slept for a while, and when I woke up I had a long hot bath. Then Gram made me a huge plate of cheese on toast, and then, finally, she got round to telling me about Lucy and Ben.

'I don't really know any details,' she explained. 'All I can tell you
20 is what I've been hearing around the estate, and you know what it's like round here. Rumours, gossip[2], someone heard this, someone heard that …' She looked at me. 'I haven't actually talked to Michelle about it yet.' I nodded. Michelle was Mrs Walker, Lucy's mum. 'I thought it best to leave it for a while,' Gram continued. 'You know,
25 let Michelle come to me when she's ready. If she's *ever* ready, that is … I don't know …' Gram sighed. 'Anyway, the story going round is that Ben was having some kind of problem with some of the boys in one of the gangs … the Crows, most people think. That Friday, a group of them waited for him to get back from school, knocked on
30 his door, made sure his mum wasn't in … and then they just started beating him up. Lucy … well, Lucy was in her room, apparently. She

---

1 wander : (here) walk in no particular direction   **2** gossip: talk about other people's private lives

heard all the noise, came out to see what was going on ...' Gram paused, looking hesitantly at me.

'Go on,' I said quietly.

She sighed again. 'There's no easy way of putting it, Tommy. They raped her. They beat up Ben, broke some of his ribs, cut his face up 5 a bit ... and then they started on Lucy.'

'Christ,' I whispered. 'How many of them were there?'

'Six or seven ... maybe more.'

'And did they all ...? You know, with Lucy ...?'

'I don't know.' 10

'Shit,' I said quietly, shaking my head with disbelief[1]. There were tears in my eyes now ... it was just such a *terrible* thing to imagine. So sickening[2], so awful ... so utterly[3] unbelievable. But the trouble was ... it *wasn't* unbelievable. It was the kind of thing that happened. It had happened before, just a few months ago. A young girl had 15 been attacked and gang-raped in a lock-up garage[4] at the back of Eden House.

It happened.

'Do the police know who did it?' I asked Gram.

She shook her head. 'No one's talking, as usual. There are lots of 20 rumours[5], and the same names keep cropping up[6] ... I think most of the gang kids know who it was. But no one's going to say anything, especially not to the police.'

'What about Ben? He must know who they were.'

'According to him, they were wearing hoods, balaclavas[7] ... he 25 couldn't see their faces.'

'What about Lucy?'

'I don't know, Tommy. Like I said, I haven't seen Michelle yet, so I don't know if Lucy's been able to identify her attackers or not.' Gram

---

1 disbelief: feeling of being unable to believe sth.   **2** sickening: disgusting
3 utterly: totally; very   **4** lock-up garage: (adj.) building for keeping cars
5 rumour: information that people talk about, which may not be true   **6** crop
up: appear; be mentioned   **7** balaclava [bælə'klɑːvə]: *Sturmmaske*

looked at me. 'No one's been arrested though ... I mean, you know how it is.'

'Yeah ...'

I knew how it was, all right. *The* number one rule in Crow Town
5 is – you *never* talk to the police. You *never* admit to anything. You *never* grass[1]. Because if you do, and you get found out, you might as well be dead.

Gram said, 'The police haven't been able to get any information from the mobile phone that hit you either. Most of what was left of it
10 had been trampled into the ground by the time they finally realized it was evidence[2], and the bits that *were* left were too badly smashed up to retrieve[3] any information. But they think that one of Lucy's attackers must have just thrown it out of the window, and you just happened to be in the wrong place at the wrong time.'

15 'No,' I said. 'Whoever threw it, they called out my name. They knew I was there. I don't suppose they expected it to actually hit me, but I'm pretty sure they threw it *at* me.'

'You'll have to tell the police, Tommy. Tell them that it wasn't an accident.'

20 I shrugged. 'What's the point? They're not going to find out who it was, are they?'

'Well, you never know ...'

We looked at each other, both of us knowing that I was right. There wasn't a chance in hell of anyone ever being charged with
25 cracking open my skull. And even if there was, even if someone *was* arrested, charged, and convicted ... what good would it do? It wouldn't change anything, would it? I'd still have bits of iPhone stuck in my brain. Ben would still have been beaten up. And Lucy ...

Nothing was ever going to make Lucy feel better.

30 After Gram had asked me at least a dozen times if I minded if she went into her room to carry on working on her new book, and after

---

1 grass on sb. (v, infml.): *jdm. verpfeifen*   **2** evidence: proof of a crime   **3** retrieve sth.: recover sth.

I'd assured her that I didn't mind at all, and that I was fine, and that she didn't have to keep worrying about me all the time ... after all that, I finally went into my room, lay down on my bed, and tried to get to grips[1] with the growing realization[2] that I knew what was happening inside my head ... and that although it *had* to be impos-   5
sible, it wasn't.

---

1 get to grips with sth.: understand and deal with sth. difficult   **2** realization: (here) insight

101

The evolution of the brain not only overshot[1] the needs of prehistoric man, it is the only example of evolution providing a species[2] with an organ which it does not know how to use.

Arthur Koestler[3]

Imagine you're trying to remember something ... anything – the last time you cried, someone's telephone number, the names of the seven dwarves[4] – it doesn't matter what it is. Just search your memory, try to remember something ... and when you've done it, try to imagine *how* you did it. How did you find what you were looking for? What did you search with? Where exactly in your brain did you search? How did you know where to look, and how did you recognize what you were looking for?

If someone asked me those questions, I couldn't answer them. All I could say was – well, I just did it. The things inside my head, inside my brain ... they just did what they do. I told myself to remember something, and the stuff in my brain did the rest.

It's my head, my brain, and it makes me what I am – but I don't have a clue[5] how it works.

And as I lay on my bed that day, listening to the distant babble[6] of soundless sounds in my head, that was the only way I could think of it: it was my head, my brain, it made me what I was ... but now there was something else in there, something that had somehow become part of me, and *it* was doing what *it* did – reaching out, finding things, an infinite number of things – and I didn't have a clue how it worked ...

But it did.

It was working right now.

---

1 overshoot (v): go beyond sth.   **2** species: classification of types of plants and animals   **3** Arthur Koestler: (1905–1983) Austrian-Hungarian writer   **4** dwarf [dwɔːf]: *Zwerg*   **5** not have a clue: not know   **6** babble: *Gebrabbel*

It was showing me bits of websites, random[1] pages from random sites – words, sounds, images, data. It was scanning[2] a world of emails, a world of texts, a world full of phone calls ... it was connecting, calculating, photographing, filming, downloading, searching, storing[3], locating ... it was doing everything that an iPhone could do. 5 And that's what it had to be – the iPhone. The fragments of iPhone that were lodged in my brain ... somehow they must have fused[4] with bits of my brain, bits of my mind ... bits of me. And somehow, in the process of that fusion, the powers and capabilities[5] of the iPhone must have mutated[6], they must have evolved ... because as 10 well as doing everything that an iPhone could do, I could also do a whole lot more. I could hear phone calls, I could read emails and texts, I could hack into[7] databases ... I could access *everything*.

All from inside my head.

I was connected. 15

I knew it now. I knew it, I knew it, I *knew* it ... but I still didn't know anything about it. I didn't know *how* it was happening. I had no control over it. It just happened ... and, like I said, it *had* to be impossible.

But it wasn't. 20

It was happening.

Other things were happening too. As I lay there, trying to digest[8] this impossible truth, I could feel a glow[9] of heat in my head, a warm tingle around my scar. It felt really weird, kind of shimmery, and I didn't like it. 25

I got up off the bed and went over to the mirror on my wall.

I didn't believe what I saw at first. It had to be something else, a trick of the light, a distorted[10] reflection ... but when I leaned in closer and stared intently at my face in the mirror, I knew that it *was* real. The skin around the wound was shimmering, vibrating almost, 30

---

1 random: with no planning or regular pattern   **2** scan sth. (v): examine sth. closely   **3** store sth.: (here) save sth.   **4** fuse with sth. [fjuːz]: join together
5 capability: ability   **6** mutate: develop; change   **7** hack into sth.: gain illegal access to sth. (e.g. a computer system)   **8** digest sth.: (here) understand sth.
9 glow (n): *Glühen*   **10** distorted: twisted and made to look strange

as if it was alive. It was radiating, glowing with countless colours, shapes, words, symbols ... all of them constantly changing, merging into each other, floating and drifting, sinking and rising, pulsating like minute[1] shoals of multicoloured fish.

5 I lifted my hand and moved a finger towards the shimmering wound ... then stopped, remembering the last time I'd touched it. The electric shock. I took a deep breath, slowly let it out, and then somehow, unknowingly, I closed something down in my head. The shimmering faded.

10 'It's OK,' I heard myself mutter. 'It's all right now. Trust yourself.'

I gently moved my finger towards the wound, hesitated for a moment, then touched it.

Nothing happened.

No shock.

15 Just a very faint tingle.

I softly ran my finger along the length of the wound, feeling the raised skin, the newly grown flesh ... and underneath it all, or maybe within it, I could feel a sensation of power. It wasn't a physical sensation, it was more like a feeling of potential ... the kind of feeling
20 you get when you touch the surface of a laptop or an iPod or something. Do you know what I mean? You can't actually feel anything, but something tells you that there's power under your fingertip, the power to do wonderful things.

That's how my head felt.

25 I took my finger away.

I looked at myself.

I shook my head.

Impossible.

I closed my eyes for a moment, opened them again, and – *click*
30 – took a picture of myself in the mirror. I viewed it, emailed it to myself, geocoded it, saved it, then deleted it.

Impossible.

---

1 minute [maɪˈnjuːt]: very small

Everything is theoretically impossible, until it is done.

Robert A. Heinlein
The Rolling Stones (1952)
http://www.quotationspage.com/search. php3?homesearch=impossible

Goodbye normality. It was nice knowing you.

110

I've been used/been abused[1]*/I've been bruised/I've been broken*

Pennywise
'Broken'

It was around seven thirty in the evening when I knocked on Gram's door and went in to see her. Her curtains were still open, and through her window I could see the orangey[2]-red glow of a distant sunset
5 fading over the horizon. Gram was sitting at her writing desk, surrounded by papers and books and ashtrays and empty coffee cups.

'How are you feeling?' she asked me.

'All right, thanks.'

'Did you get any sleep?'

10 'Yeah, a bit.'

'Are you hungry?'

'No ... no, I'm fine, thanks.'

She smiled at me. 'What's on your mind?'

'Well ...' I said, 'I was thinking of going up to see Lucy, you know
15 ... just to say hello, see how she's doing. What do you think? Do you think that'd be all right?'

'I don't know,' Gram said hesitantly. 'I suppose so ... as long as Michelle thinks it's all right ... and Lucy feels up to it. She might not, you know. I mean, I don't think she's been out of the flat since it hap-
20 pened ...' Gram looked at me. 'She might not want to see anyone, especially a boy ...'

'Yeah, I know. But I thought if I asked her mum first ... just ask her if Lucy wants to see me ... and then, if she says no, I'll just leave. I won't push[3] it or anything.'

25 'What about phoning her first?' Gram suggested.

I shook my head. 'Yeah, I thought of that, but somehow it just doesn't feel right. I'd rather just go on up.'

---

1 abuse sb.: treat sb. in a cruel way　**2** orangey: orange-coloured　**3** push sth.: (here) force people to accept sth.

'Well, all right ... but be careful, Tommy.'

'Yeah.'

As she reached out to put her hand on my cheek, I concentrated hard on not giving her an electric shock. I'm not sure how I did it, but it seemed to work. She didn't yelp[1] or snatch her hand away or anything.

'Are you sure you're all right?' she asked me.

'Yeah ...'

'Positive[2]?'

'I'm fine, Gram.'

'Well, like I said, be careful. All right?'

'Yeah,' I told her, putting on my jacket. 'I'll see you later. I won't be long.'

'Have you got your phone with you?'

'Uh, yeah ... yeah, I've got my phone.'

There were two boys in the lift when I got in. One of them was a youngish black kid from Baldwin House whose name I didn't know, the other one was a boy called Davey Carr. Davey lived on the twenty-seventh floor, and when we were at junior school he used to be my best friend. We were always hanging around together – at school, at the kids' playground, around the railway tracks and the wastegrounds[3]. Davey used to be OK. But a couple of years ago he'd started hanging around with some of the Crows, older kids mostly, and although he'd kept trying to persuade me to join them, I really couldn't see the attraction of it, and after that we'd just kind of drifted apart[4].

'Hey, Tom,' he said to me as I got into the lift. 'Y'all right?[5]'

'Yeah ... you?' I said, pressing the button for the thirtieth floor.

He nodded, smiling. But he looked a bit anxious[6].

1 yelp: scream   **2** positive: (here) sure   **3** wasteground: open land used for dumping rubbish   **4** drift apart: become less close   **5** Y'all right?: Are you ok?
6 anxious: nervous

I nodded at the other kid. He stared back at me, sniffed, then looked away.

The lift doors closed.

Davey grinned at me. 'Where you going, Tom? Anywhere exciting?'

'I'm going to see Lucy.'

His grin faded. 'Yeah?'

'Yeah ... any idea who did it?'

'What?'

'She was raped, Davey. Ben was beaten up. I was just wondering if you knew anything about it.'

He shook his head. 'Why would I know anything about it?'

I just stared at him.

'No,' he said, shaking his head again. 'No, I don't know anything ... honest. I wasn't even –'

'Hey,' the black kid said to him. 'You don't have to tell him anything. Tell him to fuck off.'

I looked at the black kid.

The lift stopped.

Floor 27.

The black kid grinned at me. 'Yeah? What you looking at?'

The doors opened.

I homed in[1] on the mobile in the kid's back pocket, and in an instant – an absolutely timeless instant – I'd downloaded and scanned everything on it. Names, phone numbers, texts, photos, videos ... everything.

'You're Jayden Carroll, aren't you?' I said to him as he walked out of the lift with Davey.

'So?' he said.

'Have you answered that text you got from Leona last night?' I said casually[2], pressing the button to close the doors. 'You know, the

---

1 home in on sth. : aim at sth. and move directly towards it   **2** casually: in a relaxed way one where she asks you if you love her?' I smiled at him. 'Better not keep her waiting too long for an answer.'

'What the fuck –?' he started to say, but the lift doors closed on him, and I carried on up to the thirtieth floor.

I knew it was a stupid thing to do, egging[1] him on like that. I knew it was pointless, and kind of pathetic[2]. But I didn't really care. It made me feel good, and that was all that mattered just then.

*

Lucy's flat was right at the end of the corridor, and as I walked down towards it, I realized how nervous I was feeling. I always felt a little bit nervous when I was about to see Lucy, but this was different. This was an anxious kind of nervousness, a fear of the unknown. What would I say to her? What *could* I say? How would she be? Would she have any interest in seeing me at all? I mean, why should she? What was so special about me? What did I have to offer her?

I stopped at the door to her flat.

The word *SLAG*[3] had been sprayed across the door in bright red aerosol[4] paint. I stood there for a while, just staring at that ugly scrawl[5], and for a moment I felt angrier than I'd ever felt before. I wanted to hit someone, to really *hurt* someone ... I wanted to find out who'd done it and throw them off the tower ...

My head was aching.

My wound was throbbing[6].

I closed my eyes, breathed slowly, calmed myself ...

'Shit,' I muttered to myself. 'The bastards ...'

I waited until my head had stopped throbbing, then I took another calming breath and reached up and rang the doorbell.

---

1 egg sb on.: encourage sb. to do sth. they shouldn't do   **2** pathetic: tragic; sad
3 slag (derog.): *Nutte*   **4** aerosol [ls]: *Spraydose*   **5** scrawl: careless and messy
writing   **6** throb (v): beat; pulsate

Lucy's mum had a history of drink and drug problems. It was mostly all in the past now – apart from the odd[1] little slip[2] now and then – but when she opened the door and looked at me, I was pretty sure that she'd gone back to her bad old ways. She looked terrible. Her skin was dull and greyish, her eyes were bloodshot[3] and slightly unfocused[4], and it looked as if she hadn't washed or combed her hair for a week.

'Hello, Mrs Walker,' I said to her. 'It's me ... Tom.' She squinted[5] at me.

'Tom Harvey,' I explained. 'Lucy's friend ...?'

'Oh, right ... yeah. Of course, Tom ... sorry. I only just woke up. I was just ... ahh ...' She rubbed her eyes. 'How are you, Tom?' She suddenly noticed the wound on my head. 'Oh, God ... of course ... your head ... you were in hospital. I'm so sorry, I forgot ...'

'It's all right,' I said. 'Don't worry about it.'

'No? Well, I mean ... I just ...' She blinked heavily. 'So when did you get home, Tom?'

'Today. This morning ...'

'Right, right ...'

'I was just wondering –'

'Did you want to see Lucy?'

'Well, only if –'

'Come in, come in ... I'll go and see if she's awake. She was sleeping ... she gets really tired.'

As I followed Mrs Walker into the hallway and shut the door behind me, I didn't feel very comfortable at all. My head was full of questions: maybe Lucy's mum wasn't in the right frame of mind[6] to decide if I should come in or not? maybe I should have waited outside? maybe I shouldn't have come up here in the first place? But it was too late to turn back now. I'd already followed Mrs Walker into the front room.

---

1 odd: (here) only happening a few times   **2** slip: small mistake   **3** bloodshot: *blutunterlaufen*   **4** unfocused: not seeing clearly   **5** squint: *blinzeln*   **6** frame of mind: (here) mood

'Just wait there a minute,' she told me. 'I'll go and see if she's awake.'

I watched her go into her bedroom (wondering why she was going into her bedroom and not Lucy's), and then I looked over at Ben, who was sitting on the settee[1] watching TV. Although the bruises on his face were fading, and the cuts were starting to heal, it was pretty obvious he'd taken a really bad beating. He was sitting kind of hunched[2] up, which I guessed was on account[3] of his broken ribs, and his left wrist was heavily bandaged.

'Hey, Ben,' I said to him. 'How're you doing?'

He stared at me. 'How d'you think?'

I looked around. The flat was a mess[4]. Empty pizza boxes on the floor, bottles, cans, dirty plates. There were piles[5] of clothes on the dining table, piles of old newspapers on an ironing board[6]. The curtains were closed. The light was dim[7].

I turned back to Ben. 'Do you want to talk about it?'

'No.'

'OK, fair enough ... but if you change your mind –'

'I said *no,* all right?'

'OK.'

Mrs Walker came out of her bedroom then. She smiled at me – a fairly vague kind of smile – and said, 'Don't be too long, Tom, all right? She's not used to seeing people yet ... she gets really tired.'

I looked at her.

She smiled again, indicating the open bedroom door with a slightly wobbly[8] jerk[9] of her head, and I guessed that meant that I was supposed to go in. I glanced back at Ben, saw that he was immersed[10] in the TV, and I went on into the bedroom.

*

---

1 settee [se'ti:]: sofa   **2** hunched up: *zusammengekauert*   **3** on account of sth.: because of sth.   **4** mess: untidiness; things lying around with no order   **5** pile (n): heap   **6** ironing board: *Bügelbrett*   **7** dim: weak   **8** wobbly: shaky; unsteady **9** jerk: quick sudden movement   **10** immersed in sth.: so fascinated by sth. you can't concentrate on other things

The curtains were closed, and the only light came from the pale orange glow of an electric heater standing on the floor. There was something about the room that made it feel like a sick person's room. The stuffy air, perhaps ... the low light, the lack[1] of energy. I
5 didn't know. It just felt like a room without any life.

Lucy was sitting on the bed with her knees scrunched[2] up against her chest. She was wearing a baggy old jumper, loose-fitting jogging pants, and big woolly socks. And as I stood there in the doorway, doing my best to smile at her, I could see straight away that she
10 wasn't the same Lucy any more. Her face was very pale, her skin very dull, and there was something about her that seemed to have shrunk[3]. It was as if her entire self – her body, her mind, her heart – was trying desperately to retreat[4] from the world. And even in the muted[5] light, I could see the depth of pain in her eyes, the faded
15 bruises on her face, and – more than anything else – I could see that she'd been through the worst thing imaginable. It was in her, it had become part of her.

She'd been violated[6].

She smiled weakly at me. 'Hey, Tom ... do you mind shutting the
20 door?'

I closed the door.

'Sorry, about the mess,' she said, looking around the room. She indicated a chair by the bed. 'You can sit down ...'

I went over to the chair.

25 'Sorry,' she said again, realizing that the chair was piled up with clothes and books. 'Let me –'

'It's all right,' I told her, clearing the clothes and books off the chair.

'Sorry,' she said once more. She smiled anxiously. 'I don't know
30 why I keep saying sorry all the time ...'

'Sorry?' I grinned.

---

1 lack of sth.: absence of sth.   **2** scrunch sth. up: (here) pull sth. up   **3** shrink: become smaller   **4** retreat from sth.: move away from sth.   **5** muted: (here) *gedämpft*   **6** violated ['vaɪəleɪtɪd]: abused; raped

She smiled weakly back at me.

I sat down in the chair and looked at her. I'd always loved the way she looked – her messy blonde hair, her pretty blue eyes, her slightly crooked[1] mouth ... I'd always liked that crookedness. It had always made me smile. And another thing that I'd always liked 5 about being with Lucy was that we could look at each other without feeling uncomfortable ... we could just be together, and look at each other, and neither of us felt self-conscious[2] about it. But now ... I realized that Lucy kept touching her hair, pretending to fiddle with her fringe[3], and I guessed that what she was really doing was 10 trying to cover up the ugly yellow bruising around her right eye. I wanted to tell her that she didn't *have* to cover it up for my sake, but I wasn't sure if it was an appropriate[4] thing to say. I mean, if she *wanted* to cover it up, if it made her feel better, who was I to tell her any different? 15

The truth is, I simply didn't know *what* to say to her. What do you say to a girl who's been raped?

What can you say?

'It's all right,' Lucy said quietly. 'I mean ... you know ...'

'Yeah,' I muttered. 20

'How's your head?' she asked.

I instinctively reached up and touched the wound. 'Yeah, it's OK ... it doesn't even hurt any more.' I looked at her, wanting to ask her how *she* was ... but I didn't know how. Instead, and kind of stupidly, I said to her, 'This isn't your room, is it? I mean, this used to be your 25 mum's room ...'

'Yeah,' she said, absently looking round. 'Well, it's still my mum's room really. I just ... well, I just couldn't sleep in my own room any more.' She lowered her eyes[5]. 'That's where it happened, you know ... that's where ... in my room ...' 30

'Oh, right ...'

---

1 crooked ['krʊkɪd]: (here) not straight   **2** self-conscious: awkward; unsure of yourself   **3** fringe: (here) *Pony*   **4** appropriate: suitable; right   **5** lower your eyes: look down

'I can't go back in there ... not yet, anyway. It makes me feel ... you know ...' She shrugged. 'So I've been staying in here.'

'It must have been terrible,' I said, without thinking. 'I mean, what happened ...'

5   'Yeah ...' she muttered. 'Yeah, it was terrible ...'

'Sorry,' I said quickly. 'I didn't mean to –'

'No, no ...' Lucy said. 'It's all right ... honestly. It happened ... there's no point trying to pretend that it didn't, is there?' She looked at me. 'It *happened*, Tom.'

10   'I know ... and I'm so sorry. I'm sorry it happened, Luce.'

'Me too,' she said sadly.

'Can you ...? I mean, do you want to ...?'

'What? Talk about it?'

'Yeah.'

15   'What for? What's the point? I mean, talking about it isn't going to change anything, is it?'

'No, I suppose not ...'

She looked at me, her eyes wet with tears now. 'I can't, Tom. I can't do it. I know I should, but I can't.'

20   'What do you mean?'

'I can't say anything ... you know, to the police. I can't tell anyone. I just can't ...'

'Yeah, I know.'

I wasn't just agreeing with her because it was the easiest thing
25 to do, I was agreeing with her because she was right. If she knew who her attackers were – and I was pretty sure that she did – her life wouldn't be worth living if she gave those names to the police. She'd have to endure an endless nightmare of threats, abuse, verbal and physical assaults[1] ... maybe even worse.

30   'And the thing is,' Lucy said quietly, her voice trembling with tears, 'the thing is ... even if I did, you know ... even if I *did* tell the police who did it, they'd still get away with it, wouldn't they?'

'Well ...'

---

1 assault: attack

She shook her head. 'Come on, Tom, you know how it works. Even if I could identify them, give the police names ... I mean, it doesn't matter how much *evidence* the police have got. DNA, fingerprints, whatever ... none of it makes any difference.' Her voice was still trembling, but now it was tinged[1] with anger too. 'All they'd have to say was that it was *consensual*[2] ... I *agreed* to it. You know, because I'm a slag ... I mean, it says so on my door, doesn't it?'

She was getting really upset now, and I was tempted to[3] get up and put my arms round her, just hold her for a while, but – again – I didn't know if it was the right thing to do.

'What about Ben?' I said to her.

'Ben?' she said, almost spitting out his name. 'What about him?'

'Well, they can't say that he *agreed* to being beaten up, can they?'

She shook her head. 'Ben won't say anything. He's too scared. He's already told the police that he couldn't see their faces because they were all wearing hoods or balaclavas.'

'Were they?'

'What?'

'Wearing hoods?'

She looked at me, hesitating. 'Some of them were ... but not the ones who actually did it.' She sniffed back tears. 'They *wanted* me to know who they were ... and they wanted me to know that they didn't *care* that I knew, because they knew there was nothing I could do about it.'

She was crying silently now, mute[4] tears pouring down her face, and all I could do was sit there, trying hard not to cry myself, feeling more helpless than I'd ever felt before. I just didn't know what to do. Should I try to comfort her? Would she *want* to be comforted? Was comfort even the right thing to consider? Or should I just sit here, listening to her cry ... should I just *be* here for her?

---

1 tinged with sth.: (here) with a small amount of sth.   **2** consensual [kən'senʃuəl]: agreed to (usu. of sex)   **3** be tempted to do sth.: want to do sth.
4 mute: silent

As I thought about all this, I could feel my wound throbbing, and I guessed there was something going on inside my head, some cyber-connected part of me that was trying to do what it thought was the right thing ...

5 But, just for the moment, I didn't want anything to do with that. Whatever it was, whatever it was doing, it wasn't right for now.

'Is your head all right?' Lucy asked me, sniffing back tears and giving me a baffled[1] look. 'Why's it doing that?'

'Doing what?' I said, suddenly embarrassed.

10 'I don't know ...' She was frowning at me, her eyes wrinkled with puzzlement. 'It's stopped now. It was kind of ...' She put her hand to the side of her head, just where my scar was, and waggled[2] her fingers. 'It was glowing, you know ... like, it was all shimmery ...' She looked at me. 'Honestly, Tom ... it was really weird.'

15 I shrugged. 'It was probably just a trick of the light or something.'

She shook her head. 'I don't think so.'

'Well, it feels perfectly all right,' I said, carelessly rubbing the wound, as if somehow that proved there was nothing wrong with it. 'So, uhh ...' I started to say, trying to think of a way to change the sub-
20 ject, but I couldn't think of anything that seemed OK to talk about.

'So ... what?' Lucy asked me.

'Nothing ...' I smiled awkwardly at her. 'I was going to ask you when you're going back to school ... but, you know ... it's a pretty stupid thing to ask.'

25 'Yeah, I don't know ...' she said distantly. 'I haven't really thought about it. I suppose I'll have to go back at some point ... maybe after the Easter holidays ... but at the moment, I just can't face it. I'm not sure I'll ever be able to face it, to tell you the truth. I just ... it's like I don't want to do *any*thing. I don't want to see anyone or talk to
30 anyone or think about anything. All I want to do is stay in here, with the curtains closed ... no, I don't even want to do that.' Her voice was a broken whisper. 'They ruined me, Tom. They totally fucking *ruined* me.'

---

1 baffled: confused   **2** waggle sth.: move sth. up and down

'Yeah ...'

'Look, you'd better go ... I'm sorry, I just ...'

'It's OK,' I said quietly, getting to my feet.

'Maybe another time ...'

'Yeah, yeah, of course ...' I looked at her. 'I could come round ₅ tomorrow, if you want ... or not. I mean, whatever you want ...'

'Yeah,' she muttered. 'Tomorrow. I'd like that ... I just need to be on my own for a bit now.'

I nodded at her, then turned and headed[1] for the door.

'Thanks, Tom,' I heard her whisper. I turned back and looked at ₁₀ her.

She smiled sadly at me. 'I mean, thanks for ... I don't know. For just listening and everything. It was ... it was ... well, you know. Thanks.'

'No problem,' I said. 'See you later, Luce.' ₁₅

'Yeah ...'

---

1 head for sth.: move towards sth.

111

There are men so godlike, so exceptional, that they naturally, by right of their extraordinary gifts[1], transcend[2] all moral judgement or constitutional[3] control. There is no law which embraces[4] men of that calibre[5]. They are themselves law.

Aristotle[6]

5　When I went back into the sitting room, Ben was still slumped[7] on the settee, watching TV, and I could hear his mum in the kitchen doing the washing up. I went over and sat down next to him.

'All right?' he grunted[8], without taking his eyes off the TV.

'No, not really,' I said.

10　He shrugged and carried on staring at the TV screen. I sat there in silence for a while, trying to ignore the fragments of online TV listings[9] in my head that I'm sure could have told me what he was watching, if I'd really wanted to know. But I didn't want to know.

'I'll tell you what,' I said quietly to Ben. 'If you tell me what you 15　did to piss off[10] the Crows, I won't tell anyone about the iPhone.'

'*What?*' he snapped[11], suddenly tearing his eyes from the TV.

'You heard me.'

'I don't know what you're talking about.'

'Yeah, you do,' I said. 'All I want to know is why the Crows came 20　round here to beat the shit out of you.' I stared at him. 'You tell me that, and I'll keep quiet about you nicking[12] the iPhone.'

Just then, his mum called out from the kitchen. 'Is everything all right in there, Ben?'

---

1 gift: (here) talent; skill　**2** transcend sth.: rise above sth.　**3** constitutional: legal　**4** embrace: include　**5** caliber ['kælɪbə]: ability　**6** Aristotle: (384–322 B.C.) Greek philosopher　**7** slump: sit in a tired, uncontrolled way　**8** grunt sth. (v): say sth. with a low, unclear voice　**9** TV listings: written information that tells you what is on TV　**10** piss sb. off (infml.): make sb. angry　**11** snap: speak angrily　**12** nick sth. (infml.): steal sth.

'Yeah, Mum,' he called back. 'I'm just talking to Tom. Everything's OK.' He turned back to me, lowering his voice. 'How do you know about the iPhone?'

Because there are bits of it stuck in my brain, I wanted to tell him, that's how. And somehow – in some kind of unreal, unthinkable, unbe- [5] *lievable way – those bits of iPhone are interacting with my brain, giving me access*[1] *to everything that an iPhone has access to, and more, and that's a whole lot of stuff. And somewhere within all that stuff is a series of codes*[2]*, or keys – some kind of security data – which in its raw state means absolutely nothing to me, but somehow (again) it's all been* [10] *filtered/ translated into something that makes sense to me, so I know that the iPhone was never sold, never registered, barely*[3] *used. I also have access to a crime report and a statement given by the manager of the Carphone Warehouse*[4] *in the High Street giving details of the theft of an iPhone on 2 March. The description of the thief in the statement is* [15] *a description of you, Ben. That's how I know that you stole the iPhone, OK?*

But, of course, I didn't tell him any of that. Instead, I said, 'It doesn't matter how I know. I just do. And if you want your mum to know too, and the police –' [20]

'My *mum?*' he sneered[5]. 'You can tell *her* what you like. I couldn't give a shit.'

'No?' I said. 'So how come you're whispering?'

He glared[6] at me for a moment, trying to look hard and scornful[7], but I knew it was just a show. All the gang kids round here are [25] scared of their mums. They'll never admit to it, of course, but no matter how old they are, no matter how vicious[8] or streetwise or emotionally dead … they're all just mummy's boys at heart. And Ben was no different.

---

1 access: admission; entry   **2** code: password   **3** barely: hardly; almost not at all   **4** Carphone Warehouse: British company selling mobile phones   **5** sneer: speak in an unpleasant way   **6** glare at sb.: look at sb. angrily   **7** scornful: showing you think a person is stupid   **8** vicious: cruel

'So,' I said to him. 'Are you going to tell me what happened? Or do you want me to go and have a word with your mum?'

He shook his head. 'I'm not giving you any names –'

'I didn't ask for any names. I just want to know what happened.'

5 'All *right*,' he hissed[1]. 'Just keep your voice down, OK?'

I stared at him. 'I'm still waiting …'

'Look,' he whispered, 'it wasn't anything to do with the phone, all right? Well, not really … I mean, I was with some of the FGH when I nicked it, but –'

10 'The FGH? What were you doing with them?'

'Nothing. Just hanging around, you know …'

'I thought you were hanging around with the Crows?'

'Well, yeah … but it started getting a bit heavy[2] with them, you know …'

15 'What do you mean?'

He hesitated.

I said, 'What do you mean, Ben?'

He sighed. 'They wanted me to stick[3] this guy, you know, stab[4] him … I don't know why. He wasn't FGH or anything, he was just 20 some kid … I think he'd dissed[5] one of the Crows, a guy called …' He hesitated again. 'Yeah, no … I can't remember who it was. But anyway, they gave me a knife and told me I had to stab this guy. Not badly or anything, just give him a little dig[6] in the leg, you know …'

'And you refused?'

25 'Yeah … I mean, I didn't want to stab anyone, for Christ's sake.' He looked at me, and all at once he wasn't the cold hard streetwise[7] kid he pretended to be any more, he was just the kid he used to be. He sniffed, wiped his nose. 'I told them I wouldn't do it,' he said.

'Is that why they came round here?' I asked him. 'Because you 30 told them you wouldn't do it?'

---

1 hiss: (here) whisper angrily   **2** heavy: (here) dangerous; intense   **3** stick sb. (infml.): stab sb. with a knife   **4** stab sb.: injure or kill sb. with a knife   **5** diss sb. (infml.): speak about sb. rudely   **6** dig (infml.): stab   **7** streetwise (adj): tough; smart

He nodded.

I could see tears in his eyes now. 'So they came round after school, and you opened the door ...?'

'Yeah,' he mumbled, wiping his eyes. 'I didn't know ... I mean, I didn't have time to think. One of them whacked[1] me in the head as soon as I opened the door, and then they were all just beating on me, kicking the shit out of me ... there were loads of them. I couldn't do anything ... I was just lying on the floor, getting my fucking head kicked in ... I can't even remember most of it. I must have passed out[2]. I didn't even know what they did to Lucy until later ...' He shook his head. 'I didn't know, Tom ... I couldn't do anything to stop them.'

'Yeah,' I said. 'Yeah, I know ... it's not your fault.'

He snorted[3] dismissively[4].

'You didn't do it, Ben,' I assured him. 'They did. They're the only ones to blame.'

'Yeah, but if it wasn't for me ...'

'You can't think like that.'

'I can't help it.'

'What about the iPhone?' I asked him.

He sniffed hard again, sniffing up snot[5] and tears. 'I don't know ... I think one of them took it out of my pocket after they'd beaten me up ... I can't really remember.' He shrugged. 'I suppose they just chucked[6] it out of the window for a laugh[7], you know ...' He looked at my head wound for the first time. 'I don't know who threw it, Tom.'

'Would you tell me if you did?'

'Probably not. I mean, you know what it's like ...'

'Yeah.'

'It won't do any good.'

'What won't?'

'Trying to find out who did it. It won't make any difference.'

---

1 whack sb. (infml.): hit sb. hard   **2** pass out: become unconscious   **3** snort: make a loud noise through your nose   **4** dismissively: showing that you think sb./sth. is stupid   **5** snot (n): *Rotz*   **6** chuck sth.: throw sth.   **7** for a laugh: for fun

'So I keep hearing.'

'Yeah, well ... it won't.'

I looked at him, my emotions torn between pity and something close to contempt.[1] Despite his stupidity in getting involved with
5 the Crows and the FGH in the first place, it really wasn't his fault that he'd been beaten up and his sister raped. And I could understand perfectly why he didn't want to name names, why he wouldn't even consider seeking[2] punishment for his and Lucy's attackers, but he was wrong about it not making any difference. It might not make
10 any difference in terms of undoing[3] what had happened to him and Lucy, but catching and punishing their attackers might just mean that someone else might be saved from the same suffering.

But then, I asked myself, *if you feel something close to contempt for Ben because of his refusal to name names, how can you not feel the*
15 *same about Lucy?*

I didn't have an answer.

I said to Ben, 'Are you getting any more trouble from the Crows?'

He shook his head. 'Not really ... just warnings, you know. Keep your mouth shut or else ... that kind of thing.'

20 'What about the FGH?'

'What about them?'

'Are you still hanging around with them?'

'No.' He looked at me. 'You're not going to do anything, are you?'

'No,' I said. 'No, I'm not going to do anything.'

25 I was really angry when I left Lucy's flat. I wasn't sure what I was angry about – Ben's feebleness[4], the Crows' brutality[5], the whole stupid thing about not being able to do anything about anything ... or maybe it was just a mixed-up mixture of everything. Like I said, I wasn't sure *what* it was, but as I left the flat and walked down the

---

1 contempt: *Verachtung* **2** seek sth.: (here) try to make sure sth. happens
3 undo sth.: cancel the effect of sth. **4** feebleness: weakness **5** brutality:
violence

corridor towards the lift, I could feel this pent-up[1] anger seething[2] away inside me, and I could feel my wound throbbing, my skin glowing, my head tingling ... and then, inside my head, I heard voices ...

Voices talking on mobiles.

There was a moment, an instant before the voices became clear [5] to me, when they seemed to be part of a vast cloud of other voices, millions and millions of people, all talking at the same time, and then, somehow, two of those voices became detached[3] from the huge swirling[4] cloud, like two single birds detaching themselves from a million-strong flock[5], and not only could I hear those two [10] separate voices with absolute clarity, I knew who they were, and where they were coming from too.

Yeah, the Harvey kid, the first voice was saying. *I think he knows her. He went up about an hour ago.*

It was Jayden Carroll, the kid I'd seen in the lift earlier on. He was [15] calling from the ground floor downstairs.

So? the second voice answered. *She ain't gonna tell him nothing, is she?*

And that was Eugene O'Neil. He was in a third-floor flat in Disraeli. [20]

I was just letting you know, that's all, Jayden said. *I thought you'd wanna –*

Yeah, all right. Is he still in there?

Dunno –

Well, get up there and find out. If he's gone, get the brother ... what's [25] *his name?*

Ben.

Yeah, right. Find out from him what Harvey wanted, and remind him again about keeping his mouth shut.

Who? Harvey? [30]

No, fuck's sake, the brother. Just tell him what we told him before. OK?

---

1 pent-up: *angestaut*   **2** seethe : (here) *hochkochen*   **3** detached: separated
4 swirl: move quickly in circles   **5** flock: large group of birds

Yeah.
Go on then. Right.
The call ended.

As I stood by the lift doors, waiting for Jayden Carroll to come up,
5 I could feel the throbbing/tingling/shimmering in my head beginning to spread. My face, my neck, my arms, my chest … everywhere
was starting to feel weird – kind of glowy, warm, buzzy[1].

Without thinking, I pulled up the hood of my jacket. The lift was
coming up now. I didn't know what I was going to do when it got
10 here, but I knew I was going to do something.

As the floor numbers above the lift doors lit up – 20, 21, 22 – I
gazed at my reflection in the shiny steel[2] of the doors. The steel was
scratched[3], graffitied[4], dirty, so my reflection wasn't all that clear,
but it was clear enough to see that the hooded figure I was looking
15 at didn't look anything like me. It didn't look anything like anything.
The face – *my* face – was pulsating, floating[5], radiating with colours,
shapes, words, symbols … my skin was alive. My face was a million
different things all at once. It was still me – my face, my features, my
skin – but everything was unrecognizable in the shimmering blur[6].

20 Before I had a chance to look any closer, the lift went *ting*, the
doors opened, and Jayden started to come out. When he saw me
standing there – a hooded figure with a nightmare face – he froze,
shocked, scared to death. I reached out to push him back into the
lift. I only intended to give him a shove[7], but when my hand touched
25 his chest, my fingers flashed[8] and I felt something jolt[9] through my
arm, and Jayden was suddenly flying backwards into the lift as if
he'd been hit with a sledgehammer[10]. As he slammed[11] back against
the lift wall and slumped to the floor with a weird kind of grunting
sound, I stepped in after him and closed the doors.

---

1 buzzy: full of excitement and movement   **2** steel: strong, hard type of metal
3 scratch sth.: cut into the surface of sth.   **4** graffiti (v): cover walls with writings
or pictures   **5** float: (here) move slowly   **6** blur (n): unclear shape   **7** shove (n):
strong push   **8** flash (v): produce a sudden light   **9** jolt (v): move violently
10 sledgehammer: *Vorschlaghammer*   **11** slam (v): crash

There was a faint smell of electricity in the lift as I hit the button for the ground floor – a hot, crackly[1] kind of smell – and for the first time I realized that the skin of my hands was shimmering too, just like my face. And the ends of my fingertips were glowing red.

The lift started to descend.   5

I looked down at Jayden. He was very pale, his face white and rigid, his hands shaking.

'You all right?' I asked him.

'Uh?'

'Are you all right?' I repeated.   10

He stared at me for a moment, then wiped his mouth and spat on the floor. 'What the fuck *are* you?'

I guessed that meant that he wasn't too badly hurt.

'I'm your worst nightmare,' I told him, moving closer.

'You what?'   15

I stood over him. 'If you go anywhere near Lucy or Ben Walker again, I'm going to make you wish you'd never been born.'

He tried to grin at me, to let me know that he wasn't scared, but his lips were too shaky for grinning. He spat again. 'I don't know who the fuck you are,' he said, 'or what the fuck you think you're doing –'   20

I wasn't in the mood for all this tough-guy talk, so I just reached down and touched him on the forehead with my finger. I felt the jolt[2] in my arm again, only this time it was a little bit stronger, and Jayden let out a screech[3] as his head jerked back and slammed against the wall.   25

'*Fuck*, man!' he screamed. 'What the –?'

'Do you want me to do it again?' I said, leaning down, reaching out for his head.

'No!' he yelled[4], cowering[5] away from me. 'No ... don't ...'

The lift was approaching the ground floor now.   30

I leaned down again and whispered in Jayden's ear.

---

1 crackly: *knisternd*   **2** jolt (n.): (here) sudden, strong feeling of energy
3 screech: loud, high scream   **4** yell: scream loudly   **5** cower: bend low because
you are frightened

'This is nothing, all right? Compared to what I *could* do to you, this is nothing. Do you understand?'

He nodded. 'Yeah, yeah ... I understand.'

'You're going to stay away from Lucy and Ben, yeah?'

5   'Yeah.'

'Good. Because if you don't, the next time I see you, you won't be getting up off the floor. All right?'

'Yeah, yeah ...'

The lift *tinged* for the ground floor. The doors opened, I gave
10 Jayden a final look, then stepped out. There was no one around. I quickly crossed over to the stairwell and started heading up the stairs.

I didn't want to think about what I'd just done. Was it right? Was it wrong? How the hell had I *done* it? No ... I couldn't let myself think
15 about it. Not yet, anyway. I just had to concentrate on climbing the stairs, getting my skin back to normal, and getting back home.

I didn't consciously know how to get my skin back to normal, but by the time I'd reached the third floor, I could already feel it cooling down, and although there were no mirrors around to check my face,
20 I could see that my hands looked like *my* hands again.

I thought about taking the lift the rest of the way, but I didn't know if Jayden would still be in there or not, and I didn't really want to see him again, so I just carried on up the stairs.

In the stairwell on the twentieth floor, three guys were slumped
25 against the wall, puffing away on crack[1] pipes[2]. They were all about nineteen or twenty, and they were all totally wasted[3].

I had to step over them to get past.

'Excuse me,' I said. 'I just need to –'

---

1 crack: strong illegal drug (cocaine)   **2** pipe: (here) glass implement used to smoke drugs   **3** wasted: (here) strongly affected by drugs

'Hey, fuck,' one of them slurred[1] at me, reaching out a grimy[2] hand. 'Gimme your –'

I flicked at his hand, my head turning on the electric, and I gave him just enough of a shock to surprise him, maybe just sting[3] him a little. He jerked[4] his hand away, cursing sharply, and at the same time he dropped his pipe from the other hand. While he scrabbled[5] around on the ground, desperately looking for his pipe – and simultaneously waggling his shocked fingers in the air – I stepped past him and climbed the last three flights[6] to the twenty-third floor.

*

No matter how weird and scary this iPhone-in-the-brain stuff was – and, believe me, it was *incredibly* weird and scary – there was no doubt that it had its advantages. I just had to hope that the more I thought about it, the more I tried to rationalize[7] it, the less weird and scary it would become.

Fat chance[8].

---

1 slur: speak very unclearly   **2** grimy: dirty   **3** sting sb.: make sb. feel a sudden pain   **4** jerk sth.: move sth. quickly   **5** scrabble: move with difficulty   **6** flight: (here) series of steps between two floors   **7** rationalize sth.: try to find a logical explanation for sth.   **8** fat chance: (here) impossible

1000

The iPhone has already taken over some of the central functions of my brain. It has replaced part of my memory, storing numbers and addresses that I once would have taxed[1] my brain with. It harbors[2] my desires ... Friends joke that I should get the iPhone implanted[3] into
5 *my brain. But ... all this would do is speed up the processing[4], and free up my hands. The iPhone is part of my mind already ... the world is not serving as a mere[5] instrument for the mind. Rather, the relevant parts of the world have become parts of my mind. My iPhone is not my tool[6], or at least it is not wholly my tool. Parts of it have become parts of me.*

David J. Chalmers[7]
Foreword to Supersizing the Mind *(2008)*
by Andy Clark[8]

10 I spent the rest of that night lying on my bed in my room, with my eyes closed, looking inside my head. It was a relatively quiet night (Crow Town is never completely silent), and I was so used to the distant sounds of the estate down below anyway – the raised voices, the muffled[9] music, the revving engines and screeching tyres[10] of
15 (probably stolen) cars – it was all just a nothing-noise to me. The flat was fairly peaceful too – just the soft tap-tapping of Gram in her room, and the occasional whispered curse. I could smell the faint drift[11] of cigar smoke from her room, and it was easy to imagine her hunched over her laptop, tapping away like crazy, with a small cigar
20 smoking away in her mouth, the ash occasionally dropping on to her clothes, burning little holes in her shirt, her trousers ... that's what she'd be cursing about.

---

1 tax sb. with sth.: (here) make sb. use up energy to do sth.   **2** harbor sth. (v): keep sth. safe   **3** implant sth.: put sth. into your body   **4** processing: procedure, course of action   **5** mere: simple   **6** tool: instrument; piece of equipment
7 David J. Chalmers: (born 1966) Australian philosopher and scientist   **8** Andy Clark: professor and author of books about cognitive science and artificial intelligence   **9** muffle sth.: make sth. quieter   **10** tyre: wheel of a car   **11** drift: *Luftstrom*

Anyway, it was quiet enough for me to just lie there in the darkness and try to make sense of the weird and scary cyberworld[1] that was growing inside my head.

It was all too much for me at first. What I knew, what I sensed, what I had access to ... it was simply too vast, too alien, too unbeliev- 5
ably colossal to comprehend. It was like suddenly realizing that you know everything there is to know. I could see it, hear it, find it, know it ... I could reach out to anywhere in the world and know whatever I wanted to know. It was all there: information, pictures, letters, numbers, words, symbols, faces, voices, bodies, hearts, thoughts, places 10
... everything. But it was far too much all at once. Too much to know. So I tried to concentrate, to focus ... I tried to make some order out of the chaos. And the best way to do that, it seemed to me, was to go back to the beginning. And the beginning of all this was the iPhone.

Everything I needed to know about iPhones – or everything I 15
already knew – came to me in an instant:

The iPhone is an Internet and multimedia enabled <u>smartphone</u> designed and marketed by <u>Apple Inc</u>. The iPhone functions as a <u>camera phone</u> (also including <u>text messaging</u> and <u>visual voicemail</u>), a <u>portable media player</u> (equivalent[2] to a video <u>iPod</u>), and an Internet client (with email, 20
web browsing[3], and WiFi connectivity[4]) using the phone's <u>multitouch</u> screen to render a virtual keyboard[5] in lieu of[6] a physical <u>keyboard</u>. The first-generation phone (known as the Original) was <u>quad-band</u>[7] <u>GSM</u>[8] with <u>EDGE</u>[9]; the second generation phone (known as 3G) added <u>UMTS</u>[10] with 3.6Mbps[11] <u>HSDPA</u>[12]; the third generation adds support for 7.2Mbps 25

1 cyberworld: virtual reality connected to the internet   **2** equivalent
[ɪˈkwɪvələnt]: comparable; equal   **3** web browsing: internet surfing   **4** connectivity: ability to connect with other programmes and computers   **5** keyboard:
Tastatur   **6** in lieu of [luː](fml.): instead of   **7** quad-band: *weltweite Netzfunktion*
8 GSM: Global System for Mobile Communication   **9** EDGE: Enhanced Data
Rates for GSM Evolution *(Ausbaustufe des GSM-Netzes)*   **10** UMTS: Universal
Mobile Telephone System   **11** Mbps: Megabits per second *(Transfergeschwindigkeit)*   **12** HSDPA: High Speed Downlink Packet Access *(beschleunigtes Datenübertragungsverfahren)*

HSDPA downloading but remains limited to 384Kbps[1] uploading as Apple had not implemented the HSPA protocol. The iPhone 3GS was announced on June 8, 2009, and has improved performance, a camera with more megapixels and video capability, and voice control.

Manufacturer	Apple Inc.
Type	Candybar smartphone[2]
Release date[3]	Original: June 29, 2007 3G: July 11, 2008 3GS: June 19, 2009
Units sold	21.17 million (as of Q2[4] 2009)
Operating system	iPhone OS[5] 3.1.2 (build 7D11), released October 8, 2009
Power	Original: 3.7V 1400mAh[6] 3G: 3.7V 1150mAh 3GS: 3.7V 1219mAh Internal rechargeable[7] non-removable[8] lithium-ion polymer battery
CPU[9]	Original & 3G: Samsung 32-bit RISC ARM[10] 1176JZ(F)-S v1.0 620MHz underclocked[11] to 412MHz PowerVR[12] MBX Lite 3D GPU[13] 3GS: Samsung S5PC100 ARM Cortex[14]-A8

1 Kbps: Kilobytes per second *(Transfergeschwindigkeit)*   **2** candybar smartphone: solid mobile phone with no moving parts   **3** release date: *Verkaufsstart*   **4** Q2: *zweites Quartal*   **5** OS: Operating System *(Betriebssystem)*   **6** mAh: milliamper per hour (capacity rate for batteries)   **7** rechargeable: *wiederaufladbar*   **8** non-removable: *nicht austauschbar*   **9** CPU: Central Processing Unit *(Prozessor)*   **10** RISC ARM: form of microprocessor   **11** underclocked: *heruntergetaktet*   **12** PowerVR: company that makes software   **13** 3D GPU: *3D Grafikprozessor*   **14** Cortex: *Prozessorkern*

	833MHz underclocked to 600MHz PowerVR SGX GPU[1]
Storage capacity[2]	Flash memory[3] Original: 4, 8, & 16GB[4] 3G: 8 & 16GB 3GS: 16 & 32GB
Memory[5]	Original & 3G: 128MB eDRAM[6] 3GS: 256MB eDRAM
Display[7]	320 × 480px, 3.5in (89mm), 2:3 aspect ratio[8], 18-bit (262,144-colour) LCD[9] at 163 pixels per inch (ppi)
Input[10]	Multi-touch touchscreen display, headset con- trols[11], proximity and ambient light sensors[12], 3-axis accelerometer[13] 3GS also includes: digital compass Original & 3G: 2.0 megapixels with geotagging[14]
Camera	3GS: 3.0 megapixels with video (VGA at 30fps), geotagging, and automatic focus, white balance[15], & exposure[16]
Connectivity	WiFi (802.11b/g), Bluetooth 2.0+EDR[17] (3GS: 2.1), USB 2.0/Dock connector[18] Quad band GSM 850 900 1800 1900 MHz GPRS/EDGE

1 SGX GPU: Graphics Processing Unit   **2** storage capacity: *Speicherplatz*
3 flash memory: *Speicherkarte*   **4** GB: *Gigabyte (Maßeinheit für Datenmengen)*
5 memory: (here) *Arbeitsspeicher*   **6** eDRAM: embedded dynamic random
access memory *(eingebetteter elektronischer Speicherbaustein)*   **7** display:
Bildschirm; Anzeigefläche   **8** aspect ratio: *Abbildungsverhältnis*   **9** LCD: liquid
crystal display   **10** input: *Ausstattung*   **11** headset control: *Kopfhörerbedienung*
12 proximity and ambient light sensors: *umgebungsangepasste Helligkeitssensoren*
13 accelerometer: *Beschleunigungsmesser*   **14** geotagging: *Angabe des augenblick-*
lichen Standorts   **15** white balance: *Sensibilisierung der Kamera an die Farbtempe-*
ratur des Lichts   **16** exposure: *Belichtung*   **17** EDR: enhanced data rate *(Schnitt-*
stelle für Bluetooth)   **18** Dock connector: *Schnittstelle zum Andocken von*
USB-Sticks und Ladegeräten

	3G also includes: A-GPS[1]; Tri band UMTS/HSDPA 850, 1900, 2100MHz 3GS also supports: 7.2Mbps HSDPA
Online services	iTunes Store, App Store, MobileMe
Dimensions[2]	Original:[3] 115mm (4.5in[4]) (h) 61mm (2.4in) (w) 11.6mm (0.46in) (d) 3G & 3GS: 115.5mm (4.55in) (h) 62.1mm (2.44in) (w) 12.3mm (0.48in) (d)
Weight	Original & 3GS: 135g (4.8oz[5]) 3G: 133g (4.7oz)

Actually, that was far more information than I needed, and most of it didn't make much sense to me anyway. But it confirmed what I'd already assumed[6]: I had WiFi capability, I could connect to the web. I had access to every single website in the world, which is a lot of
5 websites:

Web pages in the world, August 2005: 19.2 billion pages were indexed[7] by Yahoo as of August 2005.
Websites in the world, August 2005: 70,392,567 websites were indexed by Netcraft as of August 2005.
10 *Web pages per website: 273 (rounding to the nearest whole number).*
Web pages in the world, February 2007: multiplying our estimate[8] of the number of web pages per website by Netcraft's February 2007 count

---

1 A-GPS: Assisted Global Positioning System (satellite-based system to determine your location)   **2** dimensions: *Abmessungen*   **3** h/w/d/: height/width/depth   **4** in.: inch (ca. 2.54 cm)   **5** oz.: ounce (ca. 28 grams)   **6** assume: suppose; guess   **7** index sth.: arrange sth. (e.g. information) in a list   **8** estimate (n): guessed number

of websites, we arrive at 29.7 billion pages on the World Wide Web as of February 2007.

And there was even more. There were databanks, secure sites, programs and websites that were supposed to be inaccessible to unauthorized users, but my iBrain knew how to get into them.   5

My iBrain, my iSelf ...

My i.

What else did it allow me to do? Well, I could send and receive texts and calls, of course ... and, what's more, I seemed to be able to phone and text with complete anonymity. So, if I wanted to, I could   10
send texts and make calls without anyone knowing who they were from. And I could hear other calls too. I could access other mobiles – stored texts, call logs[1], address books ... whatever was there. I knew it all. I knew where the phones were. I could either triangulate[2] their signals or, with a lot of the new phones, simply locate   15
them via their GPS chips. I could reach out into the radio-waved air and pick out a single specific telephone conversation from among all the millions of others ...

What else?

I could take pictures – *click*.   20

Make videos – *click*, *whirr*.

Watch videos, watch TV, play games.

I could see every email on every computer and every phone in the world.

I could download everything downloadable ... I could do virtu-   25
ally anything.

I could overdose[3] on information.

---

1 call log: list of calls that shows the names of callers and times of calls   **2** triangulate: (here) use the locations of the three nearest phone masts to find out exactly where a mobile phone is when a call is made   **3** overdose on sth.: take more of sth. than is healthy (usu. drugs)

I opened my eyes and stared into the darkness for a while, emptying my head of everything. I was drained[1], exhausted[2]. My skull ached[3]. I was excited, confused, bewildered[4], thrilled[5] ...

This ... whatever and however it was ...

5   This was awe-inspiring[6].

A radio-controlled clock inside my head (receiving its time signal over the air from Anthorn in Cumbria[7] [MSF[8] 60kHz]) told me that it was 23:32:43.

I lifted my hands and held them in front of my face. A soft glow
10 was emanating[9] from my skin – a gentle, very pale, almost purplish light. I watched, oddly[10] unsurprised, as the glow started to shimmer, and my skin began pulsating again ... radiating, floating, swirling with the essence of everything. I didn't have to see the rest of my body to know that it was happening all over – I could feel it. And
15 now that I was witnessing it up close for the first time, I knew what it was. It was everything, the same kind of everything that I had in my head: 30 billion web pages, galaxies of words and pictures and sounds and voices ... all of it shimmering in and over and under my flesh.

20 And now I could control it.

All I had to do was switch something off in my head (I didn't know what it was), and my skin would fade back to normal; switch it on again, and the cyber-galaxies came back.

I was learning.

25 At 00:49:18 I learned that Lucy hadn't used her mobile since the attack, she hadn't sent any texts or emails, and that she had a MySpace[11] page but there hadn't been any activity on it for months. No messages, no comments, no blog entries, nothing. In fact, her MySpace profile was virtually blank – no friends, no photos, no videos,

---

1 drained: with no energy left   **2** exhausted: very tired   **3** ache: feel a continuous pain   **4** bewildered: confused   **5** thrilled: excited   **6** awe-inspiring: amazing   **7** Anthorn, Cumbria: radio station in the Northwest of England transmitting the British national time signal   **8** MSF: time signal   **9** emanate: come out   **10** oddly: strangely   **11** MySpace: free social network

no favourites, no information at all. Just her screen name – *aGirl*
– and that was it.

At 01:16:08 I learned how to hack into the personal computers of
CID[1] detectives at Southwark Borough[2] police station, and I found
out that three individuals suspected of carrying out the rape and
assault of Lucy Walker were still under investigation[3], but that the
Senior Investigating Officer, Detective Superintendent Robert Hall,
was not expecting any imminent[4] arrests.

The three individuals named were: Eugene 'Yoyo' O'Neil, Paul
'Cutz' Adebajo, and DeWayne Firman.

Other individuals suspected of being involved, but with no evidence against them, were Yusef Hashim, Nathan 'Fly' Craig, and Carl
'Trick' Patrick.

Between 01:49:18 and 02:37:08 I learned (by experimenting with
both a penknife and an old toy gun that fired plastic pellets) that
when my iSkin was turned on, my whole body was shielded with an
electric force field.

And at 02:57:44 I learned (from an article called 'Electricity is
Human Thinking', by H. Bernard Wechsler) that:

Every thought, feeling and action in *Homo sapiens*[5] originates from
the electrical signals emitted[6] by our brain cell circuits[7] ... Remember that your brain communicates with each cell of your body
through electrical impulses (hormones, enzymes and neuropep-
tides). Further, we believe Consciousness is electrically producing
mental imagery[8] in the occipital lobe[9] and precuneous[10] of your

1 CID: Criminal Investigation Department   **2** Southwark Borough: district in
South London   **3** investigation: examination   **4** imminent: likely to happen
soon   **5** homo sapiens: classification of the first modern 'intelligent' man
6 emit sth.: send sth. out   **7** circuit: (here) *Stromkreis*   **8** mental-imagery:
Vorstellungsvermögen   **9** occipital lobe: part of the brain   **10** precuneous: part of
the brain involved in memory and movement

brain. Our commonality[1] with our computer, TV, video game player, and telephone is in the use of electricity and electromagnetic fields as a source of energy.

Electricity is the movement of a charge down a wire. In our neu-
5 rons (nerve cells) the electric signal moves in the form of an Action-Potential. Inside the nerve cells is a negative charge produced by nano[2] pumps moving charged[3] Ions out of our cells. We are constantly involved in polarizing[4] and depolarizing Ions through Gates in our nerve membranes causing our muscle contractions[5] for loco-
10 motion. Impulses are sent electrically from the Brain to all parts of the body through these Action-Potentials by signaling our Central Nervous System.

Membranes have two types of proteins: Ion channels for Sodium (Na) outside the cell, and Potassium (K) inside the cell. When the
15 nerve cell receives a stimulus, it opens some of its Ion channels. The second protein is called Transporters. ATP[6] transports chemical energy within the cells for Metabolism.

And although that didn't explain how the shattered fragments of a 3.7V 1219 mAh lithium-ion polymer battery could meld[7] with the
20 organic electrical energy of my brain (or my body) to produce a level of power that was above and beyond the linear sum[8] of the two original powers, a level of power that was sufficient to produce a powerful electric shock and create a protective force field …

Well, actually, it didn't explain anything. But, to be honest, I'd
25 pretty much given up on explanations by then. I mean, Spider-Man[9] never bothered too much with explanations, did he? He just got bitten by a genetically engineered spider, acquired[10] his super-spider-powers, frowned about[11] them for a minute or two, and that was

---

1 commonality: shared characteristic or quality   **2** nano: the one billionth part of sth.   **3** charge: (here) *elektrische Ladung*   **4** polarize: split; divide   **5** contraction: *Zusammenziehen*   **6** ATP: *Adenosintriphosphat (universeller Energieträger)*   **7** meld (v): blend; merge   **8** linear sum: result when two or more things are added together   **9** Spider-Man: American superhero   **10** acquire sth.: get sth.   **11** frown about sth.: wonder about sth.

pretty much it. He didn't spend hours and hours trying to *understand* them, did he?

'Spider-Man?' I heard myself mutter. 'Jesus *Christ* ...'

I couldn't believe that I was comparing myself to a fictional[1] superhero. It was ridiculous. Absolutely *ridiculous*.   5

At 03:04:50, after forcing myself to stop thinking about the reality and non-reality of superheroes, I intercepted[2] a video being sent from a mobile phone to Lucy's mobile. It came from a girl called Nadia Moore who lived in Eden House, and she'd added a text message to the video. The message read: *jst 2 rmind u agn wat a fuckin* 10 *hor ur*[3].

I had a pretty good idea of what the video was going to show, and I didn't *want* to watch it, but I knew that I had to. So after I'd blocked it from reaching Lucy's phone, I braced myself[4], pressed the play button inside my head, and set about watching a blurred[5] and 15 shaky video of the attack on Lucy and Ben.

I can't describe the worst of what I saw.

There aren't words sick enough.

I cried so much it hurt.

I couldn't watch all of the video – there were some scenes that were 20 simply too vile[6] ... too heart-breaking to witness – but after watching most of it, I knew that the police were only partly right. The six individuals they suspected of being involved – O'Neil, Adebajo, Firman, Hashim, Craig, and Patrick – they were all definitely there, and it was definitely the first three who'd done all the really bad stuff. 25 But they weren't the only ones who'd been there. There were others. Some of them had been there from the start, and others had come later, in response to texts and calls from both Carl Patrick and

---

1 fictional: not real   **2** intercept: *abfangen*   **3** jst 2 rmind u agn wat a fuckin hor ur: just to remind you again what a fucking whore you are   **4** brace yourself: get ready for sth. unpleasant   **5** blurred: unclear   **6** vile: shocking; disgusting

Nadia Moore, who apparently were boyfriend and girlfriend (and, unbelievably, it was Nadia who'd actually done the filming). Even while the attack was going on, they were sending out texts and calling their friends, inviting them to come along – *homporn 4u*[1]*!! lovit*[2]
haha! ... cum c da fun[3]*!* – as if it was some kind of circus or something. And their friends did come along. By the time O'Neil and the others had finished with Lucy and Ben, there must have been at least six or seven others in the flat.

Some of them had their faces covered, so I couldn't make out all of them from the video, but I recognized most of them. Jayden Carroll was there, and a couple of brothers from Addington called Big and Little Jones. There were a few youngish kids – no more than twelve or thirteen years old – who I didn't know, but I'd seen them around. And Davey Carr was there too. It was Davey who'd taken the iPhone out of Ben's pocket and thrown it out of the window. He was laughing when he did it.

I wanted to delete the video, to erase it from my head. I didn't want it to be there any more ... I didn't want it to exist.

But I couldn't delete it.

Not yet.

I might need it.

Inside my head, I reached out in anger to Carl Patrick's mobile and instantly sent a text from his phone to his girlfriend's, Nadia Moore. *leona*, I wrote, *gotta cu agin*[4] *soon. ur SO xxxx hot*[5]*!! trk*[6]*xxxxx*[7]

It was a pathetic thing to do, I knew that. It was petty and stupid and utterly pointless, and it didn't make me feel the slightest bit better. But what the hell? It didn't make me feel any worse either.

At 03:41:29 Lucy logged on to her MySpace profile, opened up her blog, and started writing. As far as I could tell, it was the first time she'd ever written anything in her blog. I knew that I shouldn't be

1 homporn 4u: home-pornographic scene for you   **2** lovit: love it   **3** cum c da fun: come see the fun   **4** gotta cu agin : I've got to see you again   **5** ur SO hot: you are so hot   **6** trk: Patrick   **7** xxx: kisses

spying on her[1], and I did feel kind of sneaky[2] and ashamed of myself for doing it, but however much guilt I felt, my desire to know how she felt, to know what she was thinking, was that much stronger.

She didn't write very much.

i don't know why i'm writing this, she began, *cos i know nobody's ever* 5 *gonna read it, but i think i just need to write down what i'm feeling. i need to tell someone even if it's only me. i feel dead. i hurt. nothing's ever going to be good again. nothing means anything anymore. all the good things are gone.*

T was good and it was really nice to see him, he made me feel not 10 *so dead for a while, but tonite in the dark it all comes back and i can't see any light anywhere. there's nothing to feel. i want to hurt them, kill them. i hate them. i want them to die, to suffer. but what good would it do? they'll always have done it and i can't make that go away.*

I waited for a while to see if she wrote any more, but after about 15 fifteen minutes or so, she logged off MySpace and shut down her laptop. I waited some more, thinking about what I could do, what I should do, what I wanted to do ... and then, at 03:57:33, I closed my eyes, re-entered my cyber-head, and created a MySpace page for myself. It was almost as blank[3] as Lucy's page – i.e.[4] no pictures, 20 no information, etc. – but I did include two favourite films, *Spider-Man* and *Spider-Man 2,* because me and Lucy had watched them together once, and under the Music section I put Fall Out Boy[5] and Pennywise[6], because I knew that Lucy really liked them.

When it came to choosing a name for myself, I thought about 25 it for quite a long time, and eventually – bearing in mind the name that Lucy used on her MySpace profile (aGirl), and the fact that I

---

1 spy on sb.: watch sb. secretly   **2** sneaky: behaving in a dishonest way
3 blank: empty   **4** i.e.: (from Latin 'id est') that is   **5** Fall Out Boy: rock-band
from Chicago founded in 2001   **6** Pennywise: punk band from California
producing metallic hardcore music, founded in 1988

was, whether I liked it or not, part iPhone and part boy – I settled on the name that one of the Crows had called me earlier that day.

I called myself iBoy.

Lucy's page was set to private, which under normal circum-
5 stances meant that only her friends could send her messages (if she'd had any friends). And that meant that if I wanted her to add iBoy as a friend, I'd have to send her a request, wait until she logged on again, hope that she wanted to add me ... and I really didn't want to do all that. And, besides, these *weren't* normal circumstances
10 ... and I was iBoy, after all. All I had to do was *think* about adding myself to her friends, *think* about customizing[1] the message connection between us, making it totally private, totally instant, and totally restricted to aGirl and iBoy, and then *think* about sending her a message ... and it was done.

15 *hello aGirl,* I wrote/thought/sent, *i hope you don't mind me sending you this message, but i read your blog and i know that you didn't really mean anyone to read it, but i just wanted to let you know that if you ever feel like talking to someone, you could always talk to me. i know you don't know me, and i could be anyone, but for what it's worth[2] i'm*
20 *not anyone you shouldn't talk to. i'm not anything really, just a 16-year-old boy who doesn't understand what's going on.*

anyway, if you want to talk to me that'd be great. but if not, just don't reply or tell me to go away, and i promise you'll never hear from me again.

25 *iBoy*

At 04:17:01 I learned that my video function was on all the time, filming everything that I saw, and that all I had to do to play anything back was remember it, and then play it.

And between 04:48:22 and 06:51:16 I learned that it's really hard
30 to get to sleep when you know everything there is to know, and that

---

1 customize sth.: change sth. to suit your needs   **2** for what it's worth (infml.): just in my opinion

superpowers – no matter *how* powerful they are – are no help at all when you're crying on your own in the darkness.

1001

Few things are simple in Gangland. Your day-to-day activities, your role, your future, the people with whom you work, the people with whom you fight – all are uncertain, transient[1]. But, paradoxically, most gang members have a clearly defined perception[2] of how the drug
5 *market is structured. The best way to understand the way that market works is to imagine the process by which fruit is sold in a supermarket. In this case the producers operate in Jamaica and South America. The top gang members to whom they sell, the Elders and Faces, are the supermarket's head office. Below them are the Youngers: the branch[3]*
10 *managers. And working the supermarket's tills[4] and on the shop floor are the Shotters[5].*

John Heale[6]
One Blood *(2008)*

I slept for precisely forty-one minutes and two seconds that night (or rather that morning), and it would have been really nice to stay in bed the next day and not do anything. But I was too tired to sleep
15 by then. And, besides, I knew that if I stayed in bed, all I'd do was carry on thinking about things, and I'd just about had enough of thinking for now.

I needed to *do* something.

I went into the bathroom, turned on the shower, and then –
20 standing naked in front of the mirror – I switched on my iSkin and watched as my whole body began glowing and shifting[7]. It was an amazing sensation. The outline of my body – the defining *shape* of it – became blurred and indistinct, merging into the background, like some kind of weird super/cyber-chameleon, and when I moved, the

---

1 transient: not permanent   **2** perception: understanding; idea   **3** branch: local store representing a large company   **4** till: cash register in a store   **5** Shotter: drug dealer who sells directly   **6** John Heale: pseudonym of an investigative journalist, criticizing misleading coverage of youth crime in Britain. His book 'One Blood' is subtitled: Inside British Gang culture   **7** shift: (here) change shape

movements left fleeting[1] trails[2] in the air, making everything seem even blurrier. I stood there for a minute or two, staring at myself, and then – when I couldn't bear the weirdness any more – I switched it all off and got into the shower.

Twenty minutes later, as I was rummaging[3] around in the sitting room, looking for my shoes and my bag and stuff, Gram shuffled in, still wearing her dressing gown and slippers. From the bags under her eyes and the way that she couldn't stop yawning, I guessed that she hadn't slept much either.

'Morning, Tommy,' she mumbled, stifling[4] another yawn[5]. 'What time is it?'

'About eight,' I told her. 'Have you seen my bag anywhere?'

'What bag?' She rubbed her eyes and looked at me.

'What are you doing?'

'My school bag,' I said. 'I can't find it anywhere.'

'School?' she said, starting to wake up now. 'What are you talking about? You're not going to school.'

'Why not?'

'Oh, come *on,* Tommy ... you've only just got back from hospital, for God's sake. You were in a coma for seventeen days, and you had major surgery[6]. Or have you forgotten all that?'

I smiled at her. 'Forgotten all what?'

She shook her head. 'It's not funny ... you need to rest. The only reason Mr Kirby let you come home was because I promised him that I'd make sure you got plenty of rest.' She looked at me. 'You've got to take it easy[7] for a while, love.'

'Yeah ... but I'm fine, Gram. Really –'

'I know you are. And I mean to make sure that you stay that way.'

---

1 fleeting: lasting only a very short time   **2** trail: marks or track left behind
3 rummage ['rʌmɪdʒ]: search   **4** stifle sth.: stop sth. from happening   **5** yawn
[jɔːn]: *gähnen*   **6** surgery ['sɜːdʒəri]: medical treatment involving cutting open
the body   **7** take it easy: relax

'But I was only going to school to pick up some textbooks and stuff,' I said. 'I wasn't going to stay there all day or anything.'

'Well ... even so,' she said, hesitating slightly. 'I really don't think you should be out and about yet.'

5 It *was* only a slight hesitation, but it was enough to let me know that I was on the right track[1].

'I'll only be about half an hour,' I told her. 'I promise. Ten minutes there, ten minutes to get the books, ten minutes back.'

Gram shook her head. 'I don't know, Tommy ... why do you need
10 the books anyway? I mean, how come you're so keen on[2] learning all of a sudden?'

'Maybe it was the brain surgery,' I said, smiling at her. 'Maybe it's turned me into a budding[3] genius.'

A faint smile flickered on her face. 'It'd take more than major
15 brain surgery to turn you into a genius.'

I pulled an idiot face.

She laughed.

I said, 'So, can I go then? I promise I won't be long.'

She shook her head again, and sighed. 'You exploit[4] my better
20 nature, Tom Harvey. You know that, don't you?'

'Who me?'

'You're evil[5], you are.'

'Thanks, Gram,' I said.

She sighed again. 'Your bag's in the kitchen.'

25 When I got out of the lift on the ground floor, the postman was just coming in through the main doors. I held the lift doors open for him.

'Thanks, mate[6],' he said, getting into the lift. He looked at me. 'Harvey, isn't it?'

'Yeah ...'

---

1 be on the right track: behave in the right way   **2** keen on sth.: enthusiastic about sth.   **3** budding: promising   **4** exploit sth.: benefit from sth. unfairly
5 evil: morally bad   **6** mate (infml.): friend

He rummaged through his bag and passed me a couple of letters. 'Here you go.'

I looked at the envelopes. They were addressed to Gram – Ms Connie Harvey.

'They're not for me,' I started to say, passing them back to the postman. 'They're for my –'

But the lift doors were already closing.

'Cheers, mate,' the postman said.

It's only a ten-minute walk to school, but it was cold and rainy that morning, with an icy wind blowing around the streets, so I headed for the bus stop opposite the tower and hoped that I wouldn't have to wait too long. And I was lucky. A bus was pulling up just as I got there. I got on, showed the driver my pass, and shuffled up to the back.

The bus moved off.

It was 08:58:11 now, a bit late for going to school, so the bus was pretty empty, and I had the back seat all to myself.

I looked at the two letters the postman had given me. If, like Gram and me, you don't have much money, and you're used to getting bills and final reminders[1], you soon get to know what they look like. And I knew straight away that both of these letters were final demands[2].

I opened them up. It was no big deal, privacy-wise. I mean, I don't open any of Gram's personal letters, but she's perfectly OK with me opening anything else that's addressed to her. As she often says, most of it's just rubbish anyway. But these letters weren't rubbish. And they weren't final demands either – they were *final* final demands. One of them was from the council[3], informing Gram that she was three months behind on the rent; the other was a summons[4]

---

1 reminder: notice   **2** final demand: (here) letter saying you have just one last chance to pay for sth.   **3** council: (here) *Stadtverwaltung*   **4** summons (n): *Vorladung*

to appear at the Magistrates' Court[1] to explain why she hadn't paid her council tax.

The bus juddered[2] to a stop. We were stuck in traffic, and we'd only moved about twenty metres from the bus stop. The traffic was
5 jammed up[3] all the way along Crow Lane, and I knew it would have been a lot quicker to get off and walk, but it was cold and wet out there, and warm in here ... and it didn't matter if I was late for school anyway. No one was expecting me.

I looked through the window for a moment, gazing out at the
10 industrial wasteground that stretches between Crow Lane and the High Street. It was the same as ever: acres of cracked[4] concrete[5], piles of gravel[6], the burnt-out carcasses[7] of stolen cars and abandoned[8] skips[9] ...

A dull grey desert under a dull grey sky.
15 The bus got moving again, and I closed my eyes and thought about Gram's money problems, letting my iBrain do its stuff.

Gram didn't have an online bank account, but that didn't matter. My digitized neurons just hacked into her bank and accessed her account details, and I quickly found out that she was £6,432.77
20 overdrawn[10], her cash card[11] had been cancelled, and that she was no longer allowed to write cheques for anything. I wondered how she'd been managing for the last few months. Credit cards, maybe? I hacked into her various credit card accounts and – yes – they were all maxed out[12]. I checked the statements[13], which confirmed that all
25 she'd been using the credit cards for was day-to-day living – cash withdrawals[14], food shopping, stuff like that – and when I went back

---

1 Magistrates' Court: lower court for criminal proceedings *(Amtsgericht)*
2 judder: *holpern*   **3** jammed up: very crowded   **4** cracked: broken
5 concrete: *Beton*   **6** gravel: *Kies*   **7** carcass ['kɑːkəs]: (here) remains of a
vehicle when the rest has been destroyed   **8** abandoned: left and no longer
wanted   **9** skip (n): metal container for rubbish   **10** overdrawn: *überzogen*
11 cash card: plastic card with which you get money out of your bank account
12 max sth. out: spend all of the money in sth. (e.g. an account)   **13** statement:
(here) *Kontoauszug*   **14** withdrawal: act of taking money from your bank account

to check her bank account again, I realized that the reason she was overdrawn was not that she'd been spending too much, she'd simply not been getting enough money in. She just wasn't earning enough for us to live on.

It was a big surprise to me. I mean, Gram had never earned tons [5] of money or anything, and we'd always had to struggle to make ends meet[1], but we'd always just about managed. Now though ... well, this looked pretty serious.

The bus suddenly jerked and shuddered[2], and I opened my eyes and realized that we'd just pulled up at the school bus stop. I saved [10] all the information about Gram's finances, made a mental note to sort it out later, then shut myself down, grabbed my bag, and got off the bus.

Crow Lane Secondary[3] is a huge sprawling[4] grey place that's always looked as if it's only half finished. Bits of it are forever being refur- [15] bished[5], or torn down, or renovated, and there are so many Portakabins[6] piled up all over the place that it feels like you're going to school at a building site.

Instead of going in through the main entrance, I headed down a side street and went in through one of the workmen's gates. This led [20] me round the back of the main building towards the old sports hall, which wasn't used any more ... well, not for sports, anyway. It was supposed to have been demolished[7] years ago, but for some reason they've never got round to it, and for as long as I can remember it's been one of those places where the bad kids hang out, the kids who [25] don't want anyone to know where they are or what they're doing, the kids who don't want to go to school but can't afford to be caught on the streets.

Kids like Davey Carr.

---

1 make ends meet: earn enough money for what you need   **2** shudder: shake
3 Secondary: British school for children between 11 and 16   **4** sprawl: spread in an ugly and careless way   **5** refurbish sth.: improve sth. (usu. a room or building)
6 portakabin: small temporary building   **7** demolish sth.: destroy sth. deliberately

Davey was what they call a persistent truant[1], and he'd been caught so many times that his mum was in danger of facing prosecution[2] and a possible jail sentence[3]. And, obviously, Davey's mum didn't want to go to jail, which was why – a couple of months ago
5 – she'd given him *her* version of a final warning, which basically consisted of beating the shit out of him. After that, Davey would go to school every morning, turn up for registration, and spend most of the rest of the day hanging around in places he wasn't supposed to be. Like the old sports hall.

10   And Davey, of course, was the only reason I was going to school that morning. I had no intention of bringing home any text books. What did I need with text books? I knew everything there was to know. I could probably pass every exam in the world, at world-record speed … with my eyes closed. I could win *University Chal-*
15 *lenge*[4] on my own. I could, if I wanted to, win every quiz show on TV – *Countdown, Mastermind, Who Wants To Be A Millionaire?* I could win them all …

But for now, all I wanted to do was find Davey Carr.

It wasn't difficult. My iSenses had been tracking his mobile all morn-
20 ing, and the signal now was telling me that he was in a little room at the back of the old sports hall. And that's where I found him. He was sitting on an old wooden chair, smoking a cigarette, yapping[5] away to a couple of young Crow kids. The kids, who were hanging on his every word, clearly thought that Davey was some kind of god
25 or something.

'Hey, Davey,' I said, walking into the room. 'How's it going?'

The two young kids jumped at the sound of my voice, and even Davey looked a little bit startled[6] for a moment, but he soon relaxed when he realized that it was only me.

---

1 persistent truant: *notorischer Schulschwänzer*   **2** prosecution: *Strafverfolgung*
3 jail sentence: being forced to spend time in jail as punishment for a crime
4 University Challenge: British quiz programme on TV since 1962   **5** yap: talk in
a silly, noisy way   **6** startled: surprised

'All right, Tom?' he said casually. 'What are you doing here? I thought –'

'You can go,' I said to the two kids.

They both stared at me, and although they were only about twelve years old, their eyes were already cold and hard.   5

'Go on,' I told them. 'Fuck off.'

They glanced at Davey, he nodded, and they reluctantly sauntered[1] out. I watched them go, studying them closely, comparing them to my iMemories of the young kids in the video of Lucy's attack, but I was pretty sure that these two kids hadn't been there.   10
I waited until they'd left the room ... then waited some more. They both had their mobiles on, and I could tell from the signals that they hadn't gone anywhere – they'd stopped outside the room and were waiting to hear what happened.

'Listen, Tom –' Davey started to say.   15

'Tell them to go,' I said.

'What?'

'The two kids, they're still out there. Tell them to go.' Davey looked puzzled for a moment, trying to work out how I knew, then he just shrugged and called out,   20

'Hey! You two ... fuck off. Now!'

I heard muffled whispers, then shuffling feet ... then, from beyond the room, 'Sorry, Davey ... we was just ... we was just going, OK?'

And, with that, they were gone.

I turned to Davey. 'Fresh blood?'   25

'What?'

I shook my head. 'Nothing ... don't worry about it.' I stared at him.
'How's your conscience, Davey?'

'My what?'

'Conscience.' I closed my eyes for a moment, then opened them   30
again. 'It means the consciousness[2] of the moral quality of your

---

1 saunter: walk slowly and confidently   **2** consciousness: (here) knowledge;
understanding

own conduct[1] or intentions, together with a feeling of obligation[2] to refrain from[3] doing wrong.'

Davey frowned at me. 'What the fuck –?'

'I know you were there, Davey,' I sighed. 'And I know you threw
5 the iPhone out of the window.'

His frown deepened. 'What are you talking about?'

'I've seen the video.'

'What video?'

Sighing again, I reached into my pocket and pulled out my
10 mobile. As I selected the video player, I retrieved the video from inside my head and sent it to my mobile, and by the time I'd opened the player, the video was already there. Without saying anything, I hit play and passed the phone to Davey. He took it, watched it for a while, and then – with his face visibly paling[4] – he passed it back.

15 'Remember it now?' I asked him, deleting the video and putting the phone back in my pocket.

He nodded sheepishly[5]. 'Where did you get it from? The video, I mean ...'

'Does it matter?'

20 'No ... I suppose not.'

I looked at him. 'Christ, Davey, how *could* you? I mean, *Jesus* ... how could you *do* that?'

'I didn't *do* anything,' he whined[6].

'You were *there!* You watched them doing it ... you were *laughing,*
25 for God's sake. You think that's not *doing* anything?'

'Yeah, I know ... I just meant –'

'I know what you *meant.*' I took a deep breath and let it out slowly, trying to control my anger. Davey lit a cigarette. I sighed again. 'You used to be all right, Davey. I mean, you used to have a mind of your
30 own. What the hell happened to you?'

'Nothing.'

---

1 conduct: behaviour **2** obligation: responsibility; duty **3** refrain from sth.
(fml.): not do sth. **4** pale: becoming lighter in colour **5** sheepishly: in an embarrassed way **6** whine: speak with an annoying, high voice

'Did you think it was funny, what they were doing to Lucy? Did you think it was a really good *laugh*?'

'No.'

'So what did you think it *was* then? Did you think it was cool? Tough? Did it make you feel *good?*'   5

Davey's eyes darkened. 'You don't *know* ...'

'What? I don't know *what?*'

He shook his head. 'It's just the way it is, OK?'

'No,' I said, 'it's *not* OK.'

'Yeah, well ...'   10

I looked at him, trying to see the old Davey, the Davey who used to be my friend. 'Why didn't you try to stop them?' I asked quietly. 'Why didn't you at least *try* ...?'

'Don't be stupid,' he said. 'They would have beaten me up, wouldn't they? Same as they beat up Ben ... worse, probably. When   15 they tell you to do something, you fucking do it.'

'They told you to be there?'

He shrugged. 'I was with them, wasn't I? You're either with them or you're not. You don't get to pick and choose[1]. He puffed on his cigarette and looked at me. 'It's a different world, Tom. Once you're   20 part of it, there's nothing else. You've just got to live it.' He lowered his eyes. 'I'm sorry ... I shouldn't have thrown the phone at you.'

I stared at him in disbelief. 'You *what?*'

'I never thought it'd actually *hit* you –'

'I don't care about the fucking *phone,*' I spat[2]. 'Shit ...'   25

He looked at me, grinning. 'You've got to admit, though – it was a pretty good shot.'

I was very close to hitting him then. I really wanted to smack[3] him in the head and wipe that stupid look from his face. Not because he was grinning, not even because he'd momentarily lulled   30 me into[4] almost feeling sorry for him ... but simply because of his

---

1 pick and choose: choose only the things you really want   **2** spit sth.: (here) say sth. in an aggressive way   **3** smack sb.: hit sb. with your flat hand   **4** lull sb. into sth.: make sb. feel confident and relaxed enough to do sth.

complete lack of remorse[1] for what had been done to Lucy. I mean, how could he even *think* about apologizing to me without feeling sorry for Lucy?

It was totally unbelievable.

5   And I knew then that it was a waste of time trying to reason with him, or trying to appeal to his better side, because he didn't *have* a better side any more. I just had to treat him as nothing. I had to ignore my disgust, bury my anger, and just use him to get what I wanted.

10 I looked at him, letting him see the coldness in my eyes. 'Whose idea was it?'

'What?'

'To beat up Ben – who was behind it?'

He shook his head. 'I'm not telling you anything. I can't –'

15 'OK,' I said, taking my mobile out of my pocket. 'I'm going to ask you again, and if I don't get the answer I want, I'm sending the video to the police. And to your mum. And then I'm going to start shooting my mouth off[2], and pretty soon everyone's going to know that you've been talking to me, and that I've been talking to the police –'

20 'You wouldn't –'

I pressed a few buttons, pretending to select the video, then I keyed in a number (it was actually my own number), and said to him, 'Last chance. Whose idea was it?'

'I can't –'

25 'All right,' I shrugged, turning my attention to the phone. I moved my thumb, as if I was about to hit the send button.

'*No!*' Davey shouted. 'No ... don't, please ...'

I paused, without moving my thumb, and looked at him. 'Whose idea?'

30 'Look,' he sighed. 'It doesn't work like that, OK?'

I moved my thumb again.

---

1 remorse: feeling of guilt and regret   **2** shoot your mouth off (infml.): talk about private or secret things

'It's the *truth,* Tom,' he said quickly. 'Honestly … it's just … I mean, it's not like there's anyone in charge or anything. It's not like that.' He shook his head. 'All this stuff you see on TV about gangs, fucking Ross Kemp[1], you know … it's all a load of shit. It's just not like that. There aren't any *leaders* or rules or anything … it's just a bunch of ⁵ kids, hanging around. We just *do* stuff, you know?'

'All right,' I said. 'But one of you must have decided to beat up Ben. I mean, there must be *some* kind of hierarchy.'

'Higher what?'

'You know what I mean. Like with you and the two kids earlier ¹⁰ on – they're Crows, aren't they?'

'Little Crows, yeah.'

'And they do what you tell them?'

'Yeah.'

'And there must be other Crows who tell you what to do, and ¹⁵ you do it.'

'Well, yeah … I suppose.'

'Right. So who was it? I mean, you said just now that "if they tell you to do something, you fucking do it". So who told you and the rest of them to beat up Ben?'   ²⁰

Davey hesitated, scared to name names.

I looked at him. 'Was it O'Neil? Firman? Adebajo?'

He said nothing.

'I've got the video, Davey,' I reminded him.

'Shit,' he sighed, shaking his head. 'If they find out I talked to you ²⁵ … I'm fucked.'

'Yeah, well,' I told him. 'At least there's a chance that they won't find out. But if you *don't* talk to *me,* you're definitely fucked.'

He thought about that for a moment, then sighed again, and reluctantly started talking. 'It's Yoyo and Cutz mostly, they're the ³⁰ ones who kind of … I don't know … get stuff going.'

'That's O'Neil and Adebajo?'

---

1 Ross Kemp: British actor and investigative journalist who made a documentary series 'Ross Kemp on Gangs'

'Yeah ... they've both got older brothers, like Elders, you know ...?'

'Elders?'

'The older kids,' he explained. 'The big guys ... you know? The buyers ...'

5 'Buyers?'

'Yeah.'

'You mean they're drug dealers?'

Davey shrugged. 'Kind of ... I mean, the younger kids do most of the actual street dealing. The Elders don't go near it. I mean, they
10 never even see the gear[1]. They just take care of the business side, you know ... the money stuff.'

'Right. So what's all that got to do with O'Neil and Adebajo beating up Ben and raping Lucy?'

Davey shrugged again. 'Nothing, really ... I mean, it's just all
15 about respect and stuff. Power. You know ...?'

'No,' I said coldly. 'I don't know.'

'You can't show any weakness, all right? If you want to be something, be respected, you can't take any shit.' He looked at me. 'It's simple, really. Ben got beaten up because he said no to Yoyo. Yoyo
20 told him he had to stab this guy, and Ben refused. If Yoyo hadn't beaten him up, Yo would have looked weak. And everyone would have known it, and that would have blown Yo's chance to be like his brother.'

'And what about Lucy?' I said quietly. 'What was the simple *rea-*
25 *soning* behind ruining her life?'

Davey lowered his eyes. 'It's just ... it's what they *do*, Tom. I don't know ... I suppose part of it was to get at Ben, to hurt him, you know? But mostly ... well, it's like a power thing. They do it because they *can* ... because they know they'll get away with it.' He shrugged
30 again. 'It's just what they do.'

'And what about you?' I said coldly. 'Did you want to do it too?'

He looked at me. 'I tried to help her ... afterwards, I mean. I helped her pick up her clothes ...'

---

1 gear (infml.): (here) drugs

'You helped her pick up her clothes?'

'Yeah.'

'Well, that was incredibly thoughtful of you, Davey. I'm sure Lucy really appreciated it. Did she remember to thank you before you left?'

'Fuck off, Tom,' he said quietly. 'You weren't there. You don't know how it was.'

I didn't say anything for a moment or two. I was sick of talking to Davey now. Sick of all this stuff about power and respect and weakness and shit. It was nothing to do with anything.

I breathed in, trying to forget how I felt, and I said to Davey, 'What are their names? The brothers ...?'

'What?'

'O'Neil and Adebajo. What are their brothers called?'

'Why do you want to know?'

I just stared at him.

He hesitated for a few moments, instinctively wary of telling me, but almost immediately he realized that it was too late for keeping his mouth shut now. 'Troy O'Neil and Jermaine Adebajo,' he said.

'Right. And who do they answer to?'

'What?'

'The brothers and the rest of them. The older guys ... the Elders or whatever you call them. Who tells them what to do?'

Davey's face suddenly paled. 'No ...' he muttered. 'I mean, I don't know ...'

'Just tell me,' I sighed. 'One more name, and then I'm gone.'

'No, I can't ... not him.'

'Who?'

'He'll find out. He always does.'

I held out my mobile again. 'It's up to you, Davey. Give me the name, or I send the video.'

He was looking really worried now – blinking his eyes, nervously licking his lips – and I could tell that he was genuinely considering his options. Which made me think that whoever this guy was, the one that Davey was so frightened of, he had to be *seriously* scary.

Eventually, though, Davey looked me in the eye and said, 'Some people call him the Devil.'

'Yeah? Why's that? Has he got horns or something?'

Davey shook his head. 'It's not funny ... I mean, this is a *really* bad guy. Yoyo and the rest are *nothing* compared to him. I mean, if you think what happened to Lucy and Ben was bad –'

'Davey,' I said wearily, 'just tell me his fucking name.'

'Ellman,' he said quietly. 'His name's Howard Ellman.'

1010

Moral relativism[1] is the view that ethical standards, morality, and positions of right or wrong are culturally based and therefore subject[2] to a person's individual choice. We can all decide what is right for ourselves. You decide what's right for you, and I'll decide what's right for me. There are no absolute rights and wrongs.   5

It was still raining when I left the old sports hall, so there weren't many people around, but as I headed back[3] round the rear[4] of the main building towards the workmen's gate, I saw something going on over by the science block[5]. Two boys and two girls were arguing about something, shouting and swearing, pushing each other   10
around. I recognized three of them – Jayden Carroll, Carl Patrick, and Nadia Moore – and I guessed the other girl was Leona, Jayden's girlfriend. From the way Nadia kept waving her mobile around, shoving it into Leona's face, I assumed the argument was about the text I'd sent last night – the one that had made Nadia think that Carl   15
had been seeing Leona.

I hung back behind a pillar and watched as the argument intensified. The shouting and swearing got louder, the pushing and shoving got nastier[6], and then I saw Nadia grab[7] Leona by the shoulder and smack her across the face with her mobile. After that, every-   20
thing really kicked off[8]. Jayden grabbed hold of Nadia and shoved her into a wall, Nadia retaliated[9], scratching her nails down Jayden's face ... and then, as Jayden yelled out in pain and swung his fist at Nadia, I suddenly realized that Carl Patrick had a knife in his hand. I saw him lunge[10] at Jayden and grab his shoulder with one hand, and   25
then he just kind of pumped his other arm a few times, and Jayden

---

1 relativism: belief that truth or values are not general but can be judged only in relation to other things, e.g. your personal situation   **2** subject to sth.: depending on sth   **3** head back: go back the way you came   **4** rear: back
5 science block: *Naturwissenschaftstrakt*   **6** nasty: (here) aggressive   **7** grab sb.: aggressively and suddenly hold sb.   **8** kick off: start   **9** retaliate: strike back; get revenge   **10** lunge at sb. [lʌndʒ]: suddenly move towards sb.

staggered[1] backwards, clutching[2] at his stomach, before falling to
his knees in a puddle and slumping slowly to the ground …
   And that was it. Everything stopped then.
   Carl Patrick and the two girls didn't really do anything, they just
5 kind of stood around Jayden, looking down at him, looking at each
other … I even saw Patrick shrug, as if to say – *don't blame me, it was
his fault* …
   Which, of course, it wasn't.
   It was *my* fault.
10 I dialled 999 in my head, anonymously called for an ambulance,
then I walked back round the other side of the main building and
went out through the workmen's gate.

I knew that it wasn't really my fault. I might have unwittingly[3] caused
it by sending the text to Nadia, but that's all I'd done. I hadn't stuck
15 the knife in Jayden's belly[4], had I? I couldn't blame myself for that …
   Could I?
   I played it all back in my head, then anonymously sent the video
to DS Johnson's mobile phone, with a text message identifying Carl
Patrick as the one with the knife. And then, as I started walking back
20 towards Crow Town, I tried to forget it all. I tried telling myself that
it was no big deal, that people get stabbed around here all the time
… that you can't do anything about it, it's just how it is …
   But the words in my head sounded pretty empty. They were the
kinds of words that Davey would use – *it's just the way it is, it's just
25 what they do* – words that mean nothing. And maybe, in a funny
kind of way, that's why he used them. Meaningless words for meaningless actions.
   I stopped thinking about it then.
   Lucy was logging on to her MySpace page.

1 stagger: walk unsteadily   **2** clutch sth.: hold sth.   **3** unwittingly: *unabsichtlich*
4 belly: stomach

While I waited for her to read my message (iBoy's message), I dialled Gram's number in my head. As it rang, I suddenly realized that it'd look a bit strange if I was walking along talking to Gram without either a mobile or one of those stupid hands-free/Bluetoothy[1] things stuck in my ear, so I quickly pulled out my mobile and held it to my ear.

'Tommy?' Gram answered. 'Where are you? You're late.'

'Yeah, sorry, Gram,' I said. 'I bumped into Mr Smith, you know, my English teacher ...? He just started talking to me about stuff, and I couldn't get away. I'm on my way back now.'

'You'd better be. Where are you?'

'Just passing the garage. I'll be five minutes.'

'Right ... well, don't hang around.'

'I'll see you in five, Gram.'

Lucy had replied to my MySpace message. *iBoy,* she'd written, *i can't talk to you. please don't write again.*

And I guessed that was fair enough.

Just before I got to Crow Town, I took a quick detour down Mill Lane, a little back street that leads down to an old part of the industrial estate that isn't used any more. There's not a lot down there – abandoned warehouses and factories, vast stretches of wasteground – but it's the only place I know around here where you can't get a signal on your mobile, and I wanted to check what happened to the iStuff in my head when there wasn't any mobile reception[2].

It's not a very nice place, the old industrial estate. It's sort of grey and flat and lifeless, and it always has this weird kind of dull silence to it ... in fact, even when it's not actually silent, the whole place seems to be muffled with a cold and empty hush[3]. Although it's not used any more, there's always a lot of stuff going on down there, especially at night. A lot of the local kids hang around in the old

---

1 Bluetooth: radio technology that can connect two mobile phones, computers, etc. without wires   **2** reception: *Signalempfang*   **3** hush (n.): quietness

warehouses and factory buildings, just doing what they do – taking drugs, having sex, partying, fighting – and sometimes you hear about more serious stuff going on – gang stuff, shootings, stabbings, dead bodies.

5   So, no, it's not the nicest place in the world, and I didn't like being there, but I carried on walking – with my iBrain turned on – until I reached a point where the signal receptor[1] in my head faded[2] to zero, and then I stopped.

No signal.

10 No reception.

No iBoy.

I looked around. There was a block of old factory buildings behind me, towering[3] concrete structures with even taller brick[4] chimneys, and on either side of the road there was nothing but vast

15 stretches of wasteground. About thirty metres up ahead, I could see a disused[5] complex of industrial units and warehouses.

I tried reaching out inside my head, searching for a signal, a network, anything ... but there was nothing there.

My iHead was empty.

20 My iSkin non-functional.

The electric was off.

I walked back the way I'd come, and after about ten metres or so, everything switched back on again.

I stopped and looked around. There was no one in sight. No cars,

25 no bikes, no nothing. I stepped off the pavement and crossed over the wasteground to a blackened patch of earth – the remains of an old bonfire. I stooped down[6] and picked out some charred[7] tin cans from the ashes, then I went over and placed them on a huge slab[8] of reinforced concrete[9] that was lying nearby.

---

1 receptor: *Empfänger*   **2** fade to sth.: slowly become sth.   **3** towering: very high; impressive   **4** brick: *Ziegelstein*   **5** disused: not being used   **6** stoop down: bend your body down   **7** charred [ˈtʃɑːd]: *verkohlt*   **8** slab: block; piece   **9** reinforced concrete: *Stahlbeton*

I looked around again, making sure that I was still alone, and then – for the next ten minutes or so – I experimented with my zapping[1] capabilities. I started off by simply touching one of the cans and giving it an electric shock, zapping it right off the slab, and then I tried controlling the power – increasing it, decreasing it, moving 5 away from the cans to see if I could knock them off from a distance …

By the time I had to stop, when I saw a car cruising[2] slowly down the road towards me, I'd learned that I could control the power, although as yet my degree of control wasn't too great, and that my 10 maximum range for zapping at a distance was no more than a metre at most.

I crossed back over to the pavement just as the approaching car was pulling up at the side of the road. The front window wound down and a seedy-looking[3] guy leaned out and said, 'Hey, kid, is this 15 Crow Lane?'

I shook my head and pointed towards the estate. 'It's back there.'

He glanced at where I was pointing, then turned back to me. 'Baldwin House?'

'Second tower along.'   20

He nodded but didn't say anything. He just wound up the window, turned the car round, and drove off.

'You're welcome,' I muttered, watching him go.

Gram was working when I got home – tap-tap-tapping away – and after we'd said hello, and she'd pretended to be a bit annoyed with 25 me for staying out longer than I'd promised, I left her to her writing and went into my room.

I didn't know what I was going to do with all the information I'd got about O'Neil and Adebajo and everything else – the attack on Lucy and Ben, the gang stuff, the Elders, Howard Ellman … I didn't even 30

1 zap sth.: (here) shock sth. with an electric force   **2** cruise: pass by   **3** seedy: *schäbig*

know why I'd gone looking for it all in the first place. But as I sat at my window, looking down at the rainy-day dullness of the estate down below, I knew in my heart that I only had two options: I could either do nothing, just forget about everything and try to get on with
5 my life; or I could try my best to do something.

And maybe if I'd still been my old self – the perfectly normal, non-iPhoned Tom Harvey – maybe I might have accepted that there was nothing I could do, because the only thing the normal Tom Harvey could have done was pass on the information he'd col-
10 lected to the police, and it wouldn't have mattered how carefully or cleverly he did it, the end result would have been the same: not just the Crows, but most of Crow Town, would have turned against Lucy and her family and made their lives even more hellish than they already were. So the alternative option, of doing nothing at all,
15 would probably have been the only thing the normal Tom Harvey could have done.

But, like it or not, I *wasn't* the normal Tom Harvey any more. I was iBoy. I had the ability to do things that I couldn't do before, and there was something inside me – a part of me that I wasn't even
20 sure I *liked* – that made me feel that it was my duty, my obligation, to make the most of those abilities and try to do something useful with them. And whatever this feeling inside me was, I knew that I couldn't say no to it.

I just wished that it would be a bit more helpful. I mean, it was all
25 well and good making me feel that I had to do something ... but how about telling me what that something was?

No, it was no help at all for that. And neither was my iBrain. Deciding *what* to do was a job for my normal brain.

So I closed my eyes and just sat there – thinking, wondering, lis-
30 tening to the pouring[1] rain ...

It must have been a couple of hours later when Gram knocked on my door, waking me up, and told me that she was just nipping out

---

1 pour: (here) rain heavily

to the shops. I hadn't got much thinking done, and even the thinking I *had* managed to do wasn't very useful, or even relevant. In fact, as Gram stood in the doorway, waiting for me to answer her question – which I hadn't actually heard – I realized that I couldn't even remember what I'd been thinking about before I'd fallen asleep.   5

'Tommy?' Gram said.

I looked at her. 'Yeah, sorry ... what did you say?'

'Did you want anything? From the shops ...'

'No ... no thanks.'

'OK,' she said. 'I won't be long.'   10

'Have you got enough money?' I heard myself say.

'What?'

I shrugged. 'Nothing ... I just meant, you know ...' I rubbed my eyes, smiling wearily at her. 'Sorry, I'm still half asleep ...'

'Well, maybe you'd better get back to being *fully* asleep.'   15

'Yeah ...'

'In bed, not in your chair.'

'OK.'

'All right then. I'll see you later.'

'Yeah, see you later, Gram.'   20

I'm perfectly aware that knowing about stuff isn't the same thing as understanding it, so I knew that having access to vast amounts of information hadn't suddenly turned me into a philosophical genius or anything, but that afternoon, as I sat in my room with my eyes closed, iSearching through everything I could iSearch through,   25 looking for a way to sort out Gram's financial position, I kept seeing cyber-flashes of stuff about morals – discussion forums, philosophy websites, excerpts[1] from books – and I began to understand that the concept of right and wrong isn't as clear cut as I'd thought. When it comes to morality, there *aren't* any natural rules. There aren't things   30 that are *definitely* right or *definitely* wrong. Nothing is simply black

---

1 excerpt: quote

or white; it's all a murky[1] dull grey. Actually, come to think of it, it's more of a browny-grey kind of colour – the sort of shitty brown colour you get when you mix all the colours in a paint box together.

Of course, I was also beginning to understand that if you want to do something that you think – or even *know* – is wrong, there are all kinds of things you can do to convince[2] yourself that it's not wrong, and pretending that there's actually no such thing as 'wrong' in the first place is probably one of the easiest.

Anyway, to get to the point, I eventually realized that whichever way I chose to solve Gram's money problems – and with the growing capabilities inside my head, the possibilities were almost endless – but whichever way I picked, it inevitably meant taking money from somewhere else, money that didn't belong to me. And however much I tried to convince myself that this was OK, I knew in my heart that it wasn't.

For example, I could easily hack into the accounts and databases of all Gram's various publishers, and it would have been no trouble at all to change the sales figures, to invent more sales for Gram's books, to create a load of money for Gram that wasn't actually there. Or, even more crudely[3], I could simply hack into some super-wealthy person's bank account, someone who wouldn't miss a measly few thousand quid[4] – maybe Bill Gates[5], or Bono[6], or J. K. Rowling[7] – and take some of their money.

In short, I had the ability to steal as much as I wanted from anyone I wanted to take it from. Which, at first, was pretty exciting. I mean, I could be a billionaire, a trillionaire, an infinitillionaire ... but I soon realized that it didn't really mean very much. I mean, what was I going to do with a trillion pounds? And, more to the point, how was I going to explain where it came from?

---

1 murky: shadowy; not clear   **2** convince sb.: persuade sb.   **3** crudely: (here) not sophisticated   **4** quid (infml.): one British pound   **5** Bill Gates: (born 1955) American business magnate, former chief executive of Microsoft   **6** Bono: Paul David Hewson (born 1960) Irish musician   **7** J. K. Rowling: (born 1965) British writer, author of *Harry Potter*

In the end, what I did ... well, first of all I set up an algorithmic program.

In mathematics, computing, linguistics and related subjects, an algorithm is a sequence of finite[1] instructions, often used for calculation and data processing, in which a list of well-defined instructions for ₅ *completing a task will, when given an initial state, proceed through a well-defined series of successive states, eventually terminating in an end-state.*

And, basically, I programmed this algorithm to scan all the bank accounts in the world, rank them in terms of wealth, and remove £1 ₁₀ from each of the top 15,000. The total of £15,000 was then electronically (and totally anonymously) transferred to Gram's account as a single deposit[2]. I couldn't work out how to explain this deposit – i.e. how to invent a legitimate depositor – but I decided to leave that for later. Meanwhile, I cancelled Gram's summons for non-payment of ₁₅ council tax and, using some of the £15,000, I paid off what she owed and cleared the outstanding rent.

Yes, it was wrong.
  It was stealing.
  It was fraud[3]. ₂₀
  It was wrong.
  But I didn't feel bad about it.

I slept for a while after that (morality and algorithms are *really* tiring), and when I woke up, Gram was back, and she'd got some food, and we had some toasted sandwiches together. ₂₅
  While Gram went back to her writing, I spent some more time in my room, scanning the airwaves, listening out for any mobile calls that might tell me what the Crows were up to, but I didn't hear any-

---

1 finite: limited; restricted   **2** deposit: *Einzahlung*   **3** fraud: *Betrug*

thing particularly interesting. It was all mostly – *where are you? what you doing? you hear about Trick and Jace?*

Trick was Carl Patrick, and Jace, I assumed, was Jayden Carroll. I found out from the hospital's computer records that Carroll had suffered three stab wounds to the stomach, none of them life threatening, and that he'd undergone surgery and was now expected to make a full recovery.

Carl Patrick had been arrested.

It was 19:15:59 when I left the flat and went up to the thirtieth floor to see Lucy. I don't remember how I was feeling or what I was thinking about at the time, but whatever it was, when the lift doors opened, and I saw a group of kids along the corridor outside Lucy's flat, my head and my heart suddenly emptied.

There were about six or seven of them. They were all hooded up in the usual Crow gear, but I recognized some of them: Eugene O'Neil, DeWayne Firman, Nathan Craig. One of the ones I didn't recognize had a can of spray paint in his hand and was spraying something on the wall, and DeWayne Firman was bending down and calling out something through Lucy's letter box. Eugene O'Neil was just standing there, obviously in charge, looking mean and bad and hard as hell ... and when the lift doors opened, he looked down the corridor at me, and an ugly grin cracked his face.

As I shut the lift doors and hit the button for the twenty-ninth floor, I saw him shaking his head and smiling at me, mocking what he thought was my cowardice[1], my weakness.

But I didn't care.

He wouldn't be smiling for long.

As I got out at the twenty-ninth floor and headed back up the stairs, pulling up the hood of my jacket, my iSkin was already shimmering.

1 cowardice: lack of courage

1011

'I could be a soldier/falling in love/I could be a soldier/ I could be happy'

Shame
'Come Closer to Me'

I'd never felt the kind of rage I felt as I pushed open the stairwell door and strode[1] down the corridor towards O'Neil and the others. It was all-consuming[2], brutal[3], merciless[4] ... it felt like a volcano ₅ inside me, a force of nature, straining to erupt. But at the same time, I felt weirdly calm and controlled.

I was in control of being out of control ...

As the stairwell door slammed[5] shut behind me, all the Crows stopped what they were doing and turned in my direction. I was ₁₀ moving quickly, but not running – marching along the corridor towards them, my senses alert[6], my eyes taking in everything. I saw the shocked looks on their faces when they saw me – a shimmering, glowing, hooded figure – and I saw two of them immediately start to run, not even bothering to look back ... they just turned and sped ₁₅ down the corridor towards the lift.

I let them go.

I saw O'Neil and Firman and Craig shuffling back a few steps, keeping the kid with the spray can in front of them. And I saw him staring at me with wide-open eyes as I read the words he'd sprayed ₂₀ on the wall of Lucy's flat – *bitch*[7], *whore*[8] – and then, before I knew what I was doing, I'd grabbed the aerosol out of his hand and was spraying it into his eyes. He screamed and tried to cover his eyes, but I kneed[9] him in the balls[10] and pushed him to the ground, and

---

1 stride: take long steps   **2** all-consuming: taking up all your time and energy
3 brutal: violent   **4** merciless: unforgiving   **5** slam: close loudly   **6** alert: able to
think and act quickly   **7** bitch (infml.): offensive word for a woman   **8** whore:
prostitute   **9** knee sb. (v): hit sb. with your knee   **10** balls (infml.): testicles

as his hands left his eyes to protect his groin[1], I emptied more red paint into his face.

The other three were making a move for me now, coming up behind me and trying to pull me away from the aerosol kid, but even
5 as they reached out for me, before their hands so much as touched me, a jolt of energy surged[2] through my body, and I heard a sharp crackling sound and shocked yells of pain as the three Crow kids were electrocuted[3]. As I turned round to face them, I saw them staggering away from me, trying to shake the pain from their hands ...
10 and I could see them all staring at me with abject[4] fear in their eyes.

Behind me, I heard the aerosol kid getting to his feet. I raised my foot and kicked back at him, catching him square in the face, and then – just to make sure he didn't give me any more trouble – I quickly turned round and touched my finger to his paint-smeared
15 head. The shock I gave him was hard enough to jerk his head back, and as he crawled away down the corridor, whimpering and moaning[5], I could see that I'd given him a fingertip-sized burn mark[6] on his head.

I turned back to the other three. Firman and Craig looked as
20 if they'd had enough now, and they were already starting to edge[7] backwards towards the lift. Neither of them wanted to be the first to run, but as I moved towards O'Neil, who was still standing his ground, Firman shook his head and muttered, 'Fuck this,' and he turned and legged it[8] towards the lift. Craig didn't waste any time
25 following him.

So now it was just me and O'Neil.

He stared at me for a second, torn between running and fighting, and then – with a tough-guy crick of his neck[9] – he made his decision. He reached into his track pants and pulled out a knife. It wasn't

---

1 groin: part of the body between your legs   **2** surge: flow; rush   **3** electrocute sb.: hurt sb. with electricity   **4** abject: hopeless; miserable   **5** moan: make a sound expressing pain   **6** burn mark: *Brandmal*   **7** edge (v): (here) *zurückschleichen*   **8** leg it (v): run; escape   **9** crick of your neck: sideways movement of the neck that makes a cracking sound

much of a thing – just a stubby[1] little kitchen knife, with a blade of no more than ten centimetres – but it looked nasty enough, and just for a moment I felt a brief pang[2] of fear.

But it didn't last long.

I had faith[3] in my iPowers.   5

I smiled at O'Neil and moved towards him, holding my hands up, offering him an unguarded[4] stab at my torso[5]. The knife was shaking in his hand.

'Go ahead,' I told him. 'Use it.'

He hesitated, swallowing hard, and looked at me.   10

I moved closer. 'What's the matter?' I said to him. 'You look as if you're going to shit yourself.'

His eyes went cold, and he lunged at me, aiming the knife at my belly. I flinched[6] a little, but I knew that I was safe. My force field was on, and as the knife blade[7] struck[8] it, and sparks[9] flew, O'Neil 15
shrieked and dropped the knife to the floor. I looked down at it. It was smouldering[10], the plastic handle melted out of shape. I looked up at O'Neil. He was shaking his hand, blowing on his fingers, his face twisted in a grimace of pain.

I moved round him, positioning myself between him and the lift, 20
so now the only way he could move was back along the corridor towards the stairwell. I edged towards him, making him step back.

'What the fuck?' he said. 'Who the fucking hell –?'

'Shut up,' I told him. 'Get down the corridor.'

'What?'   25

I reached out towards him. He drew back.

'Move,' I said. 'Down the corridor.'

He backed all the way down, never taking his eyes off me, and stopped at the end of the corridor.

'Open the window,' I told him.   30

---

1 stubby: short and thick   **2** pang: sudden, strong feeling   **3** faith: belief; trust
4 unguarded: not protected   **5** torso: upper body   **6** flinch: *zucken*   **7** blade:
sharp part of a knife   **8** strike sth.: hit sth.   **9** spark: *Funke*   **10** smoulder: burn
without flame

'What for?'

'Just do it.'

He turned to the window at the end of the corridor, unlatched[1] it and opened it as far as it would go, which wasn't all that far because all the windows in the tower blocks have safety restraints[2] on them. They're there to stop the windows opening all the way so people can't jump out of them ... or throw other people out of them.

'Step away,' I told O'Neil.

As he moved back, I reached over, took hold of both restraints and shot a bolt of electricity through them. The rivets[3] popped out[4], and I yanked[5] the restraints off. Now, as I lifted the frame of the window, it opened all the way.

'Shit, man,' I heard O'Neil whisper. 'What are you doing?'

I grabbed hold of him before he could run, grasping his throat with one hand, giving him enough of a shock to stop him from struggling. It was enough to stop him from talking too. As I forced his head, and then his upper body, through the open window, all he could say was, 'Nunh ... nuhguh ... nunh ...'

I don't know how far I would have gone if Lucy hadn't suddenly appeared in her doorway, yelling at me to stop. I don't *think* I would have pushed O'Neil out of the window ... I don't think I had it in me. I think I was just trying to scare him. But I'll never know for sure. Because when I heard Lucy's voice – 'No! Don't do it!' – all the coldness, the brutality of my rage ... it all just suddenly faded away, and for a moment I really didn't know who or what I was.

I gazed down the corridor at Lucy. She was standing outside her door, with Ben in the doorway behind her, and I could see the genuine[6] concern[7] in her eyes – she really *didn't* want me to push O'Neil out of the window ... and I couldn't understand it. O'Neil had *raped*

---

1 unlatch sth.: unlock sth. (e.g. a window)   **2** safety restraints: *Sicherheitssperren*
3 rivet: metal pin holding two things together   **4** pop out: fall out suddenly
5 yank sth. (infml.): pull sth. hard and suddenly   **6** genuine: real; authentic
7 concern: worry

her. He'd done the absolutely worst thing imaginable to her. How could she possibly *not* want me to kill him?

'But you *said* ...' I heard myself say.

She frowned at me. 'What?'

'You said you wanted to hurt them, to kill them ... you wanted ₅ them to suffer ...'

She shook her head, still frowning, and I wasn't sure if that meant that she hadn't heard me, or that she had, but she didn't understand what I was saying.

While all this was going on, I must have loosened my grip on ₁₀ O'Neil, because I suddenly realized that I no longer had hold of him and he was staggering away from me, holding his throat, heading for the stairwell door.

I didn't go after him.

My rage was over now. I felt drained, exhausted, almost lifeless, ₁₅ and I wondered if I'd overdone it, used up too much power. I closed my eyes for a moment and took a few deep breaths. I could hear O'Neil running down the stairs. When I opened my eyes again and looked over at Lucy, she was still just standing there, staring at me ... and as I met her gaze, and we looked at each other across the cor- ₂₀ ridor, I saw a flash of sudden realization in her eyes. She'd remembered where my words had come from – *You said you wanted to hurt them, to kill them ... you wanted them to suffer*. She'd realized that the words were from her MySpace blog. And who was the only person who'd read her blog? ₂₅

I saw her eyes widen, and her mouth open, and I saw her lips move as she whispered to herself, *'iBoy.'*

I chose that moment to leave.

As I went through the stairwell door and started heading down the stairs, I could hear O'Neil's distant footsteps echoing on the ₃₀ steps below. He wasn't running any more, but he was still moving fairly quickly. I went inside my head and selected the video of the last few minutes, then I leaned over the railings, looking down at the dizzying[1] drop[2] of the stairwell, and zeroed in[3] on O'Neil's mobile. As I sent the video to his number, I called out his name.

'Hey, Eugene!'

As his footsteps stopped, I heard the sound of my voice echoing dully[4] around the concrete and metal of the stairwell, and then the distant sound of a ringtone[5] (Fiddy's[6] 'In Da Club').

'Answer it!' I called out.

There was a pause, then the ringtone stopped. I gave O'Neil a few moments to open the video and realize what it showed – i.e. him trying to stab me and failing, and me getting hold of him by the throat and nearly pushing him out of the window – and then I called out to him again.

'You got it?'

Another pause, then, 'Yeah ...'

His voice was a mixture of confusion and concern.

'If you go anywhere *near* Lucy again,' I shouted down to him, 'that video's going on YouTube. Do you hear me?'

Nothing. Silence.

'Do you *HEAR* me?' I yelled.

'Yeah ... yeah, I hear you. How the fuck –?'

'I'll post it on YouTube and send it to everyone you know. All the Crows, the FGH ... *every*one. Do you understand?'

'Yeah ... but –'

'No questions. You've got three seconds to get moving, and then I'm coming after you.' I started counting. 'One ... two ...'

He started running.

I waited until he'd clattered down another few flights of stairs, then I turned off my iSkin and walked back down to the twenty-third floor.

---

1 dizzying: *schwindelerregend* **2** drop (n): fall; long distance down from a high point **3** zero in on sth.: (here) log into sth. **4** dully (adv): *dumpf* **5** ringtone: sound a mobile phone makes when called **6** Fiddy: Fifty Cent, an American rapper

1100

*You don't have to be crazy to put on a shiny costume and battle evil –
but it helps.*

http://io9.com/5228906/top-10-greatest-mentally-ill-superheroes

Gram was just coming out of the bathroom when I got back home.

'I thought you were going to see Lucy?' she said to me.

'Yeah, I was ... I am. I'm just ... I forgot something.' She looked at
me, waiting for me to tell her what I'd forgotten.

'My phone,' I said. 'I left it in my room.'

'Right,' she said. 'What's that on your hands?'

'What?'

'You've got red paint on your hands.'

I looked at my hands, quickly trying to think of an explanation.
'Oh, yeah ... there was some graffiti on Lucy's door. You know ...
really nasty stuff. I tried to clean it off.'

Gram sighed, shaking her head. 'Why can't they just leave her
alone? I mean, God knows she's been through enough already.'

I shrugged. 'It's what they do, Gram.'

'I know,' she said, sighing again. 'It's just ... well, you know ...'

'Yeah.'

She looked at me. 'Is Lucy OK with you going to see her?'

'Yeah, I think so ... I mean, she *said* it was all right. And she
seemed to get *some*thing out of me being there ...' I shrugged. 'I'm
not sure what.'

Gram smiled. 'She likes you, she always has. Do you remember
that time when she asked you to marry her?'

'*Marry* her?'

Gram nodded. 'It was ages ago, you must have been about six or
seven ... the two of you were sitting on the floor in the front room,
playing with some Lego or something, and she just turned to you
and said, "Will you marry me when I'm older?"'

'Really? What did I say?'

Gram thought about it for a moment, then smiled again. 'I don't think you said anything. I think you just started crying.'

I laughed. 'Yeah, that sounds like me. I always was pretty slick[1] with the ladies.'

5 While Gram went back to her writing, I went into my room to pretend to look for my phone. I was still feeling drained, and I took the opportunity to sit down on the edge of my bed for a few moments to recharge[2] myself before I went back up to Lucy's.

As I was sitting there, going over in my mind what had happened
10 with O'Neil and the others, trying to work out if I'd made things better or worse, I sensed Lucy logging on to her MySpace page, and a few minutes later there was a message from her in my inbox.

iBoy, it said, *was that you just now?*

I messaged back: *was that who just now?*

15 *i know it WAS you,* she replied. *who ARE you?*

i'm whoever you want me to be.

I logged off.

My mind was too buzzy for resting now. I got up off the bed, got my jacket, and went back up to the thirtieth floor.

20 *Slag, bitch, whore* ... I knew that they were only words, and that words – so they say – can never hurt you, but as I stood outside Lucy's flat, gazing at those ugly words painted crudely on the wall and the door, I knew that they *did* hurt.

---

1 slick: (here) confident, cool and popular   **2** recharge: *wieder aufladen*

I held out my hand, palm[1] first, towards the wall ... and then I closed my eyes and concentrated. After a moment or two, I began to feel an energy between the wall and my hand ... a tangible[2] resistance[3], like a magnetic field. And when I opened my eyes and started moving my hand over the painted words, gently pushing the resistance into the paint, the graffiti began to flake off[4].

It didn't take long, and when I'd finished, and all traces of the graffiti were gone, I used the same scouring[5] energy to clean the remnants[6] of paint off my hands, and then I knocked on Lucy's door.

Her mum was out – she worked at the local Tesco's[7] – and Ben had gone out too, so Lucy was on her own. Which I didn't think was a good idea, especially after she'd just had a visit from half a dozen Crows. But as far as Lucy was concerned, I didn't know anything about that, so I just kept my mouth shut and made a mental note to have a quiet – and possibly threatening – word with Ben the next time I saw him.

'You'll never *guess* what just happened, Tom,' Lucy said as we sat down together on the settee in the front room.

'You won the lottery?' I said.

'No, no ... this was just now, about half an hour ago ...' She shook her head. 'God, it was so weird. I can still hardly *believe* it.'

She started telling me all about O'Neil and the others then – how she'd been really scared when she'd realized they were outside, and they'd started calling out through the letter box ... and then she'd heard another voice outside, followed by the sounds of struggling – shouts and yells, running feet – and she'd peeked[8] through the letter box and seen this *really* weird-looking kid with multicoloured skin squaring up[9] to O'Neil ...

---

1 palm: inner part of the hand   **2** tangible: able to be clearly seen or felt
3 resistance: *Widerstand*   **4** flake off: fall off in small pieces   **5** scour sth.: *etw. schrubben*   **6** remnants: leftovers; remains   **7** Tesco: largest British supermarket chain   **8** peek: look quickly   **9** square up to sb.: approach sb. aggressively

'... I mean, his skin was really shimmering, Tom. Honestly. It was like he was covered in neon tattoos or something, and the tattoos were moving ... but they *weren't* tattoos ...'

It was incredibly strange, listening to her telling me the story. Partly because I had to pretend that it was all new to me, so I had to keep going – *What? No ... really?* – and partly because Lucy seemed so enervated[1] now, so full of life, just like the old Lucy, and I didn't know how that made me feel. On the one hand, obviously, it made me feel great. I mean, Lucy seemed to be getting back to her old self again – what could possibly be wrong with that? But on the other hand ... well, there wasn't anything *wrong* with it. Nothing at all. But I suppose, if I'm totally honest, I felt just a tiny bit jealous[2]. She was so excited, so thrilled, so curious about this mysterious stranger who'd come galloping[3] to her rescue[4] ... and I wanted her to know that it was me. I wanted her to be excited about *me,* not about iBoy. And I know that sounds pathetic – and selfish and childish and whatever else you want to call it – but, like I said, I'm just trying to be honest here. And that's how I felt.

'Tom?' I heard her say. 'Are you listening?'

'Sorry,' I said, looking at her. 'I was just –'

'Do you think it's him?'

'Who?'

She sighed. 'The MySpace guy, the one I just *told* you about. Do you think it's the same person?'

'The same as who?'

'The *other* one,' she said impatiently. 'The one who tried to throw O'Neil out of the window.'

'Oh, right,' I said, pretending to suddenly get it. 'So you think this MySpace guy might be the hero guy, is that it?'

'Yeah. What do you think?'

---

1 enervate sb. (fml.): (here) make sb. feel stronger   **2** jealous: *eifersüchtig*
3 gallop: ride on a horse (used metaphorically here)   **4** rescue: act of saving sb. from a dangerous situation

I shrugged. 'Well, I don't know … I mean, this guy you saw in the corridor, the one with the weird skin … are you sure he was real?'

'Of *course* he was *real*. What else could he be?' She shook her head angrily. 'What are you trying to say, Tom? You think I made him *up?*'   5

'No … no, I didn't mean that, I just meant … maybe you were tired or something, you know …'

She glared at me. 'I know what I *saw,* Tom. I mean, if you don't believe me –'

'I believe you –'   10

'You can ask Ben if you want. He was there too. He saw him, he'll tell you. If you don't believe me –'

'OK, OK,' I said, holding my hands up. 'I *said* I *believed* you, didn't I? I believe you, Luce.'

'Yeah?'   15

'Yeah, honestly … I was just …'

'What? You were just what?'

'Nothing. I don't know … I was just being stupid. Sorry.'

She looked at me, shaking her head. 'You're such an idiot sometimes.'   20

'I know … sorry.'

She carried on glaring at me for a second or two, but she'd never been able to stay angry with me for very long, and after a while her eyes slowly softened and her face relaxed into a smile. 'Yeah, well,' she said. 'You don't have to apologize to me for being stupid. I'm 25 used to it.'

'Thanks.'

'You're welcome.'

As we sat there grinning at each other, I couldn't help noticing that she didn't look quite so withdrawn[1] as before. She was wearing 30 black jeans and a white T-shirt, no socks, no make-up, and her hair was freshly washed. She looked really good. She looked … I don't know. She just looked *good*.

---

1 withdrawn: extremely quiet and shy

'What?' she said, self-consciously[1] flicking at her hair.

'What's the matter?'

'Nothing,' I said, looking away. 'Where *is* Ben, anyway? You said he went out?'

5 'Yeah, I asked him not to, but he said it was urgent[2].'

'Urgent?'

She shrugged. 'He got a text from someone just before he went out. Maybe he had to meet them ... I don't know.' She reached down and scratched her bare foot. 'Anyway ... you should have seen this
10 guy, Tom. It was amazing. I mean, when he had O'Neil at the window, I really thought ...'

As she carried on telling me how amazing iBoy was, I tracked down Ben's mobile – he was in a ground-floor flat in Baldwin House – and I opened up his texts. There was one from someone who iden-
15 tified himself only as 'T' which just said *here now*. Ben had answered *cant*[3] *sorry*. T had written back *NOW! OR UDED*[4], and Ben, unsur-prisingly, had replied *ok 5 mins*.

I traced T's mobile – he was in the same location as Ben – but I couldn't find out anything else about him. It was a brand-new
20 phone – pay as you go, unregistered – so my iBrain couldn't tell me much about it, but my normal brain told me that T was probably Troy O'Neil.

I stayed at Lucy's until about nine o'clock, when her mum came back, by which time Lucy had finally stopped going on about iBoy
25 and we'd spent a really nice hour or so just talking to each other about not very much at all – TV programmes, school gossip, music ... just good old ordinary stuff.

As Lucy was seeing me out, I said to her, 'If anyone starts both-ering you again, just give me a call, OK? I mean, I know I'm not as
30 superheroic as your oh-so-wonderful Mr iBoy –'

---

1 self-consciously: in a nervous and embarrassed way   **2** urgent: important
3 cant: can't   **4** NOW! OR UDED: come now, or you are dead

'Shut up,' Lucy smiled, punching[1] me lightly on the arm.

I looked at her. 'I mean it, Luce. Any trouble, or even if you're just on your own or anything – call me.'

She nodded, still smiling. 'Thanks, Tom.' And then, without a word, she reached up and gently caressed[2] the scar on my head. 'It 5 tingles,' she said quietly.

'I'm Electro-Man,' I told her. 'Honestly, I'm truly shocking.'

'Yeah,' she said, grinning. 'You *wish*.'

Ben wasn't expecting to see me standing in the corridor when the lift doors opened, but I was expecting to see him.   10

'Tom ...' he said, unpleasantly surprised. 'What are you –?'

'A word,' I said, taking his arm and leading him out of the lift.

He started to pull away from me. 'I don't really have time –'

'Yeah, you do,' I told him, tightening my grip on his arm. I led him down the corridor, past his flat, and through the door into the 15 stairwell. 'Sit down,' I told him.

'What is this?'

'Sit down.'

He did as he was told, sitting down hesitantly on the steps, and I sat down next to him.   20

'What's the matter with you?' I asked him.

'What? Nothing –'

'When I talked to you yesterday, you made out like you were all eaten up with guilt about Lucy. Do you remember? You said you couldn't help thinking that it was all your fault.'   25

'Yeah ... so?'

'So how come today, twenty-four hours later, you leave her on her own in the flat after she's just been scared shitless[3] by the bastards who raped her?'

'No,' he said firmly, shaking his head. 'No, she was OK –'   30

'You left her on her *own*, for Christ's sake.'

---

1 punch sb.: hit sb. with your fist   **2** caress [kəˈres]: touch gently and affectionately   **3** scare sb. shitless (infml.) : frighten sb. very much

'Yeah, I know, but they weren't coming back –'

'How do you know?'

'Well, I mean … I didn't think they were –'

'It doesn't matter anyway,' I interrupted. 'That's not the point. You
5 left Lucy on her own.' I glared at him. 'Don't you *get* it?'

He lowered his eyes, staring sulkily[1] at the ground.

'God, Ben,' I sighed. 'You're so full of shit. You really are.'

He shrugged.

I sat there looking at him for a few moments, trying to feel some-
10 thing good about him, but I just couldn't find anything. After a while,
I said quietly, 'What did Troy want?'

His head jerked up and he stared at me. 'What?'

'Troy O'Neil. What did he want with you?'

'How do you know I was at Troy's?'

15 'Lucky guess. What did he want?'

'Nothing …'

'What did he *want?*' I repeated

Ben just shook his head again.

'Your mum's home,' I reminded him. 'Do you want me to go and
20 tell her how you stole that iPhone?'

'No,' he said quietly.

'So tell me what Troy wanted.'

He sighed. 'It's nothing to do with you.'

I started to get up, as if I was going to see his mum.

25 'No,' he said quickly, grabbing my arm. 'I didn't mean it like *that*
… I just meant …'

'What?' I said, removing his hand from my arm and sitting down
again. 'You just meant what?'

'It wasn't *about* you. Troy, I mean … he didn't want to see me
30 about you. It was about this guy …'

'What guy?'

Ben frowned. 'Shit … I don't know. It was when Yo and the rest of
them were outside the flat earlier on. This guy … shit. I don't know

---

1 sulkily: bad-tempered

what he was. He had this really weird stuff on his face ... like lights or something, but not lights. Some kind of camouflage[1] ... a mask ... I don't know. He just appeared out of nowhere and started smacking everyone around. Christ, it was *unbelievable*. And he had one of those Taser guns[2] ... you know? Those electric things, like the cops use. He was zapping the fuck out of everyone.'

'Yeah?'

'He even tried to throw Yo out the window. He probably would have if Yo hadn't chopped him one[3].'

'Really?'

'Yeah ... Yo knows karate. He chopped this guy in the neck, and the guy let him go.'

'You saw that?'

'Yeah, I saw everything. That's why Troy wanted to see me. He wanted to know all about this guy, you know ... I mean, he tried to kill Troy's brother.'

'So you told Troy everything you saw?'

'Yeah.'

'Anything else?'

'Like what?'

'Did you tell him anything else?'

'No ...'

'Are you sure?'

'Yeah, yeah ...'

'You don't *sound* very sure.'

Ben looked at me. 'I didn't tell him anything else, all right? I don't *know* anything else.'

I stared at him. 'You'd better not be lying to me.'

He shrugged.

I said, 'So what do you think Troy's going to do about this guy with the Taser?'

---

1 camouflage: (here) sth. that makes you harder to identify   **2** Taser gun: gun that gives people electric shocks   **3** chop sb. one (infml.): hit sb. with an open hand

Ben shrugged again. 'Find him, I suppose.'

'Then what?'

'Kill him, probably.'

1101

'What does he actually do?'
'I'm sorry?'
'God ... I mean, what does he actually do?'
'Well,' the vicar says slowly ... 'it's not really a question of what God
does –'   5
'It is for me.'

Kevin Brooks
Killing God *(2009)*

After I'd let Ben go back to his flat, I found myself – somewhat surprisingly – heading up the stairs instead of going back down. I didn't
consciously know what I was doing – I mean, I hadn't planned it or
anything – but I knew that the stairs led up to the roof[1], so I suppose   10
there must have been something inside me that knew what I was
doing.

Two flights up from the thirtieth floor, I came to a padlocked[2]
iron gate. It was a full-length gate, reaching from the floor to the
ceiling, and it was secured with a thick metal chain and a huge   15
brass[3] padlock[4]. I took hold of the padlock in my hand, closed my
eyes, and let the energy flow through my arm, into my hand ... and
after a moment or two, I felt things moving inside the lock. I heard
soft clicks, the sound of metal on metal ... and suddenly the padlock
sprung open.   20

I unwound[5] the metal chain and went through the gate, closing
and locking it behind me, and now I was faced with a steel-reinforced[6] door marked *NO UNAUTHORIZED ACCESS*. It was locked,
of course, but not with a padlock this time – there was a keypad[7] on
the wall. I'd need to know the security code to get in.   25

---

1 roof: top of a building   **2** padlock sth.: lock sth. with a padlock   **3** brass:
Messing   **4** padlock: *Vorhängeschloss*   **5** unwind sth.: undo sth. that has been
wrapped around an object   **6** reinforced: made stronger   **7** keypad: *Zahlentas-
tatur*

Not a problem.

I hacked into the council's database, searched through a load of security stuff relating to all the towers in Crow Town, and found the four-digit code. I keyed it in – 4514 – and opened the door. It led
5 through into a little room filled with all kinds of stuff – cupboards and shelves, pipes[1] and cables, heating controls. A metal ladder was fixed to the far wall, leading up to a padlocked hatchway[2]. I climbed the ladder, iUnlocked the padlock, then pushed open the hatchway and stepped out onto the roof.

10 The rain had stopped now, but as I closed the hatchway behind me and walked over to the edge of the roof, I could feel the cold night air breezing through my hair. I was thirty floors up, high above the ground, and I could see for miles and miles all around. Lights were glowing everywhere – lights of houses and flats, streetlights,
15 traffic lights, streams of headlights[3] – and away in the distance I could see the bright lights of London – office blocks, luxury tower blocks, streets and streets full of shops and theatres and traffic …

I'd seen it all before, of course. I saw it every day, every time I looked out of the window. But the view from up here – outside, on
20 the roof – somehow felt different. It felt wider, clearer, bigger … more *real*.

I sat down, cross-legged[4], on the very edge of the roof.

In the darkness below, Crow Town was getting ready for the night. Groups of kids were hanging around – on street corners, in
25 the shadows of the towers, at the side of the road – and others were cruising the estate in cars or on bikes. Faint sounds drifted up into the night – shouting, dogs barking, cars, music – but up here, high above the rest of the world, everything was quiet.

I gazed up into the starless night, and all I could see was a bound-
30 less[5] world of darkness and emptiness … but I knew it *wasn't* empty. The sky, the atmosphere, the air, the night … the whole world was alive with radio waves. They were everywhere, all around me, all

---

1 pipe: tube   **2** hatchway: *Hühnerleiter*   **3** headlight: large light at the front of a vehicle   **4** cross-legged: *im Schneidersitz*   **5** boundless: infinite; with no end

the time – TV signals, radio signals, mobile-phone signals ... WiFi, microwaves, VHF[1], UHF[2] ... electromagnetic waves.

They were everywhere.

And although I couldn't see them, I could sense them. I could connect to them. I knew them.   5

I closed my eyes and tuned in, at random, to a mobile-phone call: *... it's just past the post office in the High Street,* someone was saying. *You go past the post office and there's a pub, and it's just there.*

What pub? someone else said. *The George?*

No, that's on the other side of the road ...   10

And another random conversation: *... why not? You said it'd be all right if I didn't do it again.*

Yeah, I know, but you did ...

And another: *... take the fucker down, innit[3]? He can't fucking do that, I'll fucking pop[4] the fucker ...*   15

Someone, somewhere, was sending an email to someone called Sheila, telling her that unless she sorted herself out, she wouldn't be seeing her baby again. Someone else was emailing someone in Coventry from a supposedly untraceable[5] email address ... but I could trace it. *the bio[6] is easy, it read. anyone can make a germ[7] bottle and*   20
drop it in the water supply and kill 100000. the martyr would commit[8]
himself leaving no trace of j involvement.

And someone else was texting a really obnoxious[9] message to a girl called Andrea, saying all kinds of nasty things to her ...

And on the web ... God, there was a whole *world* on the web. A   25
world of so many things – good things, bad things, dull things, mad things – it was just like the real world. Just as wonderful, just as beautiful ... but also just as vile and sick and heart-breaking.

I stopped scanning.

---

1 VHF: very high frequency (used for radio)   **2** UHF: ultra-high frequency (used for TV)   **3** innit (slang): isn't it   **4** pop sb. (infml.): kill sb.   **5** untraceable: unable to be found   **6** bio: biology   **7** germ: seed; microorganism   **8** commit yourself: (here) kill yourself   **9** obnoxious: horrible

There was too much going on out there, too much bad stuff, and I didn't know how to cope with[1] it all. All the stuff I knew, but didn't *want* to know ... everything that wasn't good, that wasn't right, that wasn't fair ... I knew it. And I *knew* that I could do something about
5 it ... or, at least, I *could* do something about *some* of it. I mean, for example, I could find out who'd sent that obnoxious text message to Andrea, and why they'd sent it, and I *could* find out where they lived, and I *could* go and see them and try to persuade them that sending obnoxious text messages is a really shitty thing to do. But then
10 what about the millions of other bad things, the things that are a million times worse than sending shitty text messages – the abuses, the terrors, the sick things that people do to each other – the things that I wouldn't be able to do anything about because I'd be too busy trying to help Andrea, like terrorist plots to kill 100,000 people with
15 a biological weapon ...?

What was I supposed to do about them?

I couldn't do *every*thing, could I?

I wasn't God.

I was just a kid ...

20 And besides, I told myself, at least you're trying to do something about some of the bad stuff, the stuff that happened to Lucy ... and that's a hell of a lot more than God ever does. I mean, God does fuck all, doesn't he? He just sits there, luxuriating[2] in all his superpowers, demanding to be adored ...

25 It was 22:42:44 now, and the night was getting colder. I pulled up my hood and turned on my iSkin, warming myself with the electric heat ... and as I gazed down over the edge of the roof, I wondered what I looked like from down below – a softly glowing figure, sitting cross-legged on the top of a tower block ...

30 Like some kind of weird hooded Buddha ...

A skinny, glow-in-the-dark iBuddha.

---

1 cope with sth.: deal successfully with sth. difficult   **2** luxuriate in sth.: *sich in etw. sonnen*

Or maybe an iGargoyle[1].

I closed my eyes again and opened up my MySpace page. There were two messages from aGirl: an old one that said *have you gone?*, and a slightly longer one from five minutes ago. The longer one read:

sorry if i asked too many questions and scared you off or anything, but 5
i was just curious about you. you have to admit you're kind of unusual!
it's ok, i mean you don't have to tell me anything and i won't ask you
anything else if that's what you want. but please don't go away. we can
just talk about things.
aGirl 10

Lucy was online right now, so I wrote back:

no, it's ok, you didn't scare me away, i was just a bit busy for a while.
i'm back now. so, anyway, how are you feeling? you don't sound quite so
down as before. are things a bit better for you?

hello again, iBoy. i'm glad you're back. no, things aren't really any better 15
for me, and i don't think they ever will be, but i don't feel quite so empty
and dead anymore. i think talking helps. talking to you, of course. and
i have a friend called tom who is very kind and listens to me. can i ask
you something about the boy you nearly pushed out of the window? do
you know what he did to me? 20

yes.

were you really going to push him out?

i don't know. what would you think if i said yes?

i don't know. part of me thinks he deserves to die, but another part says
no, that's wrong. do you know what i mean? 25

---

1 gargoyle ['gɑːgɔɪl]: ugly stone figure

yes, i know exactly what you mean.

let's talk about something else.

ok. what?

where are you?

5 *i'm sitting in the sky.*

yeah, right. what's your real name?

i'll answer that if you tell me about tom.

what about him?

is he your boyfriend?

10 *no! i've known tom for ever, we grew up together. he's not my boyfriend, he's just a very close friend. i like him a lot, and i think he likes me, but i don't think he likes me in that kind of way. he just cares for me. i care for him too. he's quite a sad person, i think.*

maybe he likes you more than you think. maybe he just can't work out
15 *how to tell you.*

maybe ... what's it to you anyway?

nothing. i was just curious.

all right, so i answered your question. now you answer mine. what's your real name?

20 *you already know it. see you later.*
iBoy

I closed myself down, opened my eyes, and carefully got to my feet. I took one last look over the edge of the roof, then I turned round and went home.

1110

If I was damned of body and soul,
I know whose prayers would make me whole ...

Rudyard Kipling[1]
'Mother O' Mine' *(1891)*

Gram was in the front room watching TV when I got back. She looked as pale and worn out as ever – her face too thin, her eyes too
5 tired, her skin too old for her age. She wasn't that old – fifty-four last year – but her life hadn't been easy, and the years of struggle had taken their toll[2].

She'd spent most of her life on her own.

In the same way that I'd never known my father, my mum had
10 never known hers. Her father had been just as unknown and absent as mine. So Gram had spent most of her adult life as either a single mother, bringing up her daughter on her own, or as a single grand-mother, bringing up her dead daughter's son on her own. And she'd done all this while trying to make a living from something which
15 neither paid very much nor gave her any enjoyment at all.

So I guess she was entitled[3] to look a bit worn out.

'Hey, Gram,' I said, sitting down next to her. 'What are you watching?'

'Just the news,' she said, muting the TV and smiling at me. 'How's
20 Lucy?'

'OK, I think ... well, kind of OK, you know ...'

Gram nodded. 'And how about you? How's your head?'

'Fine ... no problems.'

'Are you sure?'

25 'Yeah ...'

'No dizziness or anything?'

---

1 Rudyard Kipling: (1865–1936) English writer of short stories, novels, poems, most famous as the author of *The Jungle Book*   **2** take your toll: (here) have a bad effect   **3** be entitled to do sth.: have a right to do sth.

'No.'

(Just a world of wonder and madness.)

'Any headaches?'

'No.'

(Just phone calls and emails and texts and websites ...) 5

'You haven't been hearing any voices then?'

I looked at Gram. 'What?'

She smiled. 'It was a joke, Tommy.'

'Right ...' I said. 'Yeah, very funny.'

She put her hand on my knee. 'I'm glad you're OK, love. Really. I 10
was so worried when you were in hospital ... I thought, you know ...
I thought ...' Her voice trailed off[1], and she wiped a tear from her eye.
And I knew she was thinking about my mum, her daughter ... and I
could barely imagine how hard it must have been for Gram when I
was in hospital, and she was sitting with me, not knowing whether 15
I was going to live or die ...

I put my arms round her neck and rested my head against hers.
'Don't worry, Gram,' I said quietly. 'I'm going to be absolutely fine, I
promise.'

She smiled at me through her tears. 'You'd better be.' 20

'Trust me ... I plan on living until I'm at *least* as old as you.'

She laughed, playfully slapping my leg, and then she took a tissue from her pocket and started wiping the tears from her face.
There were so many things I wanted to ask her then, things about
my mum, but I knew that she wouldn't want to talk about it. Gram 25
never liked talking about what happened to Mum. It was just too
much for her, I think. Too painful, too sad ... and I understood that.
Or, at least, I tried to. I mean, it was mostly OK ... I didn't really mind
too much. And most of the time I didn't *need* to know any more than
the facts – i.e. that my mum had been killed by a hit-and-run[2] driver 30
when I was six months old.

That was enough for me ... Most of the time.

---

1 trail off: (here) become gradually quieter and then stop   **2** hit-and-run: *Fahrer-
flucht*

But sometimes, like now, it *wasn't* enough.

Sometimes, for whatever reason, I felt the need to know more.

'Gram?' I said quietly.

She sniffed. 'Yes, love?'

5 'Was it the same ... with Mum, I mean?'

She looked at me. 'The same as what?'

'Did she ...? I mean, was she in hospital for a while, like me ... or was it, you know ... was it quick?'

Gram held my gaze[1] for a second or two, then she turned away 10 and looked down at the floor, and for a while I thought she wasn't going to answer me. But then, after sniffing and wiping her nose again, she said, very softly, 'She didn't suffer, Tommy. It was very quick. She wouldn't have known what was happening.'

'She died straight away?'

15 Gram nodded. 'Georgie ... your mum, she was going to work ... she got off the bus, started to cross the road, and a car just came out of nowhere and ran her over. She died instantly. She wouldn't have known anything, thank God ...'

Gram's voice was broken with tears, and I could see her hands 20 trembling.

'I'm sorry, Gram,' I said. 'I didn't mean to –'

'No, no,' she said quickly, looking up at me. 'It's all right, Tommy ... it's just me ... it's just ...'

She couldn't finish what she was trying to say. She smiled sadly 25 at me, wiped another tear from her eye, and as she gently took my head in her arms and gave me a long hard hug[2], I could feel her shaking all over.

Later on, after we'd had something to eat and watched the end of a late-night film together, I asked Gram if she'd ever heard of Howard 30 Ellman, the man that Davey had told me about, the one they called the Devil. Her reaction was totally unexpected. At first, she didn't do

---

1 hold sb.'s gaze: make eye contact with sb. for a long time   **2** give sb. a hug: put your arms around sb.

anything – she just sat there, completely still, staring straight ahead … not even breathing – and for a moment or two I wondered if she'd actually heard me. But then, very slowly, she turned to face me, and I could tell by the look on her face that she had heard me. She looked stunned[1] – totally and utterly stunned. It was as if she'd just heard the worst news in the world.

'What's the matter, Gram?' I said. 'Are you all right?'

'What?' she whispered.

'Are you OK? You look terrible.'

She blinked, frowning at me. 'Sorry …? I was … uh … I was miles away. What did you say?'

'Howard Ellman … I asked you if you'd ever heard of him.'

'Why …? I mean …' She cleared her throat. 'Why do you want to know about him?'

I shrugged. 'No reason, really. It's just that Davey told me he's the one who runs[2] all the local gangs … well, he doesn't actually run them, but he pretty much pulls all the strings[3].'

Gram nodded, smiling tightly at me. 'So why are you asking me about him? Why would I know someone like that?'

'I don't know … I just thought you might have heard of him, that's all. I mean, you've lived here a long time, you know a lot of people, you hear a lot of stuff …' I shrugged again. 'It doesn't matter, Gram. It's not important or anything. I was only asking …'

She nodded again, her eyes fixed on mine, and for a moment I thought that she was going to tell me something, that she wanted to tell me something … something really important …

But I was wrong.

She just glanced at her watch and said, 'You'd better get off to bed now. It's getting late. I'll see you in the morning, all right?'

*

---

1 stunned: (here) amazed; astonished   **2** run sth.: manage sth.; be in charge of sth.   **3** pull the strings: control events or people

A few minutes later, as I was closing the door to my room, I looked back down the hallway and saw Gram sitting bolt upright[1] on the settee. She was perfectly still, her hands laid flat on her knees, and she was staring straight ahead, staring at nothing. She looked as if she'd just seen a ghost.

1 bolt upright: very straight

1111

The Devil tempts that he may ruin and destroy ...

Saint Ambrose[1]

If you know where to look, and how to look, and if you have the ability to look wherever you want, the cyberworld is full of places where you can find out all kinds of things about all kinds of people. There's the National DNA[2] database, the General Register Office (births, marriages, deaths), the national identity register, the NHS[3] detailed care record, the Driver and Vehicle Licensing Agency[4], the Identity and Passport Service ... the list is almost endless. And if, like me, you can hack into these places without any problems at all, it's not too difficult to find out all there is to find out about someone.

But that night, as I lay on my bed in the darkness, searching through every search engine and hacking into every database that I could think of, I couldn't find any current information about Howard Ellman at all. At least, not the Howard Ellman that I was looking for. There was a Howard Ellman in San Francisco, a lawyer; another one who'd written a book called *Arthroscopic[5] Shoulder Surgery*; another one who was 'an accomplished[6] designer and licensed[7] architect' ... there were hundreds of Howard Ellmans all over the world, but none of them had any links with Crow Town. I scanned millions of emails, billions of texts ... nothing. I checked telephone records, council tax, gas and electric, the electoral roll[8], bank and credit card accounts ... nothing. Even when I tried different spellings of the surname – Elman, Elmann, Ellmann – I still couldn't find anything.

Nothing current[9], anyway.

---

1 Saint Ambrose: (337–397) Archbishop of Milan   **2** DNA: chemical in cells of animals and plants that carries genetic information   **3** NHS: National Health Service; *staatliche Krankenkasse*   **4** Driver and Vehicle Licensing Agency: *Führerschein- und Kraftfahrzeugzulassungsstelle*   **5** arthroscopic: related to a certain method of surgery on joints   **6** accomplished: talented; expert   **7** licensed: *zugelassen*   **8** electoral roll: *Wählerverzeichnis*   **9** current: (here) recent

It was only when I hacked into the Police National Computer (PNC) and accessed Ellman's criminal record that I finally found out something about him. The information wasn't exactly up to date – the last entry was dated July 2002 – and it wasn't particularly
5 detailed either ... but it was detailed enough to convince me that Davey hadn't been exaggerating when he'd said that Ellman was 'a *really* bad guy'.

Name: *Howard Ellman*
Ethnic type: *Caucasian*[1]
10 **Height:** *1.85m*
Weight: *83kg*
Eye colour: *Pale blue*
Distinguishing[2] **marks/tattoos, etc.:** *None*
Address: *Unknown*
15 **Date of birth**: *10/01/1971*
Place of birth: *Addington House, Crow Lane Estate, London SE15 6CD*
Occupation: *Unknown*
Registered vehicles: *None*
20 **Convictions**[3]/**Cautions**[4]/**Arrests:** *Arrested Sept 1989, March 1990, April 1992 for aggravated assault*[5], *all charges subsequently dropped. Arrested March 1993, Oct 1995, July 2002 for sexual assault*[6], *complaints*[7] *withdrawn, charges dropped*[8].
Additional comments: *Suspected involvement in funding/ import/*
25 *supply*[9] *Class A drugs, as yet unproved. Also possible involvement in organized prostitution, arms smuggling, illegal money lending, people trafficking*[10]. *Known variously as 'The Devil', 'Hellman', or 'HellMan',*

---

1 Caucasian: member of a race of people with pale skin   2 distinguishing: individual; unique   3 conviction: (here) fact of having been found guilty of a crime in court   4 caution: (here) warning   5 aggravated assault: *schwere Körperverletzung*   6 sexual assault: *sexuelle Nötigung*   7 complaint: claim that sb. has done sth. illegal   8 drop charges: *Anschuldigungen fallen lassen*   9 supply: (here) selling   10 people trafficking: smuggling people illegally into a country

this individual is highly dangerous and should be approached with extreme caution at all times.

There were no photographs in the PNC file, but there was a link to the computerized custody records[1] at Southwark Borough Police Station, and when I accessed these I found a JPEG image of a mug shot[2] of Ellman which I guessed had been taken when he was in his early twenties. It showed an angular[3]-faced man with a thin mouth, a shaved head, and staring, soulless eyes. There was no trace of emotion in his face: no fear, no anger ... nothing at all. It was the face of a man who could take a life as easily as taking a breath.

In the darkness of my room, in the light of the darkness inside my head, I studied that face for a long time. And the more I stared at it, the more I wondered how much Howard Ellman had to answer for, how much pain he'd caused, how much suffering ...

I remembered Lucy's anguished words: *They ruined me, Tom. They totally fucking ruined me.*

And I wondered how many other lives Ellman was responsible for ruining.

It was 03:34:42 when I left the flat and quietly closed the door. I tiptoed[4] down the corridor, paused to put my shoes back on, then carried on down to the lift.

My iSkin was glowing.

My hood was up.

My heart was stone cold.

---

1 custody records: *Häftlingsregister*   **2** mug shot: picture of an arrested person's face taken by the police   **3** angular: thin and bony   **4** tiptoe (v): (here) walk quietly, trying not to be noticed

10000

*'The end may justify the means as long as there is something that justi-
fies the end.'*

Leon Trotsky

The estate was unusually quiet as I crossed the stretch of grass
between Compton House and Crow Lane. The towers, the streets,
5 the empty black sky ... everything was bathed in that dead-of-night
silence that makes you feel like you're the only living thing in the
world.

The night was cold. My breath was misting[1] in the air, my hands
were icy, and I could feel the soft crunch[2] of frost beneath my feet.
10 But I didn't care.

Hot or cold ... it didn't make any difference to me. I was in that
state of controlled brutality again – in control of being out of control
– and the only thing I could feel was an overriding and irresistible
sense of purpose. Get there, find them, find him ... get there, find
15 them, find him ... get there, find them, find him ...

I walked on – across the grass, through the gate in the railings,
along Crow Lane – and as I approached the entrance to Baldwin
House, the sound of voices began to break through the darkened
silence. Raised voices, laughter, the soft rumble[3] of an idling[4] car
20 engine ...

I couldn't see anyone yet, but it wasn't hard to guess what kind of
people the voices belonged to – I mean, they were hanging around
Baldwin House at quarter to four in the morning ... they weren't
going to be choir boys, were they?

25 I heard the car engine revving, a dog snarling, another shout of
laughter, and then – as I turned off Crow Lane and into the square
around Baldwin House – I saw them: half a dozen or so gang kids, all
in hoods and caps, hanging around a VW Golf in front of the tower-

---

1 mist: (here) turn into fog or steam   **2** crunch: cracking noise made when sth.
breaks   **3** rumble (n): low, continuous sound   **4** idling: (here) *leerlaufen*

block doors. A skinny Doberman[1] and a Staff[2] with a spiked collar[3] were skulking[4] around the car, neither of them on leads[5]. A couple of the kids were quite young – twelve or thirteen – but most of them were about seventeen or eighteen.

I didn't recognize any of them.   5

The dogs noticed me first, and as they both started running at me, barking and snarling[6], the kids all stopped whatever it was they'd been doing and turned to see what was happening. They saw me walking towards them – my skin shimmering, my hooded face a pale glow of radiating light – and they watched, confused, as the 10 two dogs suddenly sensed something about me that scared the shit out of them. They skidded to a halt[7] about two metres away from me, their ears flat, their tails between their legs, and then they both sloped off[8], whimpering[9] quietly.

'What the fuck?' one of the kids said.   15

As I carried on walking towards them, a tall black guy with a knife scar on his cheek moved towards me, blocking my way.

'Hey, fuck,' he said. 'What you –?'

I didn't stop walking. I just raised my arm, placed my hand on his chest, and blew him off his feet with a surge of electricity. As he 20 lay on the ground – his hooded top smoking, his legs twitching – I stepped to the side and laid my hand on the bonnet[10] of the Golf. The engine was still running. The kid in the driver's seat was staring open-mouthed at the tall black guy on the ground. I pressed my palm against the metal of the Golf's bonnet, twitched something in 25 my hand – some kind of nerve or something – and shot a spark of electricity through the bonnet. Nothing happened. I tried it again, and this time the spark ignited[11]. A burst of orange flashed under the bonnet, something went *WOOF!* and suddenly the car was in flames.

---

1 Doberman: very big and dangerous dog   **2** Staff: Staffordshire bull terrier
3 spiked collar: *Stachelhalsband*   **4** skulk: *herumstreunen*   **5** lead: leash or chain for a dog   **6** snarl: make a noise like an angry dog   **7** skid to a halt: stop suddenly   **8** slope off: walk away slowly and unconfidently   **9** whimper: *winseln*
10 bonnet: (here) metal part on the front of a car, covering the engine   **11** ignite: burn; explode

As the kid in the car scrambled out[1], and the others quickly backed away, I left them to it and carried on into Baldwin House.

Troy O'Neil's flat was at the end of the corridor on the ground floor. Number Six. The front door – which was made of reinforced steel –
5   was guarded by a full-length metal grill[2]. I'm sure I could have got through both the door and the grill if I'd wanted to, but instead I just reached up and rang the bell. Light was showing through the edges of the door, so I guessed that O'Neil was in, and probably awake.
I waited.
10   Orange light from the blazing[3] Golf was flickering through the corridor window, and I could already smell the faint stink of burning rubber in the air. From inside the flat, I heard a ringtone (2Pac's[4] 'Hit 'Em Up'). Inside my head, I tuned in and listened to the call. It was from one of the kids outside, calling O'Neil.
15   *Yeah?* he answered.
You know that weird kid? The one done your brother? He's here, man. He just fucking –
Yeah, I know.
O'Neil ended the call.
20   I scanned the flat for other mobiles.
There were three of them, including O'Neil's.
I rang his number.
He answered, angrily. 'I just fucking told you –'
'Are you going to open your door, or what?' I said.
25   'Eh?'
'I'm not waiting all night.'
'Who's this?'
I saw an eye appear at the peep-hole[5] in his door. I waved at him.
'Is that you?' he said.
30   'Is what who?'
'What?'

---

1 scramble out: get out quickly   **2** grill: rows of thin metal pieces   **3** blaze (v): burn   **4** 2Pac: (1971–1996) American rapper   **5** peep-hole: *Türspion*

I sighed. 'Just open the door, for Christ's sake.'

There was a pause then. I heard the phone's mouthpiece[1] being covered, muffled voices, and then the metallic clack of locks being unbolted[2]. After a few seconds, the inner door opened, and through the metal grill I saw Troy O'Neil standing in the doorway. He looked a lot like his brother – mixed race, tall, with dead-looking eyes – and I guessed he was in his early twenties. He had his phone in one hand, and the other hand was stuffed in his pocket.

'What d'you want?' he said to me.

I smiled at him. 'Can I come in?'

He frowned at me. 'What the fucking hell are you?'

'Let me in, and I'll tell you.'

He stared at me for a moment, and then – with a shake of his head and a suck of his teeth[3] – he unbolted the metal grill, swung it open, and moved to one side to let me in. His right hand, I noticed, never left his pocket, and as I stepped through into the hallway, I wondered what kind of weapon he was holding. A gun or a knife? And I started wondering then if my electric force field was strong enough to protect me from a bullet ... but I quickly realized that it was too late to start worrying about that.

As O'Neil pulled a pistol from his pocket, a figure moved out from behind the door and put a knife to my throat, and at the same time a door on my right opened and a fat Korean guy came out holding a rifle[4] in his hands.

O'Neil grinned at me, waggling the pistol in my face.

'You're not so fucking smart now, are you, eh?' I stared at him.

The Korean guy – who was only about five feet tall, but seriously fat – was just standing there, pointing the rifle at my head, and who-ever it was with the knife at my neck was making a weird kind of panting[5] noise in his throat. I couldn't see him without turning my

---

1 mouthpiece: part of the phone into which you speak   **2** unbolt sth.: unlock sth.   **3** suck your teeth: (here) make an annoyed sound with your tongue against your teeth   **4** rifle: large gun   **5** pant: *schnaufen; keuchen*

head, and I couldn't turn my head without the blade of the knife digging into my skin, but I guessed it was probably Jermaine Adebajo.

I kept my eyes on Troy O'Neil.

He moved closer, peering curiously into the shimmering whirl
5 of my face.

'What *is* all that?' he said. 'I mean, how do you *do* it?'

'Do you want to see what else I can do?' I said quietly. Before he could answer, I tensed[1] myself – from within – and then, almost immediately, I released the tension and blasted[2] out a surge of
10 power. It came out from all over my body, a blinding white *CRACK!* that knocked O'Neil and Adebajo and the Korean guy off their feet and sent them all flying. O'Neil and Adebajo smashed back against the hallway walls and crumpled to the floor, and the fat Korean guy was blown back through the bedroom door.

15 I waited a while, just looking down at their smouldering bodies, but none of them got up. The barrel[3] of O'Neil's pistol had fused[4] together at the end, and the blade of Adebajo's knife had buckled[5] and melted.

I leaned down and checked O'Neil for a pulse.

20 He was still alive.

So was Adebajo.

I closed the front door, locked and bolted it, then went into the bedroom and checked the Korean. He looked a bit worse than the other two – blood coming out of his ears and his nose – but he was
25 still breathing too. The rifle was still gripped in his badly burned hands.

I went over to the window and looked out to see what was happening with the burning Golf. Nothing was happening. There was no one around. The car was just burning away, thick black smoke
30 drifting up into the night, and nobody gave a shit about it.

---

1 tense sth. (v): *etw.anspannen* **2** blast: explode **3** barrel: *Gewehrlauf* **4** fuse [fjuːz]: join because of heat **5** buckle: become crushed

I went into the kitchen and found a roll of insulation tape[1] in a cupboard under the sink, then I went back out into the hallway and got to work.

After I'd tied up Adebajo and the Korean guy and locked them in the bedroom, I dragged[2] O'Neil into the front room, tied him to a chair, and then I just sat down and waited for him to wake up. 5

The room was filled with all kinds of drug stuff – bags of white powder, bags of brown powder, blocks of cannabis, carrier bags[3] full of grass[4] and pills. There was clingfilm[5] for wrapping, scales[6] for measuring, spoons and knives and syringes[7] and foil[8] ... piles of cash 10 all over the place.

I wondered how much money they made here. And how come, if they had so much money, they didn't find somewhere nicer to live? I mean, even by Crow Town's standards, this place was a hovel[9]. Dirty walls, dirty windows, greasy[10] carpets, foul air ... the whole place 15 stank.

O'Neil groaned.

I looked at him and saw that his eyes were beginning to open. I waited a few seconds, just enough time to let him recognize me, then I leaned forward and spoke to him. 20

'Howard Ellman,' I said. 'Where does he live?'

'Munh?'

'Howard Ellman,' I repeated. 'I want to know where he lives.'

O'Neil just looked at me for a moment, not quite sure what was happening, and then – suddenly realizing that he was tied to the 25 chair – he started struggling. Wriggling[11] and writhing[12], cursing and spitting, trying to break free ...

---

1 insulation tape: *Isolierband*   **2** drag sb./sth.: pull sb./sth.   **3** carrier bag: plastic shopping bag   **4** grass (infml.): cannabis   **5** clingfilm: transparent plastic wrap that sticks to surfaces   **6** scales: instrument for weighing things   **7** syringe [sɪˈrɪndʒ]: needle for injections   **8** foil: thin metal sheet used for wrapping **9** hovel: small, dirty building   **10** greasy: slippery and fatty   **11** wriggle: twist and turn with quick movements   **12** writhe [raɪð]: move around in pain

I touched his knee, giving him a short sharp shock. He yelped, stopped struggling, and stared wide-eyed at me.

'Listen to me,' I said to him. 'Just tell me where Ellman is, and I'll let you go.'

5 'What?'

'Ellman. I just want to know where he is.'

O'Neil shook his head. 'Never heard of him. Now you'd better fucking –'

I zapped him on the knee again, harder this time, and once he'd
10 stopped screaming and shaking, I said to him, 'I'm going to keep doing this until you tell me what I want to know, and each time it's going to get worse. Do you understand?'

He glared at me, trying to show me that he wasn't scared, but I could see the fear in his eyes. I reached out towards him again. He
15 jerked away, rocking from side to side in the chair.

'Just tell me where he lives,' I said.

He shook his head. 'I don't know ... nobody knows.'

'I don't believe you.'

'I don't *know*,' he spat. 'It's the fucking *truth*.'

20 I didn't *want* to believe him, but the way he said it – the passion in his voice, the fear in his eyes – I was pretty sure that he was telling me the truth.

'What about a phone number?' I said.

O'Neil shook his head. 'He doesn't give it out.'

25 'So how do you get in touch with him?'

'You don't ... if he wants something, he gets in touch with you.'

'How?'

'He'll send someone ... or maybe get someone to call. One of the kids, usually.'

30 'What kids?'

He shrugged. 'The kids, you know ... the little fuckers who want to be Crows.' O'Neil looked at me, a bit more confident again now. 'You'll never find him, you know. Not unless he wants you to. And then you'll wish you hadn't.'

35 'Yeah?'

He grinned. 'You've got no fucking idea what you're dealing with. When he finds out what you've done tonight –'

'How's he going to find out?'

O'Neil hesitated for a moment, then he just shook his head and shrugged again. I raised my arm and moved my hand towards his face, palm first. I let the energy flow into my skin, feeling it pulse and burn, and I could see my hand glowing with heat as I moved it ever closer to O'Neil's face. His skin was reddening now, his forehead dripping sweat, and he was starting to panic – straining backwards[1], arching[2] his neck, trying to get away from the heat.

'No!' he screamed. 'No! Please, don't … *please* …'

I paused, my hand a few centimetres from his face.

'How's Ellman going to find out I've been here?'

'He won't … I won't say *nothing*,' O'Neil spluttered[3]. 'I *promise* … I won't tell him –'

'Yeah, you will. I *want* you to tell him.'

I heard the siren[4] then. Faint at first, but rapidly getting louder. I got up, went over to the window and looked out. Beyond the burning Golf, I could see the flashing blue lights of two police cars speeding down Crow Lane. I knew that no one in Crow Town would have called them, especially about something as trivial[5] as a car on fire, so I guessed that they were on their way to somewhere else. But, just to be on the safe side, I tuned in to the police radio frequency and simultaneously hacked into the communications system at Southwark Borough Police Station to find out what was going on. And it took me less than a second to discover that I was wrong – they *weren't* going somewhere else, they were answering a call from a passing motorist about a burning car outside Baldwin House.

'Shit,' I muttered as the two patrol cars turned off Crow Lane and started racing down towards the square with their lights and sirens blazing.

---

1 strain backwards: pull or stretch backwards   **2** arch (v): bend; curve
3 splutter: make a spitting sound   **4** siren: sound of a police car   **5** trivial: not important

I knew that I was probably safe enough staying where I was, that the police were probably just going to check out the Golf, make sure it was nothing more serious than just another burning car ... then they'd probably just wait for the fire service to arrive and leave it to
5 them. The last thing the local police would want to do at four o'clock in the morning was to go round Baldwin House knocking on doors, waking people up.

So, yeah, I was *probably* safe enough staying where I was ...

In this stinking flat.

10 Surrounded by drugs and guns ...

And drug dealers ...

Electrocuted drug dealers.

One of whom was tied to a chair.

No, I realized, *probably* wasn't good enough. If by any chance the
15 police did find me in here, I'd have a lot of explaining to do.

I had to get out.

I moved away from the window and quickly went over to a table in the middle of the room. It was piled high with clear polythene[1] bags filled with what I assumed was heroin and cocaine. I picked up
20 two bags of each and put them in my pockets.

'Hey!' O'Neil called out. 'What the fuck are you doing?' Ignoring him, I reached out and picked up a small black automatic pistol from the table and put it in my pocket with the drugs.

Car doors were slamming outside now.

25 Police radios were squawking[2].

It was time to go.

I turned to O'Neil and said, 'Tell Ellman I'm coming for him.' And before he could answer, I walked out of the room, went down the hallway, opened the flat door and left.

30 As I headed down the corridor towards the fire exit, I called 999 from my iBrain.

---

1 polythene: *Kunststoff*   **2** squawk: make a harsh sound like a bird

It was answered almost immediately. 'Emergency. Which service?'

'There's been a murder,' I said, pushing open the fire door. '6 Baldwin House, Crow Lane –'

'Just a moment, sir. I need to know –'   5

'It's on the ground floor, 6 Baldwin House,' I repeated. 'The Crow Lane Estate. Someone's been shot.'

I ended the call.

The fire door opened out to the rear of Baldwin House – a concreted jungle of weeds[1] and wheelie bins[2] and broken syringes and dog shit   10
– and from there I headed south, away from the tower, scrabbling down a shallow grass slope[3] to a makeshift[4] path that led me along a dip[5] in the fields all the way back to Compton.

By the time I'd crept back into the flat and tiptoed down to my room, the police officers dealing with the burning car had been alerted   15
to a possible fatal shooting at 6 Baldwin House, and they'd sealed off[6] the area and were waiting for additional officers and an armed[7] response team[8] to arrive.

As I got undressed and climbed into bed, tired and drained, I wondered what the police would think when they finally smashed   20
O'Neil's door down and found that there was no dead body, no murder, just three slightly battered[9] drug dealers, all of them tied up, and a flat full of drugs and guns.

Would the cops care that they'd been wrongly tipped off[10]?

Did I care whether they cared or not?   25

I didn't know.

I didn't care.

---

1 weed: (here) wild plant   **2** wheelie bin: dustbin on wheels   **3** slope: *Abhang*
4 makeshift: not permanent   **5** dip: (here) low ground   **6** seal sth. off: prevent
people from entering sth.   **7** armed: with guns   **8** response team: police team
called in to deal with serious, dangerous situations   **9** battered: injured   **10** tip
sb. off (infml.): warn sb. about illegal action

I lay down in the darkness and tried to think about myself and
what I'd just done – my violence, my rage, my savagery[1] – but I
couldn't seem to find anything in me to feel anything about it. I knew
that I'd done it, and I knew that there was a reason for doing it, and
5 I knew that – despite the validity of that reason – I still ought to be
feeling some degree of shame or remorse[2] or guilt or something …
   But there was nothing there.
   No feelings at all.
   Just me and the darkness …
10 And iBoy.
   Us.
   Me.
   And i.
   We lay there in the silence and thought about ourselves. What
15 were we doing? And why? What were we trying to achieve? And
how? What was our goal[3], our plan, our aim, our desire?
   What was our *reason*?

The heart has reasons that reason cannot know.

Blaise Pascal[4] (1623–1662)
http://www.quotationspage.com/quote/1893.html

It was 04:48:07.
20 We closed our eyes and waited for the sun to rise.

---

1 savagery [ˈsævɪdʒri]: cruel and violent behavior 2 remorse: bad feeling about
sth. you did wrong 3 goal: (here) aim; purpose 4 Blaise Pascal: French philosopher

10001

A fugue[1] state is a dissociative memory disorder[2] characterized by an altered[3] state of consciousness and an interruption of, or dissociation from, fundamental aspects of an individual's everyday life, such as personal identity and personal history. Often triggered[4] by a traumatic[5] life event, the fugue state is usually short-lived (hours to days), but can 5 *last months or longer. Dissociative fugue usually involves unplanned travel or wandering, and is sometimes accompanied by the establishment of a new identity.*

I know what happened over the next ten days or so. I know what I did, and at the time I was perfectly aware of what I was doing. I was 10 there. It was me. I was myself. I knew exactly what I was doing and why.

But now, when I try to recall[6] those days (without the aid of my iMemories), all I can remember are bits of things that don't seem to belong to me. 15

Fragments.

Snapshots.

Disconnected[7] moments.

... in my room, sitting on the floor beneath the open window. Rays[8] of afternoon sunlight are streaming in over my head, lighting up 20 motes[9] of dust. My eyes are closed and my iBrain is buzzing with a thousand million words. It's listening to phone calls. Reading emails and texts. It's scanning Crow Town's underworld for anything it can use, anything incriminating ... names, places, times ... anything at all. 25

It's a god, seeing everything, hearing everything.

1 fugue [fjuːg]: psychological description of a state where memories are partially forgotten **2** memory disorder: *Gedächtnisstörung* **3** altered: changed
4 trigger sth.: start sth. **5** traumatic [trɔːˈmætɪk]: shocking; disturbing
6 recall: remember **7** disconnected: *unzusammenhängend* **8** ray: (here) line of light **9** mote: small particle

It's not me.

It's an automatic police informant[1] application: searching the airwaves, scanning the words, finding the bad guys – the thieves, the dealers, the muggers[2], the runners[3], the soldiers, the shooters, the shotters. It finds them all and automatically grasses them up to the cops.

All of them.

The application in my iBrain doesn't care who they are or what they're doing – it targets[4] them all: eleven-year-old wannabe[5] gangsters, delivering drugs and guns on bikes; gang kids – Crows and FGH – fighting each other just for the hell of it[6]; and the older kids, the ones who used to be wannabe gangsters, the ones who used to be gang kids and muggers, the ones who now spend their lives doing what they've always wanted to do – dealing drugs, making lots of money, living the life ... beating and killing and shooting and raping ...

The application in my iBrain doesn't care why they do it. It doesn't care if they're poor or uneducated or bored or addicted or troubled or lonely or if they simply don't know any better. It doesn't care if they come from dysfunctional[7] families, if they have no one to guide them, no one to help them, no one to show them what life can really be like. Nor does it care if they're none of these things, if they're rich and well educated and they do know better.

It doesn't give a shit.

But it doesn't dislike them or blame them for anything either. It doesn't make judgements. They're just things to it.

It has no feelings.

It just does what it does.

And I just let it. Because I'm just doing what I feel I have to do: for Lucy, for Gram, for me ...

---

1 police informant: *Polizeispitzel*   **2** mugger: person who attacks others in the street and steals their money   **3** runner: (here) person who sells drugs in small quantities   **4** target sb.: aim at sb.   **5** wannabe sth. (infml.): (here) person who wants to be sth.   **6** for the hell of it: just for fun   **7** dysfunctional: (here) with lots of problems

For all of us.
I'm just doing it.

... iBoy at night, patrolling Crow Town with his iSkin on. He's breaking up drug deals and fights. He's burning cars and melting bikes and scaring the shit out of little Crow kids. He's mugging the muggers, stealing their guns and their knives and machetes[1] ...

... creeping into a flat in Eden. It's 03:15:44. A drunken mother is asleep in her bedroom, her two boys sleeping in the room next door. I move through the darkness, a palely glowing ghost, and I find a rucksack in the kitchen. I take Troy O'Neil's automatic pistol from my pocket, wipe it clean, and slip it into the rucksack.

Walking away from Eden House, I call the police.

'Flat 3, fourteenth floor, Eden House,' I tell them. 'Yusef Hashim. He's got a gun. It's in a rucksack in the kitchen.'

... and other flats, other nights, other sounds of sleeping. The pale ghost plants a bag of heroin here, a bag of cocaine there ...

... timeless iHours spent working on the computer in my head: sending false texts and photoshopped pictures, posting videos on YouTube, spreading malicious[2] lies in chat rooms and blogs. Lies become rumours, rumours become facts: Nathan Craig's a grass; Big and Little Jones are terrorists; DeWayne Firman has posted a Facebook message calling Howard Ellman a queer[3] ...

... Sunday 11 April, 19:47:51. Tom Harvey is sitting on a bench at the kids' playground, thinking about Lucy. He hasn't been to see her for nearly a week ... and he knows that it's iBoy's fault. iBoy and Lucy have got into a routine of sending each other at least a couple of MySpace messages every day, and Tom keeps forgetting that *he's* not

---

1 machete [mə'ʃeti]: big knife   **2** malicious: mean; evil   **3** queer: (here) offensive word for a gay person

iBoy, that *he's* not talking to Lucy all the time, but that she doesn't know that. So she'll be wondering why Tom hasn't been round to see her.

Or maybe she won't …?

5 It's really confusing for Tom, flipping from iBoy to himself all the time, trying to remember who he is and what he's supposed to be. And when he thinks about Lucy, it almost feels as if he's cheating on her with himself … or maybe it's the other way round? As if she's cheating on him, but she doesn't know that the other boy she's see-
10 ing (or at least talking to on MySpace) isn't actually another boy at all, it's Tom.

He closes his eyes.

There's a new MySpace message from Lucy.

hey iBoy, have you heard about all this stuff going on round the estate?

15 *what stuff?*

you know, all the gang kids getting arrested and beating each other up and everything. it's been in the local papers. all the dealers are get-ting busted[1] *and there's rumours about some kind of superman going round kicking the shit out of the crows and fgh. do you know anything*
20 *about that?*

me? why would i know anything?

yeah, ha ha! why would you? btw[2] *ben told me nathan craig got beaten up yesterday. it was pretty bad, apparently. some of the older kids found out he grassed up a deal and they beat the crap out of him.*

25 *yeah?*

---

1 get busted (infml.): (here) be arrested by the police   **2** btw: by the way

yeah. and the cops caught yusef hashim with a gun. and dewayne's disappeared, no one's seen him for days. funny. it seems like everyone who had anything to do with what happened to me is running into a lot of bad luck.

really? must be some kind of karma[1].   5

yeah, well ... just be careful, OK?
aGirl xxx

i'm always careful. see you later.
iBoy xxx

It's just then, after iBoy has logged out of MySpace, that Tom looks   10
up and sees a bunch of FGH kids walking along Crow Lane. He
knows they're FGH because most of them are wearing Adidas gear,
which is an FGH thing. There's about eight or nine of them, and
they're heading south, away from the playground and down towards
Fitzroy House. Most of them are around sixteen or seventeen, but   15
there's a few younger kids too, and there's also a couple of girls.
   It's the girls that draw Tom's attention.
   They're both about thirteen or fourteen, both dressed in short
skirts and skinny little tops, and they're both trying very hard to look
as if they're enjoying themselves – shouting and laughing, messing   20
around[2] with the boys – but there's something about them that
doesn't seem right to Tom. He isn't sure what it is, but he can sense
something wrong about the whole situation. The way the boys are
looking at the girls, their eyes cold and empty, even when they're
smiling at them. The way the girls keep looking at each other, look-   25
ing for reassurance[3], as if to say – this is just a bit of fun, isn't it? And
the way some of the boys keep looking back down the road, while

---

1 karma: (here) when bad things happen to people who have behaved badly
2 mess around: act in a silly way   **3** reassurance: support; encouragement

the others are keeping the girls surrounded, blocking[1] them in as they walk along ...

It just isn't right.

Tom gets up off the bench and starts following them. He doesn't 5 recognize any of them, and he's pretty sure that none of them know him – they're FGH, and the FGH don't usually mix with the kids from his end of the estate – so he doesn't bother turning on his iSkin for the moment, he just follows them as Tom.

Nothing much happens for a while.

10 The boys and girls keep walking, and as they get closer to Fitz-roy House, the girls start getting a bit edgier[2]. They try stopping and turning back once or twice, but the boys just grab them and pull them along. They're all still laughing and smiling, even the girls, and Tom starts to wonder if he's made a mistake. Maybe it is just a bit of 15 fun? Maybe the girls are just playing hard to get[3], and the boys are just playing hard? *Or maybe,* he suddenly thinks to himself, *maybe it's just you. Maybe you're just a hopeless and pathetic romantic who believes in treating people with respect. I mean, you were brought up by a single grandmother who writes old-fashioned love stories for a liv-* 20 *ing, weren't you? And she did used to read you those love stories at bedtime ...*

Christ, he thinks, pausing for a moment, is that what this is all about? The whole knight in shining armour/ superhero thing – putting wrongs to right, saving fair maidens, slaying evil dragons – is 25 that what I'm trying to do?

It isn't a comfortable thought. In fact, it's kind of embarrassing. And for a moment or two, Tom seriously considers turning round and going home. Why not? Just forget about the two girls, they'll be perfectly all right. Just forget about them. Forget about everything. 30 Just turn round, go home, and spend the night with Gram watching crappy[4] TV.

---

1 block sb. in: not allow sb. to move freely   **2** edgy: (here) nervous   **3** play hard to get (infml.): *sich zieren*   **4** crappy (infml.): of very bad quality

And he's just about to do it, he's just about to turn round and start heading back home …

But then he sees the van.

It's a white Transit, and it's speeding down Crow Lane from the north side. As it approaches the FGH boys, four of them suddenly grab the two girls and start dragging them over to the side of the road. At first, the girls just think that the boys are messing around again – just playing rough, having a laugh. So the girls screech and curse a bit, and they struggle and fight against the four boys, but they don't do it with any real sense of urgency. They still think that it's all just a game. But Tom knows that this isn't a game any more. He can tell by the sudden change in the boys' demeanour[1] – their mouths set tight, their movements quick and furtive[2], their eyes darting[3] around, looking for witnesses[4] …

Tom's iSkin is on now, and he's already running when the van pulls up at the side of the road. The back doors swing open and two more FGH kids jump out of the back and start helping the others as they bundle[5] the girls towards the van. The girls have finally realized that this is deadly serious. They're being dragged into the back of a van by a dozen or so young men, and no one's laughing any more. They're panicking now, trying desperately to get away. They're kicking and writhing, squirming[6] and struggling, trying to scream for help … but two of the boys have their hands clamped[7] hard over the girls' mouths.

iBoy is running as fast as he can now, his feet slapping hard on the pavement. He's about ten metres away from the van when one of the younger boys spots him and yells out a warning to the others. They stop and turn to face iBoy, and when they see what's running towards them – some kind of fluorescent mutant[8] in a hood – they all just stand there for a second or two, too stunned to do anything.

---

1 demeanour [dɪˈmiːnə] (fml.): behavior   **2** furtive: *verstohlen*   **3** dart: move quickly and suddenly   **4** witness: person who sees a crime and can give evidence   **5** bundle sb.: push sb.   **6** squirm: make small twisting movements **7** clamp: hold   **8** mutant: living thing with a change in its genetic structure

But then one of them – a really nasty-looking guy with deathly[1] white skin – barks out[2], 'You lot get 'em in the van! The rest of you get this fucker!' And the sound of his voice spurs[3] the rest of them into action.

5 Six of them turn and form a line behind the nasty-looking guy, blocking iBoy's way to the Transit, while the others carry on man-handling[4] the girls into the back of the van. iBoy knows that he doesn't have much time now. If they get the girls into the van and drive them away, it'll be too late.

10 So he doesn't waste any time thinking about what to do, he just does it.

He keeps running, heading straight for Nasty, and just as he reaches him, just as Nasty is pulling a knife from his pocket, iBoy screams like a madman and throws himself at Nasty and blasts out
15 a huge burst of power. An ear-splitting *CRACK!* rips[5] through the air, and just for a moment everything disappears in a blinding flash of electric blue. The power and heat of it is so intense that it singes[6] the hairs on the back of iBoy's arm.

He stands there for a few seconds, waiting for the after-image of
20 the flash to fade from his eyes, and then he looks down at the bodies on the ground. There are seven of them. Some are still semi-con-scious – groaning weakly, coughing and spluttering, rubbing their eyes – but most of them have been knocked out. They're just lying there on the ground, perfectly still. Nasty has taken the worst of it.
25 He's lying on his back, about two metres away from iBoy, his face burned red and his eyebrows smouldering. His nylon hooded jacket has melted into his skin, and he's bleeding from his ears, nose, and mouth.

iBoy looks up at the others – the ones at the back of the van with
30 the girls. The two nearest to him are on their knees, holding their

---

1 deathly: looking dead   **2** bark sth. out: say sth. with a loud, aggressive voice
3 spur sb. into sth.: encourage sb. to do sth.   **4** manhandle sb.: lift sb. who
doesn't want you to touch them   **5** rip: (here) move quickly and violently
6 singe sth. [sɪndʒ]: burn sth. slightly

heads in their hands. Another two are already running off towards Fitzroy House. And the last two are still holding the girls, but not making any effort to move.

'Let them go,' iBoy says.

They let them go, and the two girls stagger towards iBoy.   5

'You OK?' he asks them.

'Yeah ... I think so,' one of them says, gazing around at the bodies on the ground.

The other one doesn't say anything. She's crying.

'Where do you live?' iBoy asks the first one.   10

'Disraeli.'

'Are you all right to get back on your own?'

She nods.

'Sure?'

'Yeah ...'   15

'Go on then,' he says gently. 'You'll be all right now. Just go straight home, OK?'

She looks at him, hesitating, and iBoy can see the questions in her eyes – who are you? what are you? what have you done to these boys?   20

'I think you'd better get your friend home now,' he says to her. 'She's pretty shaken up[1].'

'Yeah ... yeah, of course,' the first girl says, moving over to her friend and putting her arm round her. She says a few comforting words to her, wipes some tears from her face, then turns back to   25 iBoy. 'Thanks,' she says, smiling. 'I mean, whoever you are ... thanks.'

He smiles back at her.

She nods, turns round, and the two of them start walking back.

iBoy watches them for a moment, making sure that they're both OK, then he turns back to the two boys at the van. They haven't   30 moved.

'You waiting for something?' he says to them.

They shake their heads.

---

1 shaken up: upset and frightened

'Well, fuck off then.'

They run.

iBoy walks round to the front of the van. The driver's door is open, but there's no one inside. Whoever was driving must have run
off at some point. iBoy leans in, pulls the keys from the ignition, and drops them to the ground. He puts his finger to the ignition and gives it a quick zap. The dashboard glows, the engine roars, then sparks start crackling[1] and popping under the bonnet. Within a few seconds, smoke starts rising from the engine and flickering blue
flames begin to appear.

iBoy shuts the van door, spits on the ground, and walks away.

He doesn't look back.

---

1 crackle: make a burning sound

10010

CROW LANE 'SUPERHERO'

Local police are concerned[1] at reports of a so-called 'superhero' fighting crime on the Crow Lane Estate. Witnesses have described several incidents[2] in which a mysterious figure has been seen taking the law into his own hands in the vicinity[3] of the notorious[4] high-rise estate. 5
One resident, who wishes to remain anonymous, told the Southwark Gazette how she was recently saved from a mugging by 'a masked man in a hooded costume'.

'He just appeared out of nowhere,' she said. 'There was a bright blue flash, which blinded me for a moment, and the next thing I knew the 10
muggers were running away.' When asked if the police condoned[5] the 'superhero's' deeds, a spokesman said, 'While the intentions of this individual may be good, the way he's going about them is wrong. The police strongly advise[6] against all forms of vigilante action[7], and we would urge this person, whoever he is, to let the police do their job.' 15

http://www.southwarkgazette.co.uk/home/090410/local

When I woke up on Monday, I felt as if I'd just woken up from a very long and intensely vivid dream. It was a really strange sensation, because I knew that the things in my head that felt like dream memories were actually real memories – memories of the last ten 20
days. And I knew that I hadn't been dreaming for the last ten days …

But I still felt as if I had.

I lay in bed for a while, trying not to think about it, trying instead to just feel perfectly normal … but it's hard not to think about something when you're lying in your bed, just staring at the ceiling, 25
acutely[8] aware that you're trying not to think about something …

---

1 be concerned at sth.: be worried about sth.   **2** incident: event   **3** vicinity:
neighbourhood   **4** notorious: famous for being bad   **5** condone sth.: tolerate
sth.   **6** advise: warn; recommend   **7** vigilante action [ˌvɪdʒɪˈlænti]: *Selbstjustiz*
8 acutely: highly; extremely

and it's even harder to feel perfectly normal when it's perfectly obvious you're not.

So, in the end, I gave up.

I got out of bed, took a shower, and got dressed.

5 When I went into the kitchen, Gram was sitting at the table, holding what looked like a bank statement in her hand.

'Morning, Gram,' I said, sitting down. 'How are you –?'

'What's this, Tommy?' she said sternly.

'Sorry?'

10 'This,' she repeated, waving the bank statement at me.

'Fifteen thousand pounds, deposited anonymously into my bank account on the thirty-first of March.' She glared at me. 'Do you know anything about it?'

'Me?' I said, feigning[1] surprise and indignation[2], while at the
15 same time mentally[3] kicking myself for forgetting all about it. 'I don't know what you're talking about.'

'I'm talking about this,' she said, passing me the statement and pointing out the deposit. 'Look ... see? Someone's put fifteen thousand pounds into my account.'

20 I smiled at her. 'Well, that's good, isn't it?'

She glared at me again. 'Not if I don't know who it's from or what it's for.'

I shrugged. 'Does it matter? I mean, money's money –'

'Yes, Tommy. It *matters*.'

25 I looked at the bank statement. 'Maybe it's from your publishers,' I suggested. 'A bonus or something ...'

'A *bonus?*'

I shrugged again. 'I don't know, do I?'

'It's not from my publishers, I've already checked. And the bank
30 can't tell me who it's from either.' She looked at me. 'Are you *sure* you don't know anything about it?'

---

1 feign sth.: pretend sth.   **2** indignation: anger   **3** do sth. mentally: do sth. in your imagination

'Why would I?'

Gram hesitated.

'What?' I asked her.

She looked me in the eye. 'You'd tell me if you were in any trouble, wouldn't you?'

'Trouble? What kind of trouble?'

She shook her head. 'Look, I know how hard it is ... around here, I mean. It's so easy to get mixed up[1] with the wrong kind of people –'

'Gram,' I said, genuinely confused. 'I really don't know what you're talking about.'

She reached across and put her hand on mine. 'Just tell me the truth, Tommy. Did you get that money from somewhere and put it into my account?'

I shook my head. 'Where would I get that kind of money from?'

'Where does *anyone* get that kind of money from in Crow Town?'

I stared at her. 'You think I'm selling drugs?'

She shrugged. 'I'm just asking –'

'Christ, Gram,' I said angrily. 'You really think I'd do that?'

'So, you're not?'

'No,' I sighed. 'I'm not.'

'And you're not thieving[2] or anything either?'

I sighed again. 'How can you even think anything like that?'

'I'm sorry, Tommy,' she said. 'But it happens ... it can happen to anyone. Even someone like you. I mean, I *know* that you're a really good person, a really decent[3] person, and I *know* that you love me ... but I also know that *because* you love me, you'd do almost anything to help me. And if you knew that I was in financial difficulties ... well, you might do the wrong thing to help me. Do you understand what I'm saying?'

'Yeah ... yeah, of course I understand. But I haven't done anything wrong.'

---

1 get mixed up with sb. (infml.): be involved with sb.   **2** thieve (infml.): steal
3 decent: honest; good

Gram looked at me, nodding her head, then she picked up some letters from the table. 'This,' she said, showing me one of the letters, 'this is confirmation[1] that my council tax arrears[2] have been paid off[3]'. She put down the letter and showed me another one. 'And this
5   is a statement showing that I'm all up to date on the rent payments'. She looked at me. 'Did you know I owed[4] all this money?'

'No,' I lied.

'Did you pay these bills?'

'No.'

10   'Are you sure?' I nodded.

Gram sighed. 'Well, someone did, and it wasn't me'.

I couldn't think of anything to say then, so I just sat there, trying to look innocent.

Gram sat there in silence for a while too, just looking at the let-
15   ters, occasionally shaking her head ... and then, eventually, she said to me, 'Look, Tommy, I'm sorry if I've upset you or offended you or anything, but I had to ask. It's not that I don't trust you, because I do. And even if you were mixed up in something illegal, I'd still love you'. She smiled at me. 'And, besides, you *have* been acting a bit strangely
20   recently'.

'What do you mean?'

'Well, you're either in your room all day, doing God knows what, or you're out all the time ... especially at night. And you seem so preoccupied[5], so worried about things, and you look really tired –'

25   'I've been studying'.

'Studying?'

I nodded. 'In my room ... at the library. I've missed a lot of school, so I thought I'd try to catch up a bit on my own'.

Gram frowned at me. 'Really?'

30   'Yeah ... what's the matter? Don't you believe me?'

---

1 confirmation: statement or note showing that sth. is correct   **2** arrears [ə'rɪəz]: debts that are not paid back at the right time   **3** pay sth. off: pay all the money owed for sth.   **4** owe sth.: have to pay sth. back   **5** preoccupied: thinking about lots of things

'Well, I'm not saying that I don't *believe* you –'

'Test me.'

'Sorry?'

'You can test me. I'll *prove* to you that I've been studying.'

She laughed. 'You don't have to *prove* anything.' 5

'No, go on,' I insisted. 'I've been studying British post-war history. Ask me a question.'

'Don't be silly, Tommy. I believe you.'

'Post-war history,' I repeated. '1946 to the present day.'

'I'm not going to –' 10

'Any question you like.'

'All right,' Gram sighed wearily. 'If you insist –'

'I do.'

'OK, let me think a minute ...'

While she thought of a question to ask, I went inside my head 15
and opened up Google. I was feeling kind of sick of myself now, wishing that I'd never got into this whole stupid lying thing ... wishing
that I could just tell Gram the truth. The whole truth. But I couldn't,
could I? How could I tell her the truth? How could I tell her that her
grandson wasn't normal any more, that he had extraordinary pow- 20
ers, and that he was using those powers to seek out[1] and punish
the world of people who'd beaten and raped Lucy – the world of the
O'Neil brothers, the world of Paul Adebajo and DeWayne Firman,
the world of Jayden Carroll and Yusef Hashim and Carl Patrick ... the
world of Howard Ellman. 25

How could I tell Gram that?

And how could I tell her that her grandson was afraid that he
was not only beginning to lose any sense of compassion[2] he may
once have had, but also that he was beginning to lose his mind ...?

How *could* I tell her that? 30

I couldn't, could I?

I just couldn't.

And I hated myself for that.

---

1 seek sb. out: look for and find sb. with great effort   **2** compassion: kindness

'Who was the Prime Minister in 1956?'

I looked at Gram. 'What?'

'You asked me to ask you a question,' she said. 'About post-war history.'

5   'Oh, right ... yeah.'

'That's my question – who was the Prime Minister in 1956?'

I looked inside my head at a website of British Prime Ministers:

... Eden replaced Winston Churchill as prime minister in April, 1955. Later that year he attended a summit conference at Geneva with the
10 *heads of government of the USA, France and the Soviet Union ...*

'Sir Anthony Eden,' I said.

Gram looked surprised. 'Very good.'

'He was succeeded by Harold Macmillan on 10 January 1957,' I added, 'and he spent his later years writing his memoirs, which were
15 published in three volumes between 1960 and 1965. He also wrote an account of his war experiences called *Another World* which was published in 1976.' I smiled at Gram. 'He died in 1977.'

Gram shook her head in disbelief. 'You really *have* been studying.'

'I told you, didn't I.'

20 'I'm impressed.'

You shouldn't be, I thought.

'Yeah, well,' I said, looking at the clock on the wall. 'I'll be off to the library again now, if that's OK.' I grinned at her. 'Get some more studying done.'

25 She nodded. 'I'd better get to work myself.'

'How's it going?' I asked her.

'Not bad ...' She smiled at me. 'Maybe my publishers might even give me a *bonus* for this one.'

'Very funny,' I said.

30 She grinned.

I got to my feet. 'I'll see you later, OK?'

'OK ... but don't stay out too long. You are looking tired.'

'I'll be back in a few hours,' I said, heading for the door. 'I promise.'

'And Tommy?'

I stopped and looked back at her. 'Yeah?'

'I'm sorry … sorry I doubted you.'

'You don't have to apologize, Gram. Honestly … it's OK.'

'I know. But I *am* sorry.'   5

I felt too bad to say anything else to her. What could I say? She was apologizing for not trusting me, but she had every *right* to mistrust me. I was lying to her. I was betraying her trust[1]. I should have been apologizing to *her* …

I very nearly told her the truth then.   10

I was so sick of lying to her and making her feel bad about herself that I'd just about decided that no matter how difficult it would be, I simply had to tell her the truth.

But then, just as the words were beginning to form in my mind, the doorbell rang, and before I had a chance to say anything, Gram 15 had got up from the table, gone out into the hallway and opened the door.

'Oh, it's you,' I heard her say. 'What do you want?'

'Good morning, Ms Harvey,' a vaguely familiar male voice said. 'Is your grandson in?'   20

It took me a moment to recognize the two men who followed Gram into the kitchen. The last time I'd seen them was at the hospital, when I'd only just woken up from another dream that wasn't a dream, the non-dream about Lucy – *A 15-year-old girl has been raped by a gang of youths on the Crow Lane Estate* – which, understandably, 25 had left me feeling slightly confused at the time. Now, though, as the two men stood there looking down at me, smiling their supposedly comforting smiles, I wasn't too confused to remember them. The tall fair-haired one – the one with the tobacco-stained teeth and bad skin – was DS Johnson. The other one – who was so unremarkable- 30 looking that he didn't really look like anything – was DC Webster.

'Hi, Tom,' Johnson said. 'How's it going?'

---

1 betray sb.'s trust: lie to sb. who believes you because they like you

I looked at Gram.

She half-shrugged. 'Sorry, Tommy ... they want to ask you some questions. You can say no, if you like.'

I looked at Johnson. 'Questions about what?'

Without asking, he sat down at the table. 'So, Tom,' he said over-casually[1], 'how's the head? That's a nice-looking scar you've got there.' He smiled, winking[2] at me. 'The girls are going to like that, you know.'

'Yeah,' I said. 'They all love a guy who's had brain surgery, don't they?'

His smile faded, and for a moment he looked a little embarrassed. He sniffed and cleared his throat. 'All right,' he said. 'Well, the reason we're here ...' He looked up at Gram. 'Would you like to sit down, Ms Harvey?'

'Nice of you to ask,' Gram said, 'but I'm all right here, thanks.' She looked at Webster, who was standing behind Johnson with an open notebook and a pencil in his hands. 'Would *you* like to sit down?' she asked him.

'No,' he mumbled, glancing at Johnson. 'No ... I'm all right here, thanks.'

Johnson frowned at Gram, not sure if she was being sarcastic or not, then – after a quick glance at DC Webster – he turned back to me. 'So, as I was saying, the reason we're here ... well, basically, we'd just like to ask you a few more questions about your accident –'

'It wasn't an accident.'

'No, I know ... well, actually, we don't know if it was an accident or not, but we're assuming it wasn't. We think the mobile phone that caused your injuries was probably thrown out of the window during the attack on Lucy and Ben Walker.'

'Yeah,' I said. 'It was.'

'You saw it being thrown?'

---

1 over-casually: too relaxed   **2** wink at sb.: close one eye quickly to show you are sharing a joke with sb.

I nodded. 'I couldn't see who threw it, though. The sun was in my eyes. All I could see was someone at the window.'

'Can you describe them?'

I shook my head. 'They were too far away.'

'Was it a man? A boy?'   5

'A boy, I think.'

'Black or white?'

'I don't know.'

'How old?'

'I couldn't tell.'   10

'OK ... but you definitely saw a boy at the window, and you think he threw the phone at you?'

'Yeah.'

'What time was this?'

'Ten to four.'   15

Johnson raised his eyebrows. 'That's very precise.'

I shrugged. 'I remember looking at my watch just before it happened. It was ten to four.'

He nodded. 'Right. So you'd just left school?'

'Yeah.'   20

'And where were you going?'

'Home.'

'Right ... you were coming here?'

'Yeah.'

'OK.' He glanced at Webster, who was busy writing down every-   25
thing I was saying, then he looked back at me. 'Were you aware at the time that an assault was taking place in a flat on the thirtieth floor?'

'No.'

'You didn't find out until later?'   30

'That's right.'

'Remind me again how you found out about the attack.'

'It was when I was in the hospital,' I told him, looking him in the eye. 'I was in the toilets and someone had left an old copy of the

Southwark Gazette behind. There was a report about the attack in the paper.'

Johnson nodded, looking at Webster. Webster flicked through his notebook, checked something, then nodded back at Johnson.

5 Johnson turned back to me.

I said to him, 'Have you caught them yet?'

'Sorry?'

'The kids who raped Lucy – have you caught them?'

He hesitated for a moment, then said, 'I'm afraid we can't reveal[1]
10 any details of an ongoing[2] investigation –'

'You haven't caught them.'

He sighed. 'We're doing our best, Tom. But with these kinds of cases ... well, it's difficult. You know what it's like around here. People won't talk to us. They're afraid.' He looked at me. 'You know Lucy
15 Walker, don't you?'

I nodded. 'We grew up together.'

'I believe you've been visiting her recently. Is that right?'

'Who told you that?'

'How is she?' he asked, ignoring my question. 'How's she holding
20 up?[3]'

I shrugged. 'As well as can be expected, I suppose.'

He looked at me. 'Has she talked to you about what happened?'

I glanced at Gram, not sure what to say.

She turned to Johnson. 'Whatever Lucy and Tommy have talked
25 about, that's their business. Now, have you got any more questions? Because if you haven't –'

'I'll let you know when we're finished, Ms Harvey,' Johnson said, turning away from her and looking at me. 'I'd like to ask both of you about a series of incidents that have occurred in Crow Lane over the
30 last week or so.'

'Incidents?' Gram said. 'What incidents?'

---

1 reveal sth.: make sth. known   **2** ongoing: continuing; happening now   **3** How are you holding up?: (here) How are you?

Johnson kept looking at me. 'A number of the individuals that we suspect were either involved in or have information about the attack on Lucy and Ben have recently been subjected to varying degrees of assault.'

I frowned at him. 'Can you say that again, please? In English.' 5

Johnson stared at me. 'You heard me. Someone's been taking the law into their own hands. Do you know anything about that?'

'No,' I said.

He looked at Gram. 'Ms Harvey?'

She looked puzzled. 'You mean someone's been attacking the 10 boys you suspect of raping Lucy?'

'Well, it's not quite as simple as that ... and because no one's talking to us, most of the information we have is sketchy[1] to say the least. But we think that someone, probably someone local, might be targeting anyone who has connections with the local street gangs.' 15 He looked at me again. 'So we think it's probably someone who has some kind of grudge[2] against the gangs ... someone seeking revenge, perhaps.'

I laughed quietly. 'What? And you think that might be me or Gram?' 20

Johnson shrugged. 'I'm just asking if you know anything, Tom. That's all. You're friends with Lucy ... maybe you know someone who might want to punish the people who hurt her. Can you think of anyone like that?'

I slowly shook my head. 'No ... no one springs to mind. And, 25 anyway, how would they know who did it? I mean, how would they know who to punish?'

Johnson shrugged again. 'Your guess is as good as mine. Maybe Lucy told them, or Ben ... or maybe they witnessed the attack themselves but are too afraid to tell us. Or perhaps they've just been lis- 30 tening to all the rumours going round the estate. Or maybe they

---

1 sketchy: vague; not precise   **2** grudge against sb..: feeling of anger or dislike towards sb.

don't know who did it, they're just assuming it was the Crows or the FGH –'

'This is all getting a bit ridiculous, isn't it?' sighed Gram.

Johnson looked at her. 'You think so?'

5 'I do.'

'Why's that, Ms Harvey?'

'Well, firstly ...' Gram held up a finger. 'The gangs are *always* fighting each other. It's what gangs do – they beat each other up, stab each other, shoot each other. They've been doing it for hundreds of 10 years, and they'll carry on doing it until they're all gone ... which won't ever happen. So I don't see why you suddenly seem to think that any of it *means* anything. I also don't understand why you're wasting your time looking for someone who's attacking the bad guys, when you still haven't found the bad guys yourself.'

15 'Well ...' Johnson started to explain, 'as I said before –'

'And secondly,' Gram said, holding up another finger, 'even if there is some kind of vigilante out there, which I very much doubt, I don't see what that's got to do with us.' She stared at Johnson. 'Do I *look* like I'm capable of terrorizing gangsters?'

20 Johnson shook his head. 'I never said –'

'Do you think Tommy's capable? I mean, he's still recovering from a life-threatening operation, for God's sake. And even if he wasn't ... well, look at him. He couldn't terrorize a fly.' She smiled at me. 'No offence[1], Tommy.'

25 'None taken.'

She turned back to Johnson. 'So, unless you've got anything more relevant –'

'A number of youths were assaulted near Fitzroy House yesterday evening,' he said sternly, turning to me. 'Two of them are still in 30 hospital, one in a critical condition. During the assault, a van was set on fire. We have a witness who saw you at the children's playground minutes before the attack. Do you deny[2] being there?'

'No, I was there.'

---

1 no offence (infml.): not meant to insult   **2** deny sth.: say that sth. is not true

'Hold on, Tommy,' Gram said. She turned to Johnson. 'What's going on here? You can't just –'

'Yes, I can, Ms Harvey. Your grandson is a potential[1] witness to a very serious assault that may end up as a murder case. I need to ask him some questions. All right?'   5

Gram looked at me.

'It's OK, Gram,' I said.

'Are you sure?' I nodded.

Johnson said to me, 'Did you see what happened?'

'No.'   10

He tutted[2] and sighed. 'Come *on*, Tom ... you were there. I *know* you were there –'

'Yeah, I was at the playground,' I said. 'But I wasn't there for long, and I didn't see anything happening at Fitzroy House. I didn't go anywhere near there.'   15

'You didn't *see* anything?' he said incredulously. 'How could you *not* see anything? There were about a dozen FGH boys, and six of them got knocked out, so there must have been a hell of a fight ... and even if you didn't see that, a van was set on fire, for God's sake. Do you seriously expect me to believe that you didn't *see* anything?'   20

'I didn't,' I said simply.

He took a deep breath and let it out slowly. 'Can I see your hands, please?'

'What?'

'Your hands ... please. I'd like to see the palms of your hands.'   25

'What for?' asked Gram.

Johnson sighed. 'Please, Ms Harvey. We can either do this here, with no fuss, no bother, or I can take Tom down to the station with me. It won't take a minute. All I'm trying to do is eliminate[3] Tom from our enquiries[4]. Believe me – if he's innocent, he's got nothing   30 to worry about.'

Gram looked at me. 'It's up to you, Tommy.'

---

1 potential: possible   **2** tut [tʌt]: make a disapproving sound   **3** eliminate sb.: exclude sb.   **4** enquiry: official procedure to find out information

I shrugged and said, 'I don't mind,' and I held out my hands, palms up, for Johnson to study. He didn't touch them, he just leaned down and looked very closely at them. I think he even sniffed them too.

'Turn them over, please,' he said.

5 I turned them over.

'What happened there,' he said, pointing to a patch of singed[1] hair on the back of my forearm.

'Nothing,' I shrugged. 'I got too close to the fire, that's all.'

'What fire?' Johnson said, glancing over at the radiator[2] against

10 the wall.

'At Lucy's,' I told him. 'She's got an electric heater. I sat too close to it.'

He stared at me for a few moments, disbelief showing in his eyes, and then eventually he said, 'Thank you ... now, just a few more

15 questions, and I promise that's it. All right?'

'Yeah, fine.'

'Right ...' he said, hesitating slightly. 'I need to know ... and I realize that this might sound a bit strange ... but I need to know if you own a mask.'

20 'A mask?' I said. 'What do you mean?'

'A mask ... you know, a toy mask. Superman, SpiderMan, anything like that.'

Gram laughed. 'Is that who you're looking for – Superman?' She laughed again. 'You really think Superman's going to move from

25 Gotham City[3] to Crow Town?'

'That's Batman, Gram,' I said.

'What?'

'It's Batman who lives in Gotham City, not Superman.'

'Really? Where does Superman live then?'

30 'I don't know.'

'Metropolis,' Webster said.

We all turned and looked at him.

---

1 singed: burnt   **2** radiator: room heater   **3** Gotham City: fictional American
city from *Batman*

Blushing[1] slightly, he said, 'Superman lives in Metropolis.'

'For Christ's sake,' Johnson sighed. 'Can we please stay in the real world?' He looked at me. 'If you could just answer the question, Tom.'

'Sorry,' I said, grinning. 'What was it again?'

'Do you own any masks?'   5

'No,' I said, still grinning. 'I don't own any masks.'

'Would you mind if DC Webster took a quick look in your room?'

'No, no problem.' I turned to point out which way my bedroom was, but Webster was already leaving the kitchen. Gram started to follow him, but Webster said, 'It's all right, Mrs H. I'll be fine, thanks,'   10
and he shut the kitchen door behind him.

As I turned back to Johnson, he said to me, 'Do you know what a Taser is, Tom?'

In an instant, an article from a website flashed into my head:

A Taser is an electroshock weapon that uses electrical current to dis-   15
rupt[2] voluntary[3] control of muscles. Its manufacturer, Taser Inter-
national, calls the effects 'neuro-muscular incapacitation[4]' and the
device's mechanism 'Electro-Muscular Disruption (EMD) technology'.
Someone struck by a Taser experiences stimulation of his or her sen-
sory nerves and motor nerves[5] resulting in strong involuntary muscle   20
contractions ...

'Yeah,' I said. 'I know what a Taser is.'

'Have you ever seen one?'

'No.'

'Do you know anyone who owns one or has seen one?'   25

'No.'

'Aren't you curious as to why I'm asking you about Tasers?'

'Not really, no.'

---

1 blush: become red in the face   **2** disrupt sth.: disturb sth.; interrupt sth.
3 voluntary: done willingly   **4** incapacitation: inability to work or move properly
5 sensory ... motory nerves: *sensorisches und motorisches Nervensystem*

He didn't say anything for a while then, he just sat back in the chair, crossed his arms, and looked at me. I could almost hear his mind ticking over[1] – trying to work out if I was telling him the truth or not ... and if not, why not? Did I know anything? Was I too scared to tell him anything? What could I be hiding? *Who* could I be hiding?

I emptied my head, emptied my eyes, and stared back at him.

After a minute or two, DC Webster came back in. Johnson glanced at him, his eyebrows raised expectantly[2], but Webster shook his head – letting him know that he hadn't found any superhero masks or Tasers in my room.

Johnson sighed and got to his feet. 'All right, Tom. That'll be all for now, thank you. We'll be in touch.'

'I'm sorry you had to go through all that,' Gram said to me after she'd shown Johnson and Webster out. 'Are you OK? You look really tired.'

'Yeah ... I am a bit. I've got a really bad headache coming on too. Maybe I'll go back to bed for a while.'

'I think you should. Have you still got enough of those painkillers[3] that Mr Kirby gave you?'

I nodded.

She said, 'OK, well, take two of those and get yourself off to bed. Do you want me to get you anything else before you go?'

'No, thanks,' I said, getting up.

She gave me a hug and a kiss on top of my head, and I went down the hall to my room.

I really *was* tired. All those questions, trying to work out how to answer them ... and all that lying to Gram too. It had really drained all the energy out of me.

That and the last ten days.

---

1 tick over: keep working slowly   **2** expectantly: expecting certain results
3 painkiller: pain-reducing drug

As I lay down on the bed, there were so many things I had to think about, so many unknowns – what did Johnson know? what did he suspect? what did he think? what was I going to do about the money in Gram's bank account? what was I going to do about *every*thing? – and I knew that I ought to start looking for answers right now. I ought to start scanning and hacking and searching and listening ...

But as soon as I closed my eyes, that was it.

I fell into a deep and dreamless sleep.

10011

No one saves us but ourselves. No one can and no one may. We ourselves must walk the path.

Buddha

I must have been even more tired than I thought, because when I finally woke up – and when my brain finally started working prop-
5 erly – I realized that it was 11:26:54 on the following day.

I'd slept for almost twenty-four hours.

And I *still* felt tired.

But at least the dreaminess/non-dreaminess seemed to have gone.

10 In fact, I almost felt quite normal.

Almost ...

In the kitchen there was a note from Gram telling me that she'd gone shopping, and that she'd be back in a couple of hours.

I made myself some toast.

15 Ate it.

Made some more (I was *really* hungry).

Ate it.

Drank some orange juice.

Put the TV on ...

20 Turned it off.

Then, not quite ready to do anything else yet, I went over to the window and gazed down at the estate below. It was a really nice day – clear and bright, birds singing, the sun shining – and even the estate itself seemed a lot less depressing than usual.

25 There wasn't much going on down there. A bunch of little kids were messing around on bikes, an old man in a battered old hat was walking his dog, and across Crow Lane a group of young girls were dancing and singing along to their iPods.

There was something about the estate that felt kind of strange
30 – but strange in a good way. It's hard to describe, but it felt both

familiar and unfamiliar at the same time, as if, somehow, everything about it was the same as ever – the same buildings, the same roads, the same colours, the same shapes – but something else, something that was above and beyond the physical reality of the estate, had changed.   5

Or maybe it was just the weather ...?

Or just me ...?

Or maybe it was nothing at all?

Just one of those days ...

After a while, I went back into my room, lay down on my bed, and –   10 somewhat reluctantly – closed my eyes.

I didn't really want to do any cyber-surfing/iBoy stuff today. I was sick of it all now, to tell you the truth. Sick of knowing everything, sick of not knowing anything. Sick of hurting people. Sick of all the secrecy and the lies and the utter[1] pointlessness of what I was trying   15 to do ... whatever that was.

And that was the thing ... what *was* I trying to do? Destroy the Devil and all his cohorts[2]? Rid the world of all violence and evil? Turn Hell into Paradise?

That was never going to happen, was it?   20

For a start, as Gram had said, gangs are *always* fighting each other – it's what they do. They fight, they rape, they kill. They've been doing it for hundreds of years, and they'll carry on doing it until they're all gone ... which won't ever happen. Because there'll always be gangs of some kind or other – tribes[3], families, religions, nations, football   25 supporters – because, quite simply, humans are social animals. We naturally form ourselves into groups. We seek protection and security in groups. We find safety and status and purpose in groups. And,

---

1 utter: total; complete   **2** cohort: member belonging to a group of supporters
3 tribe: clan; ethnic group

in order to reinforce[1] everything we get from our group, we fight and kill and rape individuals from other groups.

It's what humans do.

How could I possibly hope to change that?

5 And another thing ... even if all I was trying to do was flush out[2] Howard Ellman – and maybe that was all I was trying to do – what was I going to do with him when I found him? Or when he found me? Would I kill him? Lock him up for ever? Beat him up? Fry his brains[3]? Was I capable of doing any of that? Did I have it in me? And,
10 whatever I did, did I really think it would actually make any difference? Whatever I did to Ellman, would it make other people stop doing terrible things?

Of course it wouldn't.

And besides all that, I was sick of everything because I just
15 wanted to be normal again. I wanted to be a normal kid, doing normal things – going to school, worrying about spots[4], being happy or miserable or crazy about things that don't really matter. I didn't want to be different. I didn't want to know everything. I didn't want to have a mutant brain that was constantly evolving, constantly
20 soaking up more and more information, constantly giving me a growing sense of wisdom ...

I mean ... wisdom?

I was sixteen years old – what did I want with *wisdom*?

I just wanted to be normal.

25 And I wanted to be normal with Lucy too. I wanted to be Tom Harvey with her. Not iBoy, just Tom. I wanted her to be as excited by the real me as she was by the fake me who talked to her on MySpace. I wanted her to like me for what I was. I wanted us to be stupid and funny and embarrassed together. I wanted her to be how she used to
30 be, and me to be how I used to be. I wanted us to be us.

But, like everything else, it wasn't going to happen, was it?

---

1 reinforce sth.: (here) emphasize sth.   **2** flush out sb.: force sb. to reveal themselves   **3** fry sb.'s brains (infml): injure and possible kill sb. with electricity
4 spot: (here) *Pickel*

I wasn't *just* Tom any more. I wasn't how I used to be.
And neither was Lucy.

hey iBoy – did you see the story in the gazette? you're famous! a super-
herosuperstar! and i know you! but don't worry, your secret's safe with
me.   5
aGirl xxxxxx

iBoy didn't reply.
I wouldn't let him.
I was Tom ...
I was losing my mind.   10

To take my lost mind off everything for a while, I stopped thinking
consciously about things and concentrated instead on letting my
iBrain check the facts – the straightforward[1], no-nonsense, on-or-
off facts – about what I'd been doing over the last ten days ...
    What iBoy had been doing.   15
    What we'd been doing.
    What we'd done.
    Who we'd done it to ...
    Where they were now.
    In what condition ...   20
    And so on.
    It was as pointless as everything else, but I went ahead and did it
anyway. And this, in short, was what I came up with:

– In the last seven days, reported crime on the Crow Lane Estate
   had fallen by 67%.   25
– Yusef Hashim had been arrested for possession of an unlicensed[2]
   firearm[3] and was currently out[4] on bail[5].

1 straightforward: easy; uncomplicated   **2** unlicensed: not registered
3 firearm: gun   **4** out: (here) free; not in prison   **5** on bail: *auf Kaution*

- Nathan Craig was in hospital, recovering from a ruptured spleen[1] and three broken ribs.
- Carl Patrick had been arrested and was currently in police custody[2] for stabbing Jayden Carroll.
5 - Jayden Carroll had been discharged from hospital after undergoing minor surgery on his stomach.
- DeWayne Firman had disappeared following the publication of grossly insulting comments about Howard Ellman on his Facebook page.
10 - Paul Adebajo had been arrested for possession of, and intent to supply, Class A drugs.
- Big and Little Jones were under investigation by the Counter Terrorist Unit[3] after a video on YouTube appeared to show them planning a suicide bombing.
15 - Troy O'Neil, Jermaine Adebajo, and the fat Korean guy (whose name was Sim Dong-ni, or just Dong to his friends) were being held in police custody awaiting trial[4] for various offences, including possession of Class A drugs, intent to supply, and possession of unlicensed firearms.

20 And so on, and so on, and so on ...

I'd done a lot.

We'd done a lot.

But had we really achieved anything? No.

Had we turned Hell into Paradise? No.

25 Had we found Howard Ellman?

No.

Had we made Lucy Walker feel any better?

Perhaps ...

Had I started to think that she was falling in love with iBoy ...?

30 Shit.

---

1 ruptured spleen: *Milzriss*   **2** in custody: not able to leave the police station or prison   **3** Counter Terrorist Unit: *Antiterroreinheit*   **4** trial: *Prozess*

10100

... wholly to be a fool
while Spring is in the world
my blood approves[1],
and kisses are a better fate
than wisdom ...   5

E. E. Cummings[2]
'since feeling is first' (1926)

At 19:45:37 that evening, freshly showered and dressed in clean
clothes, I was standing outside Lucy's door, with my heart beating
hard, hoping that everything was going to be perfect.

I'd been busy all afternoon.

I'd got everything ready.   10

And now all I had to do was do it.

I took a deep breath ...

Slowly let it out.

Then reached up and rang the bell.

I was planning on being kind of cool when Lucy answered the door. 15
You know, like it was no big deal, I was just calling round ... just
wondering if, by any chance, you'd be interested in ... blah blah blah
...

It didn't happen that way, of course.

Instead, when she opened the door and said, 'Hey, stranger,' and
I opened my mouth to say, 'Hi,' something got caught in my throat 20
and I started coughing and retching[3] like a lunatic[4]. By the time I
finally managed to get some air into my lungs, my face was bright
red and I was dripping sweat all over the place.

Very cool.

'Are you OK?' Lucy asked me.   25

1 approve: (here) feel good   **2** E. E. Cumminngs: (1894–1962) American poet
3 retch (v): *würgen*   **4** lunatic: maniac; mad person

'Yeah – *hack!* – yeah … I'm all right, thanks. Just …' I coughed again – *hyack!* 'Just a bit of a cough, you know …'

Lucy smiled. 'You want to stop smoking your gran's cigars.'

I grinned at her. 'Yeah …'

5 She stepped back, opening the door to let me in.

'Uh, yeah …' I muttered, suddenly unsure how to say what I wanted to say (even though I'd been practising all afternoon). 'Listen, Luce,' I said. 'I was wondering if you'd like to … well, you know … I just thought we might …'

10 'Are you coming in or not?' she said.

'Well, the thing is …'

'What, Tom?' She frowned at me. 'What's going on?'

'Nothing …' I took another deep breath, trying to calm myself down. *Just take it easy,* I told myself. *Stay calm. Just open your mouth*
15 *and say it.* And that's what I did. I looked at Lucy, opened my mouth and said, 'Do you fancy[1] a picnic?'

She stared at me. 'A *what?*'

'You won't have to go anywhere,' I told her. 'Well, you'll have to go *some*where … but we won't have to leave the tower.'

20 She shook her head. 'I don't get it …'

'I know … I mean, I know it sounds kind of strange, but it'll be all right. Honestly … trust me. You'll be perfectly safe.'

'But where …?'

'I can't tell you, can I? It's a surprise.'

25 She shook her head again. 'A *picnic?*'

I smiled at her. 'Yeah … sandwiches, crisps, Coke …'

'I don't know, Tom,' she said anxiously. 'I mean, it's a really nice thought and everything, and it's not that I don't want to *be* with you … but, you know … I just … I just don't think I'm ready yet.'

30 'Ready for what?' I asked gently.

'Anything … going out, being with people …'

---

1 fancy sth.: want sth.

'Yeah, but you won't *be* going out,' I assured her. 'And the only people you'll be with is me. I promise. There won't be anyone else near us. I guarantee it.'

'I don't see how you can.'

'Trust me, Luce.'   5

She looked down at the floor, her face worried, her eyes sad ... and for a moment I seriously started to doubt myself. Maybe this wasn't such a good idea, after all. Maybe I was just being selfish, thoughtless, uncaring ...

But then Lucy said, very quietly, 'I won't have to leave the tower?'   10

'No.'

'And I definitely won't see anyone else?'

'Guaranteed.'

She slowly looked up at me. 'What kind of sandwiches?'

Lucy's mum was out at work, but Ben was in, so Lucy told him that   15 she was going out with me for a while, and that she wouldn't be long. She put on a coat and one of those knitted[1] woollen hats with ear flaps[2], and then – after I'd checked to make sure that the corridor was empty – I started leading her along to the stairwell.

'All right?' I asked her.   20

She nodded hesitantly. 'Yeah ... I'm just a bit ... I don't know ... this is the first time I've been out since it happened ...'

'I know.'

She smiled at me, anxiety showing in her eyes. 'Where are we going?'   25

I smiled back. 'Follow me.'

I led her through the stairwell door and up the two flights of steps to the padlocked iron gate. I'd already been up earlier and unlocked it, so I just pushed it open, guided Lucy through to the steel-reinforced door, and locked the iron gate behind us. As I reached up to   30 the keypad on the wall, tapped in the security code, and opened the door, Lucy gave me a puzzled look.

---

1 knitted ['nɪtɪd]: *gestrickt*   **2** flap: piece of cloth that hangs loose

'Don't ask,' I said to her. 'This way.'

I ushered[1] her into the little room, closing the reinforced door after us, and went over to the ladder on the wall. Again, I'd already been up and unlocked the hatchway, so all we had to do now was
5 climb the ladder and we'd be out on the roof.

I looked at Lucy. 'Still OK?'

'Yeah, I think so ...'

'Are you all right with ladders?'

She looked up at the hatchway. 'Does that go where I think it
10 goes?'

'You'll soon find out. Do you want me to go first?'

'OK.'

I climbed the ladder, pushed open the hatchway and stepped out onto the roof, then I reached back down to help Lucy up.
15 'All right?' I said to her.

'Yeah ...'

'I really like your hat, by the way.'

She grinned at me. 'Do you always do this when you're trying to impress a girl? Give her a ladder to climb, then compliment her on
20 her choice of hat?'

'It usually works for me.'

As she reached the top of the ladder, I took her hand and helped her up through the hatchway onto the roof.

'Wow,' she said quietly, getting to her feet and looking around.
25 'This is *amazing*. You can see for ever ... I mean, I know I've seen it all before, but ...'

'It feels different up here, doesn't it?'

'Yeah ...' She looked at me. 'You're full of surprises, Tom Harvey.'

'I do my best,' I said. She smiled at me.
30 'Are you hungry?' I asked.

'Why? Is there a restaurant up here or something?'

'It's a picnic, remember? I invited you to a picnic.' I pointed towards the middle of the roof. 'See?'

---

1 usher sb.: show sb. where to go

She gazed over at where I was pointing, and when she saw what was there, her eyes lit up and her face broke into the most wonderful shining smile. 'Oh, Tom,' she cried. 'That's *fantastic* ... it's so *beautiful*.' She turned to me, still smiling like a child on Christmas morning. 'Did you do all that for me?' 5

I looked over at the picnic table that I'd set up in the middle of the roof, and although it was a pretty ramshackle[1] affair – an old fold-away[2] table and chairs I'd found in the spare room, a red and white tablecloth, a candle on a saucer, some paper cups and plates, sandwiches, crisps, a big bottle of Coke, half a packet of chocolate 10 digestives[3] and the remains of a fruit cake that Gram had made the week before – I had to admit that Lucy was right, it really *did* have a certain kind of raggedy beauty to it.

'Yeah,' I said, turning back to Lucy. 'Yeah ... I did it for you.' I could feel myself blushing slightly now, but I didn't mind. 'Do you really 15 like it?'

She put her hand on my shoulder, leaned in towards me, and kissed me lightly on the cheek. 'I *adore* it,' she said, looking into my eyes. 'Really ... I absolutely *love* it. Thanks, Tom.'

She kissed me again, another quick peck[4] on the cheek, and then 20 we just stood there for a while ... just the two of us, high above the rest of the world, alone together in the dying light of a crimson[5] sunset ...

It was everything I'd ever wished for.

And in that moment, nothing else mattered. 25

It was just the two of us ... just Lucy and me. Just like it used to be.

Lucy smiled and said, 'Shall we eat?'

I bowed my head[6]. 'If Madam so wishes. Table for two, is it?'

'Please.' 30

'Follow me, m'lady.'

---

1 ramshackle ['ræmʃækl]: in a bad condition   **2** fold-away table: *Klapptisch*
3 digestive: (here) biscuit   **4** peck (infml.): quick kiss   **5** crimson: red   **6** bow
your head [baʊ]: bend your head down

I led her over to the picnic table and held out the chair for her to sit down.

'Thank you, I'm sure,' she said.

'You're very welcome.'

5   I sat down and reached for the bottle of Coke. 'Coca-Cola?'

'Don't mind if I do.'

I poured a small amount into a paper cup and offered it to her to taste. She took the cup, sniffed the Coke, rolled it around in the cup for a while, then took a tiny sip[1].

10   'Mmm ...' she said, swallowing. 'Delightful, thank you.' She held out her cup and I filled it up. I poured myself a cup, then offered her the plate of sandwiches. 'There's cheese,' I explained. 'Or ... cheese spread[2]. Or, if you'd prefer, there's the sandwich of the day.'

Lucy grinned. 'And what might that be?'

15   'Cheese.'

She laughed and took a couple of sandwiches. 'Did you make these yourself?'

I nodded. 'Cheese is my speciality. It was also the only thing left in the fridge.'

20   I opened a packet of crisps for her.

'Cheese and onion?' she said.

'Yep[3].'

'Excellent.'

For the next few minutes, we just ate. It was really nice ... just sit-
25 ting there in the growing darkness, eating and drinking, not having to say anything, both of us unable to wipe the stupid smiles off our faces. The night was getting a little colder now, with a chilly breeze drifting across the roof, but we both had our coats on, and I don't think either of us were really bothered.

30   After a while, Lucy took a rest from chewing and said to me, 'So ... what have you been doing recently? I haven't seen you for a while.'

'Yeah, I know ... I'm sorry, I kept meaning to come round, but stuff just kept getting in the way.'

---

1 sip: tiny amount of a drink   **2** cheese spread: *Streichkäse*   **3** Yep (infml.): yes

'Stuff?'

I touched my head and shrugged, kind of ambiguously[1] ... which I knew was a pretty crappy thing to do. But I just didn't know what to say, and I didn't want to lie to her ... and, in a way, it was the stuff in my head that had got in the way of me going round to see her.   5

'Right ...' Lucy said, nodding uncertainly at me and slowly putting a crisp in her mouth. 'Right ... I see.'

She chewed quietly on the crisp for a while ... which baffled me. I mean, how can anyone chew quietly on a crisp? And then she looked at me and said softly, 'It's really quiet up here, isn't it?'   10

'Yeah,' I agreed. 'The whole estate seems pretty quiet at the moment.'

She nodded, and for a moment or two she was silent again, concentrating on getting the last few crisp crumbs out of the packet. She licked[2] her finger and ran it round the inside of the packet, sucked[3]   15
the bits off her finger, then upended[4] the packet into her mouth.

'Finished?' I asked her, smiling.

She grinned. 'I don't like wasting any.'

I watched her as she twisted the empty crisp packet into a bow[5] and placed it under the Coke bottle to stop the breeze blowing it   20
away. She stared at the table top for a few seconds, thinking about something, then she looked up at me.

'Can you keep a secret?' she said.

'Yeah ...'

'Well ... you know all this stuff that's been going on round the   25
estate, all the arrests and everything?'

'Yeah.'

'And you know there's all kinds of rumours going round that there's some kind of vigilante out there ... some guy in a costume?'

'Yeah.'   30

---

1 ambiguously: with different possible meanings   **2** lick: touch with your tongue
3 suck sth.: *etw. ablutschen*   **4** upend sth. [ʌp'end]: turn sth. upside down
5 bow (n): (here) *Schleife*

She looked at me. 'Well ... I think it's that kid I told you about, the one who calls himself iBoy. Remember?'

'The one who tried to throw Eugene O'Neil out of the window?'

'Yeah ...'

5　'The MySpace guy?'

'Yeah. I think it's him.'

'Who?'

'The vigilante,' she said impatiently. 'The one who's been doing all this stuff round the estate. I think it's iBoy.'

10　'Really?'

'Yeah ... I mean, we talk to each other quite often on MySpace, and although he hasn't actually admitted it's him, he hasn't denied it either.'

'So what are you trying to say? You think this iBoy kid is some 15 kind of superhero or something?'

'No, of course not. But he definitely exists. I saw him, remember. I was there when he sorted out O'Neil and the others ...' She shook her head in disbelief at the memory. 'He zapped them, Tom. I mean he really zapped them. And he was wearing some kind of mask ... 20 honestly.'

'I believe you.' I cut a couple of slices of fruit cake, passed one to Lucy, and started eating the other one myself. 'What do you think he is then?'

'I don't know –'

25　'And why do you think he's doing it? I mean, do you think he's doing it for you, like he's some kind of guardian angel[1] or something?'

She was about to bite into the fruit cake, but she paused in mid-chomp[2], lowering the cake and looking intensely at me. 'What?'

'What?' I echoed. 'What did I say?'

30　Her voice was quiet. 'Why would you think he'd be doing anything for me?'

'Well ... you know ... I mean, he went after O'Neil and Firman and Craig, didn't he?'

---

1 guardian angel: *Schutzengel*　**2** mid-chomp: in the middle of a bite

'So?'

I suddenly realized that I wasn't supposed to know who'd raped Lucy, or who'd been there when it had happened. She hadn't told me. I looked at her, trying to hide the hesitation in my mind. 'I just meant, you know ... he helped you when O'Neil and the others were outside your flat. iBoy, I mean. He was helping you, wasn't he?'

'Yeah, but –'

'Well, that's all I meant. He was helping you, and he got in touch with you on MySpace ... so, you know ... maybe it's possible that he's doing some of these things for you.'

Lucy's eyes were fixed steadily[1] on mine. 'Right ... but how would he know?'

'Know what?'

'How would he know who to go after? I mean, I know the only information I'm getting about any of this is what Ben tells me, but it seems like a lot of the people who were there when it happened ... you know, when me and Ben were ... when I was ... well, you know what I mean.' She swallowed hard, trying not to cry. 'A lot of those kids who were there ... well, they're the ones who've been getting beaten up or arrested or whatever.'

'So maybe this iBoy really is your guardian angel?' I suggested.

'Yeah, right,' said Lucy, biting into her fruit cake.

'Have you told anyone else about this?'

She shook her head, her mouth full of cake.

'What about the police?' I asked. 'Have they been to see you?'

She nodded.

'What did you tell them?'

She swallowed. 'Nothing.'

'Same here.'

She raised her eyebrows. 'The police have been to see you?'

'Yeah ...'

'Why?'

---

1 steadily: without moving

I touched the scar on my head. 'I was there, wasn't I? I mean, when they attacked you and Ben, I was there. Well, I was sort of there. The police wanted to know if I saw anything.'

'How could you have seen anything? You were thirty floors below.'

5 'I know ... and I was lying on the ground with an iPhone stuck in my skull.'

She laughed, then almost immediately she said, 'Sorry, I don't know why I'm laughing. It's not funny.' She looked at me. 'So the police just came to see you about that? They didn't ask you anything
10 about the vigilante?'

'Yeah, they asked me about that too.' I shrugged. 'Apparently a bunch of FGH kids were attacked last week by our friendly neighbourhood Mystery Kid, and someone saw me sitting around the kids' playground a few minutes before it happened. So, you know,
15 the cops just wanted to know if I saw anything.'

'Did you?'

'No.'

'What were you doing at the playground?'

'Not much ... just hanging around, you know.'

20 She smiled. 'On your own?'

'Yeah.'

'Did you go on the swings?'

I shook my head. 'They were all broken.'

Lucy grinned. 'Yeah, I bet they were.'

25 'They were ... what are you grinning about?'

'You were always scared of going on the swings.'

'No, I wasn't.'

'You were. When we were kids ... you always had an excuse for not going on the swings – your gran wouldn't let you, they didn't
30 look safe, you had a bad back –'

'Yeah, well, they weren't safe, were they? Kids were always falling off and cracking their heads open.'

Lucy laughed. 'I went on them.'

'Yeah, but you never went on the whizzy-round[1] thing, did you?'

'The whizzy-round thing?'

'Yeah, you know – the wooden roundabout thing that whizzes round really fast?' I smiled at her. 'You never went on that.'

Lucy shrugged. 'It made me dizzy.'   5

'You were scared of it.'

'Yeah, but I was a little girl. Little girls are allowed to be scared.' She looked at me, her eyes sparkling. 'What's your excuse?'

I held my hands up. 'All right, I admit it. I'm a wimp. Always have been, always will be.'   10

Lucy shook her head. 'You're being too hard on yourself, Tom. You're not a wimp.'

'Thanks.'

'You're more of a nerd than a wimp.'

I gave her a pained look. 'Now you're going too far. I mean, wimp-   15
iness I can accept. In fact, I kind of like being a wimp. But calling me
a *nerd* ...?' I shook my head. 'That hurts, Luce. Honestly ...' I put my
hand on my heart. 'It gets me right here.'

'In that case,' Lucy said, 'please accept my humblest[2] apologies[3].'

'Apologies accepted.'   20

She smiled. 'Actually, I kind of like wimps too.'

'You're just saying that to make me feel better.'

'No, really ... I do. I'd rather be with a wimp than a non-wimp any
day.'

'A *non*-wimp?'   25

She grinned. 'You know what I mean.'

'All right,' I said. 'Name one.'

'One what?'

'A wimp who you like ... name one.'

'Apart from you?'   30

I shook my head. 'It's no good trying to distract me with cheap compliments.'

---

1 whizzy-round: *eine Art Karussel*   **2** humble: modest   **3** apology: statement
saying that you are sorry

'It wasn't cheap.'

'Come on,' I said. 'Name that wimp.'

'OK ... all right, let me think. Right ... a wimp that I like ...'

As she gazed up at the night sky, trying to think – or maybe just
pretending to try to think – of a wimpy guy who she really liked, I did
my best not to stare at her, but it was really hard. She looked so good
– all muffled up[1] in her coat and hat, with cake crumbs on her lips
and crisp-dust on her fingers ... and I wondered if I could really let
myself think that this game we were playing was perhaps something
more than just a game. Were Lucy's joke compliments actually *real*
compliments? Was it really possible that she liked me as more than
just a friend?

'Spider-Man,' she said suddenly.

'What?'

'Spider-Man ... a wimp I really like.'

'He's not a wimp,' I said. 'Spidey's really tough.'

'Yeah, no ... I don't mean *Spider-Man*, I mean the other one, the
real one, what's-his-name, you know ...' She clicked her fingers, trying to remember the name.

'Peter Parker[2]?'

'Yeah, that's it. Peter Parker. He's a wimp, isn't he?'

'Yeah ...'

'And I like him.'

'No, you don't. It's Tobey Maguire[3] that you like.' She shrugged.

'Same thing.'

I laughed. 'It's not the same thing at all. Peter Parker, the fictional
character ... yeah, *he's* a wimp. But Tobey Maguire is a Hollywood
film star. He's rich and famous and –'

'Very attractive.'

---

1 muffled up: wrapped tightly in order to keep warm   **2** Peter Parker: main
character in *Spider-Man*; a high-school student who turns to crime-fighting after
developing spider-like powers   **3** Tobey Maguire: (born 1975) American actor

I pulled a face. 'You think so? He's a bit kind of loopy[1]-looking, isn't he?'

'Loopy?'

'Yeah, you know, that loopy kind of lop-sided[2] face he's got –'

'No,' Lucy said. 'He's really cute[3]. And he's sexy. Do you remember that bit in the first film when he's hanging upside down in the rain and he kisses what's-her-name –'

'Mary Jane Watson[4]. MJ.'

'Yeah ... I mean, that's a really sexy kiss.'

'Only because he's still got his mask on, so you can't see his face.'

'You don't *have* to see it. You already know how cute and sexy he is.'

'Mary Jane doesn't know.'

'Who cares about Mary Jane?'

'I think you'll find that a *lot* of people care about Mary Jane, especially when she's kissing the aforementioned[5] upside-down Spider-Man in the rain, and her shirt is all wet and clingy[6].'

Lucy laughed, shaking her head and wagging her finger at me. '*Now* who's getting their characters and actors mixed up?'

'What?' I said innocently.

'It's Kirsten Dunst's[7] rain-soaked shirt that you care about, not Mary Jane's.'

I shrugged. 'Same thing.'

We both started giggling then, and it felt really good – just sitting there, looking at each other, laughing and giggling like two little kids ... but then, after a while, I think we both slowly realized that the stuff we'd just been talking and laughing about was the kind of stuff that maybe we *shouldn't* have been talking and laughing about. Because although we'd only been messing around and enjoying ourselves, and although we'd only been talking about sex in a totally

---

1 loopy: strange; crazy   **2** lop-sided: irregular; uneven; unequal   **3** cute: attractive; pretty   **4** Mary Jane Watson: girlfriend of Peter Parker   **5** aforementioned [ə,fɔː'menʃənd]: as said before   **6** clingy: wet and sticking to the body, showing its shape   **7** Kirsten Dunst: (born 1982) American actress

superficial and unsexual way, that still didn't change the fact that we *had* been talking about sex. And now that she'd realized it, that, for Lucy, was just too much.

It was too close.

5   Too raw[1].

Too confusing.

And now she was just sitting there, not smiling any more, just looking down sadly at her hands in her lap as she twisted and picked at a paper tissue.

10   'I'm sorry,' I said quietly. 'I should have realized ...'

'It's OK,' she said, trying to smile at me. 'It's not your fault. I just ...' She shrugged. 'Sometimes it goes away for a while, you know? I actually forget about it ... at least, I'm not *aware* that I'm thinking about it. But then ...' She shook her head. 'It always comes back. It's

15 like it's never *not* there. And even when I *do* forget about it for a few minutes, there's always *some*thing that brings it back to me. Something on the TV, you know, a sex scene or something, or just some guy in a hood who reminds me of them ... I mean, God, you wouldn't *believe* how hard it is to watch TV without seeing a guy in a hood.'

20 She smiled shakily[2] at me. 'They're *every*where.'

I self-consciously pulled down my hood. Lucy laughed. 'What did I tell you?'

'Sorry ...'

'Actually, I hadn't even noticed yours until now.'

25   'Sorry,' I said again.

'No, it's fine. Really.' She frowned to herself. 'It's weird that I didn't notice it before, though ...'

'It's probably just the way that I wear it,' I suggested, smiling.

'What – on your head, you mean?'

30   We were starting to get back to each other again now. It didn't quite feel the same as before – we were quieter now, less boisterous[3] – but that was OK. In fact, I really quite liked it. It somehow made

1 raw: (here) painful   **2** shakily: (here) uncertainly   **3** boisterous ['bɔɪstərəs]: animated; lively

me feel as if we knew each other a lot better. And I think Lucy was OK with it too.

'All right?' I said to her.

She smiled. 'Yeah.'

'Do you want anything else to eat?'   5

She shook her head. 'I'm stuffed.'

'Do you want to go for a walk?'

'Where to?'

'How about the edge of the roof?'

Lucy looked over at the edge, then back at me. 'You sure it's not   10
too far?'

'I can call a taxi, if you want.'

'No,' she said. 'It's a nice enough night. Let's walk.'

I'd never had a girlfriend before ... well, not a proper girlfriend anyway. I mean, I'd been out with a few girls, you know, I'd gone on a few   15
dates – to the pictures, to see a band, that kind of thing. But although
I'd quite liked the girls I'd been out with, I hadn't been absolutely
crazy about any of them or anything, and so I'd never really given
all that much thought to what I was expected to do with them, or
to what I *thought* I was expected to do ... and, no, I don't mean that   20
in a sexy/sexual/sexist kind of way. I just mean the stupid stuff, you
know ... like knowing if it's OK to hold hands or not, and whether it's
expected ... and, if it *is* expected, when do you do it? And how? And
what if you make the first move[1], but it turns out that it's *not* OK ...
what do you do then?   25

That kind of stuff.

And it was that kind of stuff that I *thought* I'd be thinking about
as I got up from the picnic table and walked over to the edge of
the roof with Lucy. Because I *was* crazy about her. I always *had*
been crazy about her. And now here we were, finally on some kind   30
of date together ... although, admittedly[2], it wasn't the most tradi-
tional of dates. But still, we'd had a meal together, and we'd talked

---

1 first move: first step   **2** admittedly: *zugegebenermaßen*

and laughed and suffered about stuff together, and now we were
going for a walk together ... and I'd dreamed of this moment so
many times. I'd pictured it, imagined it, lived it ... worried about it.
Should I hold her hand? Should I put my arm around her? Should I
5 try to be cool about things? Should I do this, or do that, or try this,
or try that ...?

But the strange thing was, now that it was actually happening,
none of this stupid stuff even entered my mind. I just got up and
walked across the roof with Lucy, not worrying about anything, not
10 caring about anything, just knowing that we both felt OK – walking
side by side, as close to each other as we wanted to be ... it all felt
perfectly natural.

'What are you smiling about?' Lucy asked me.

I looked at her. 'Was I smiling?'

15 'Yeah, like an idiot.'

I grinned at her.

She smiled back at me.

'Careful,' I said, reaching out and touching her arm. She stopped,
realizing that we were nearing the edge of the roof.

20 'Wow,' she said softly. 'It's a long way down.'

'Are you OK?' I asked her. 'Not dizzy or anything?'

She looked at me. 'Is that meant to be a joke?'

'No,' I grinned. 'Honestly ... I mean, some people don't like heights,
do they? I was just checking that you were OK, that's all.'

25 'Yeah,' she said, smiling. 'I'm fine.' She looked down over the edge
again, not saying anything, just looking and thinking.

'Shall we sit down?' I suggested.

'Why? Are you feeling dizzy?'

'You know me,' I said, lowering myself cross-legged to the ground.
30 'Tommy the Wimp.'

She smiled and sat down beside me, and then we just sat there
in silence for a while, both of us gazing out over the estate at the distant lights of London. Streetlights, traffic lights, headlights ... office
blocks, tower blocks, shops and theatres ...

35 It was all a long way away.

'Is that the London Eye?' Lucy said after a while.

'Where?'

She pointed into the distance. 'There ... by the river.'

I couldn't see it, and just for a moment I thought about logging on to Google Earth in my head to help me find it ... but that was iStuff, and iStuff didn't belong here. So I didn't.

'I can't even see the *river*,' I told Lucy. 'Never mind the London Eye.'

She smiled, but I could tell that her mind was on something else now. She'd stopped looking into the distance and had turned her attention to the more immediate surroundings of the estate down below, gazing around at the streets, the towers, the low-rises, the kids' playground ...

'It's funny, isn't it?' she said quietly, her voice full of sadness.

'What's that?'

'Knowing that they're all out there somewhere ... you know, the boys who raped me. They're all out there ... living their lives, doing whatever it is they do ...' She breathed out wearily. 'I mean, they're all just *out* there ...'

'Some of them will be in cells now,' I said. 'Or in hospital.'

Lucy looked at me, her eyes wet with tears. 'You know, don't you?' she said. 'You know who they are.'

I nodded. 'Most of them, yeah.'

'How do you know?'

I shrugged. 'People talk, you know ... you hear rumours. It's not too difficult to work out the truth.'

'The truth ...?' she said, her voice barely audible. 'I'm the only one who knows the *truth*.'

As she looked away from me and went back to gazing down at the estate, I could have kicked myself for being so stupid. Not that I'd *meant* to imply that I knew what she'd been through, but still ... it was just so thoughtless, such a brainless thing to say.

I really *was* an idiot.

'Sorry, Tom,' Lucy said.

I looked at her, not sure I'd heard her right. 'What?'

'I know you didn't mean anything ... and I didn't mean to snap at you –'

'No, please,' I said, 'I'm the one who should be saying sorry. Not you. I just didn't think, you know ... I just opened my big stupid mouth and –'

'You haven't got a big stupid mouth.'

I stared at her. She was smiling again.

'It's OK,' she said. 'All right?'

'OK.'

'All right.'

We went back to our silent gazing for a while, watching the lights, the sky, the stars in the darkness. I could hear the wind sighing in the night, and there were a few faint sounds drifting up from the estate – cars, voices, music – but, all in all, everything was still pretty quiet. And even the sounds that *were* breaking the silence didn't seem to have any menace[1] to them.

They were just sounds.

'Does it make any difference?' I said quietly to Lucy. She looked at me.

'Does what make any difference?'

'All this stuff that iBoy's done ... or whoever it is that's doing it. You know, making O'Neil and Adebajo and the rest of them suffer ... I mean, does it make you feel any better?'

She didn't answer for a while, she just stared at me, and for a moment or two I thought she was going to say – 'It's *you*, isn't it? It's you ... you're iBoy,' – and I started to wonder how that would make me feel. Good? Embarrassed? Ashamed? Excited? And that made me wonder if perhaps, subconsciously, I *wanted* her to know that it was me, that I was iBoy, that I was her guardian angel ...

'I don't know, Tom,' she said sadly. 'I really don't know if it makes any difference or not. I mean, yeah ... there's a bit of me that gets something good out of their suffering ... you know, I really *want* them to feel pain ... I want them to fucking *hurt* ... because they

---

1 menace: threat; danger

deserve it … God, they deserve everything they fucking get …' Her voice had lowered to an ice-cold whisper. 'So, yeah, it makes a difference in that way. It gives me something that part of me really needs …' She sighed. 'But it never lasts very long. I mean, it's just not enough … it *can't* be enough. It can't take anything away.' She looked at me. 'Nothing can take anything away.' ₅

'They'll always have done it …' I said quietly.

She nodded. 'And whatever happens, nobody can change that.'

As we sat there looking at each other, alone together in the boundless dark, I found myself thinking about an old Superman ₁₀ film that I'd seen on TV at Christmas. I'd only been half-watching the TV at the time, so I couldn't remember all that much about it, but there was a bit in the film where Superman's so busy saving the lives of other people that he doesn't have time to save the life of Lois Lane[1], the girl he loves. And when he finds out that she's dead, he ₁₅ gets so distraught[2] that he flies up into the atmosphere and starts whizzing in circles around the Earth, and he flies so fast that somehow the Earth begins to slow down, and eventually it stops spinning altogether and begins to rotate[3] in the opposite direction, making everything go back in time, allowing Superman to go back into the ₂₀ past and prevent Lois Lane from dying.

Which was all pretty ridiculous, of course.

But I couldn't help thinking that if only I could do that, if only I could go back in time … well, then I really *could* change things for Lucy. I really *could* make everything all right again. ₂₅

But I knew that was never going to happen. This was the real world, not a movie. And in the real world, no matter how impossible things might be, they're never quite impossible enough.

'What are you thinking about, Tom?' Lucy asked me.

'Nothing …' I shrugged. 'You know, just stuff …' ₃₀

She smiled. 'There's a lot of stuff to think about, isn't there?'

'Yeah …'

---

1 Lois Lane: Superman's girlfriend   **2** distraught: very upset   **3** rotate: turn round; spin

'And it's always ... I don't know. It's like it's never straightforward, is it? It's never just *this* or *that*. Do you know what I mean?'

'Yeah.'

'There's always two sides to everything. You feel good about
5 something, but you still feel bad. You like something about someone, but you don't *want* to like it.' She looked thoughtfully at me. 'Two sides, you see? Even the stuff we were talking about earlier, you know ... Tobey Maguire's cute, Kirsten Dunst's sexy ... I mean, that's OK – kissing and stuff, people looking sexy ... it's just kind of nice.
10 But then there's the *other* side of it, the other side of sex – the bad side, the shit, the fucking *awful* things that people do ...' She shook her head. 'I just don't *get* it, you know?'

'Yeah ...'

She sighed again. 'And it's the same with people too ... you think
15 you know them, you think you know exactly what they're like ...' She looked slowly at me.

'But maybe you're wrong ... maybe you've always been wrong, and maybe this person who you *thought* you knew ... well, maybe they've got another side to them. A side you're not sure about.'

20 'Right ...' I said tentatively[1].

Lucy looked at me for a long moment, her eyes never leaving mine, and then she smiled. 'Or maybe I'm wrong about that too?'

I smiled back at her. 'Don't ask me. I haven't got the faintest idea what you're talking about.'

25 'You never do, do you?'

'Never do what?'

She laughed, and I grinned at her, and then we just sat there in silence for a few moments, smiling at each other in the darkness ... and I knew in my heart that this was how it was supposed to be. This
30 was everything I could ever want, everything there was to want.

This was *it*.

After a while, Lucy looked at her watch and said, 'I'd better get going, Tom. Mum'll be back soon.'

---

1 tentatively: not confidently

'OK.'

We both got to our feet then, and as we stood there at the edge of the roof, looking out into the darkness, I remembered the last time I'd been up here – all on my own, with my hood up and my iSkin glowing ... a softly glowing figure, sitting cross-legged on a cold stone roof, thirty floors up ...

Like some kind of weird hooded Buddha ...

A skinny, glow-in-the-dark iBuddha.

Or maybe an iGargoyle.

It was so much better now.

'Tom?' Lucy said. I turned to her.

'Thanks,' she said quietly, looking at me. 'This has been a really wonderful night. I'll never forget it.' She moved closer to me, put her hands to my face, and kissed me softly on the lips.

God, it felt good.

So perfect, so *right* ...

It felt so good, I nearly fell off the roof.

'OK?' she whispered.

I couldn't speak. I couldn't even smile. It was all I could do just to breathe. Lucy moved her hand to my head and gently stroked my scar with her fingertips.

'It feels warm,' she said quietly.

'Warm ...' I muttered.

She smiled at me. 'Come on, we'd better go ... before you start drooling[1].'

She held my hand as we walked back across the roof to the hatchway. I helped her down the ladder, then we held hands again as we went out through the doors, down the stairs, and along the corridor to her flat.

'Thanks again, Tom,' she said. 'That was really nice.'

'Thank *you*,' I said.

---

1 drool: *sabbern*

She smiled and kissed me on the cheek. 'Are you coming round tomorrow?'

I nodded. 'If it's OK with you.'

'It's perfectly OK with me.'

5   'Good.'

She smiled again and opened the door. 'I'll see you tomorrow then.'

'Yeah.'

I waited for her to close the door, and then I just stood there for a
10 while, smiling the biggest, floatiest[1], stupidest smile in the world ... and then, breathing in a breath of pure satisfaction, I turned round and started heading back to the roof to clear all the picnic stuff away.

Just before I got to the stairwell, I heard Lucy's door opening.

'Tom?'

15   I turned round and saw her leaning out through the doorway.

'Be careful,' she said.

I smiled at her. 'I'm always careful.'

She gave me a long thoughtful look, almost frowning at me, then she smiled again, nodded her head, and went back into the flat.

1 floaty: (here) rising into the air

10101

My name is Legion[1]; for we are many.

New Testament, Mark 5:9

After I'd cleared away the picnic stuff from the roof and lugged[2] it all back to the flat – and after Gram had virtually *forced* me to tell her how it had all gone with Lucy – I went to my room and lay down in the dark and tried not to think about anything. I didn't want to *think* at all – I just wanted to feel what I was feeling ... and nothing else. I just wanted to lie there with Lucy.

The memory of her sunset eyes.

Her lips.

Her smile. Her face.

Her kiss ...

It was all I'd ever wanted. All I'd ever needed.

I knew that now.

Nothing else mattered. Revenge, punishment, retribution[3] ... none of it mattered. My iPowers, my abilities, my *knowing* ... none of it was *me*. It was iBoy. And I wasn't iBoy – I was Tom Harvey, a perfectly normal sixteen-year-old kid, with no major problems, no secrets, no terrors ... no story to tell. Just a kid, that's all. With hopes and dreams ...

And a girl to think about ...

iBoy could never dream.

He could never make a wish come true.

But Tom Harvey could.

iBoy *had* to go.

It was the only way I could get back to being Tom Harvey again, and being Tom Harvey was the only way I was ever going to be with Lucy. And that was my dream, and I needed it more than anything else.

Tomorrow, I decided.

---

1 legion: mass; multitude   **2** lug sth.: carry sth. heavy   **3** retribution: *Vergeltung*

I'd do it tomorrow.

First thing in the morning, I'd tell Gram everything – what had happened to me, what I could do, what I'd done, what I knew – and then, with her help, I'd tell everyone else who needed to know. The
5 police, Mr Kirby, Lucy …

It wasn't going to be easy, of course. The police were going to want to interview me about all the stuff I'd done, the damage I'd caused, the people I'd hurt, and how I'd hurt them … and I was probably going to be arrested and charged … if, that is, they actually believed
10 me. Which was by no means guaranteed. But once I'd explained everything to Mr Kirby, and maybe proved to him and the police what I could do with my iBrain … maybe then Mr Kirby could start working out how to get inside my head and get rid of[1] whatever it was I needed to get rid of in order to get me back to normal again …

15 Maybe.

And Lucy …?

God, what was *she* going to think? I mean, even if she did already have a sneaking[2] suspicion[3] that I might have some connection with iBoy – and, after tonight, I was pretty sure that she suspected *some*-
20 thing – how was she going to react when she found out that it really was me who'd done all those things? And, even worse, that it was me she'd been talking to on MySpace … me, pretending to be someone else. Lying to her. Betraying her trust. *Using* her …

She'd hate me. Wouldn't she?
25 She'd hate me, despise[4] me, and I'd lose her …

I'd lose her by trying to be true.

But the only way I was ever going to be with her was *also* by trying to be true.

Lucy was right, I thought to myself then. There *are* always two
30 sides to everything.

---

1 get rid of sth.: take sth. away   **2** sneaking: (here) secret; quiet   **3** suspicion: (here) idea   **4** despise sb.: hate sb.

I spent the next few hours just lying on my bed, thinking as hard as I could, racking my (ordinary) brain[1], trying to work out how to be true without losing everything ... and maybe if I'd had more time, I might just have come up with an answer.

But I didn't.

I never got the chance.

It was 02:12:16 when the doorbell rang. I was still lying on the bed, still fully dressed, still chasing circles[2] inside my head, and I'd been lying there in the silent darkness for such a long time by then that some kind of inertia[3] had set in. My head was dead. My body was ten thousand miles away. I wasn't really aware of myself any more. But when the doorbell rang, I was instantly wide awake.

Something was wrong.

It had to be.

The doorbell only rings at two o'clock in the morning when something is wrong.

With my iBrain already scanning for nearby phones, I jumped off the bed and ran out into the hallway. Gram was just coming out of her room, and it was obvious from her sleep-scrunched[4] face and her messed-up hair that the doorbell had woken her up.

'Tommy?' she said sleepily, tightening the cord on her dressing gown. 'What's going on?'

'I don't know ...' The bell rang again.

Gram looked at me, slightly worried now. 'Who could it be at this time of night?'

'I don't know.'

She started moving towards the door. 'Well, I suppose we'd better see –'

'Hold on, Gram,' I said, moving ahead of her. 'I'll deal with it.'

---

1 rack your brain: think very hard   **2** chase circles: *sich gedanklich im Kreis drehen*   **3** inertia [ɪˈnɜːʃə]: lack of energy   **4** sleep-scrunched: (here) marked with the signs of sleeping (i.e. folds of pillows)

'No, Tommy –' she started to say, but I was already at the door now. My iBrain had picked up the presence of four mobile phones in the corridor outside, all of them switched[1] to silent.

'Who is it?' I called out.

5 There was a moment's silence, a muffled whisper, and then I heard Lucy's voice.

'Tom ...?'

She sounded desperate[2].

'Tom, don't – *ummf*...'

10 I didn't stop to think, I just grabbed the door handle, unlocked the door, and yanked it open ... and there they all were: Lucy, Eugene O'Neil, Yusef Hashim, a big black guy I'd never seen before ...

And Howard Ellman.

Lucy was barefoot, dressed only in a long white nightgown, so I
15 guessed she'd just been dragged out of bed. Her face was streaked[3] with tears, she had an ugly red cut just below her right eye, and her mouth was sealed[4] with a strip of black tape[5]. Yusef Hashim had a gun to her head. The gun, an automatic pistol, was taped to his hand and wrist with black insulation tape, and his hand and the pistol
20 were tightly fixed to Lucy's head with more insulation tape. Hand, pistol, Lucy's head ... all taped together, like some kind of nightmare repair job.

I stared at Lucy, unable to move.

She was petrified[6].

25 And so was I.

'Hello, Thomas,' Ellman said softly. 'I hear you've been looking for me.'

I stared at him, unable to speak.

'Just so you understand,' he said, smiling calmly. 'Hashim's finger
30 is taped over the trigger of the gun, OK? So if you try zapping him, or me, or anyone else ... if you go anywhere near her, if you try call-

---

1 switch to sth.: change to sth.   **2** desperate: extremely worried and anxious
3 streaked with sth: marked by sth.   **4** sealed with sth.: closed tight with sth.
5 tape: sticky strip of plastic   **6** petrified: so scared you stand still

ing the police ... if you do *anything* that I don't like, Hashim's going to pull the trigger and your girlfriend's brains are going to be splattered[1] all over the place. Do you understand?'

'Yes,' I said quietly. 'I understand.'

I saw his eyes glancing over my shoulder then, and as I turned to see what he was looking at, I saw Gram picking up the phone in the hallway.

'*No*, Gram!' I shouted. '*No* ...'

Ellman pushed past me, shoving me into the wall, and strode over to where Gram was standing. Without a moment's thought, he snatched the phone from her hand, ripped out the cable, then cracked her across the head with the phone. She didn't make a sound, she just crumpled to the floor and lay still, her head streaming with blood.

'You fucking *bastard*,' I spat, lunging at Ellman.

'Hash,' he said quickly.

A muffled cry of pain stopped me in my tracks, and I turned round to see that Hashim had rammed[2] Lucy's head against the wall and was digging[3] the barrel of the gun into her head.

'I warned you,' Ellman said to me. 'You make another move, your bitch is dead.'

As I turned to face him, breathing heavily, he just smiled at me.

I looked down at Gram. Her face was very pale, and she was breathing shallowly[4]. Through gritted[5] teeth, I said to Ellman, 'She needs help.'

He shrugged. 'It's up to you – you can help her all you want ... as long as you don't mind having a girlfriend with no head.'

I heard the flat door closing then, and I looked down the hallway to see Lucy being dragged into the front room by Hashim, with O'Neil and the black guy following them.

---

1 splatter sth.: splash sth. (usu. a liquid)   **2** ram sth.: push sth. hard   **3** dig sth. into sth.: put sth. against sth. else and push it hard   **4** breathe shallowly: *flach atmen*   **5** gritted: *knirschend*

I gazed down at Gram again, then back at Ellman. 'Can I at least get her into her room and make her comfortable?'

Ellman smiled, shaking his head. 'You've only got yourself to blame, you know. If you'd left things alone, none of this would be
5   happening.'

I stared desperately at Gram. Her poor grey hair was matted[1] with blood now, and she looked so small and weak ...

I'd never felt more helpless in my life.

'Get in there,' Ellman told me, nodding his head towards the
10   front room.

When I went into the front room, Hashim and Lucy were standing over by the window, and O'Neil and the black guy were just hanging around by the door.

Ellman told me to sit down.
15   I looked over at Lucy.

'I'm *so* sorry,' I said to her.

She couldn't answer me.

'Don't worry –' I started to tell her.

'Sit *down!*' Ellman barked.
20   I sat down on the settee, and he sat in the armchair opposite me. He hadn't changed very much from the photograph I'd seen of him in his police record. He was about fifteen years older, of course, so his face wasn't quite so young-looking as before, but apart from that, he looked pretty much the same. The same shaved head, the
25   same angular face, the same soulless eyes. His eyes – described in the police record as pale blue – were actually so pale that they were almost transparent, like the blue of a distant sky. He was dressed in an expensive black suit, an equally expensive black T-shirt, and shiny black crocodile-skin shoes.
30   My iBrain told me that in the inside pocket of his suit jacket he had a BlackBerry Bold 9700[2].

---

1 matted with sth.: (here) covered with sth.   **2** BlackBerry Bold 9700: popular type of smartphone

'All right,' he said calmly, lighting a cigarette. 'This is how it's going to go. I ask you a question, you give me an answer. If you don't give me an answer, or if you lie to me, the bitch gets it. OK?'

'Yeah.'

'Good.' He puffed on his cigarette. 'All right, first question. You're the kid who calls himself iBoy, right?'

'How do you know –?'

'Just answer the fucking question.'

I glanced over at Lucy. Her eyes were on me, but I couldn't tell what she was thinking. I looked back at Ellman.

'Yeah,' I told him.

'You're iBoy, yeah?'

'Yeah.'

'And it's you that's been going round Crow Town fucking things up?'

'Yeah.'

'Stirring up[1] all kinds of shit.'

'Yeah.'

'Why?'

'Why?'

'Yeah, why? I mean, what's in it for you?'

'Nothing.'

He shook his head. 'No one does anything for nothing.'

'I'm just doing what I think is right,' I told him.

He laughed. 'What the fuck is that supposed to mean?'

I nodded at O'Neil. 'He raped Lucy. Him, Hashim, Adebajo ... the rest of them. They raped her, for Christ's sake. They fucking *raped* her.'

Ellman shrugged. 'And your point is?'

There was nothing in his eyes, nothing at all. No feeling, no sympathy, not a shred[2] of humanity. This man was sick. There was no point in talking to him.

'Forget it,' I sighed, looking away. 'It doesn't matter ...'

---

1 stir up: (here) cause problems   **2** shred: very small piece

'You want revenge, is that it? You want payback[1]? Is that what this is all about?'

'Yeah, if you say so ...'

'Well, is it or not?'

5 I said nothing.

Ellman suddenly leaned forward and yelled into my face. 'Fucking *answer* me ... *NOW!*'

'Yes,' I said slowly, looking right at him. 'Revenge ... that's what it's all about. Revenge, punishment, retribution. You're just as much to

10 blame for what happened to Lucy as the ones who actually did it –'

'Yeah? And how d'you work that one out?'

'You tempt people to ruin and destroy –'

'*What?*' he said, frowning at me.

'You ruin people, you and your world ... you ruin lives.' I shrugged.

15 'So, yeah, I've been going round the estate stirring up all kinds of shit, because I knew that'd piss you off, and that eventually you'd come looking for me ... and I guess it worked. Because here you are.'

Ellman smiled. 'And now what? You're going to kill me?'

'If I have to.'

20 He laughed, looking over at O'Neil and the others. 'You hear that? He says he's going to kill me if he has to.' They laughed along with him, and then he turned back to me. 'OK,' he said. 'Next question. This iBoy thing ... what's that all about?'

I shrugged again. 'Nothing, really ...'

25 'Nothing?'

'It's just a bit of fun, you know ... dressing up like a superhero, wearing a costume and a mask so no one knows who I am.'

'Where is it?'

'Where's what?'

30 'The costume, the mask. Where are they?'

'Why?'

---

1 payback: (here) act of hurting sb. who has hurt you

'That's not an answer, that's a question.' He nodded over at Hashim. Hashim jabbed the pistol into Lucy's head again. She winced[1], but didn't make a sound.

'All right,' I said to Ellman, holding my hands up. 'All right, please don't hurt her any more.'   5

'Where's the costume and the mask?' he repeated.

'There isn't any costume,' I sighed.

'What?'

'No costume, no mask. Honestly ... it's just me.'

Ellman stared at me for a moment, then he looked over at O'Neil.   10
'Check his room, Yo. And all the other rooms too. See if you can find any of this iBoy shit – costume, mask, Taser, any kind of tech[2] stuff.'

O'Neil went out, and Ellman turned back to me. 'So, it's just you, yeah?'

I nodded.   15

Ellman smiled. 'You want to show me what you mean by that?'

I didn't have any choice now – I had to show him the truth. If I didn't, if I tried to hide what I was, what I could do ... well, I didn't even want to think about what Ellman would do to Lucy.

I just couldn't risk it.   20

'Look,' I said to Ellman, and I turned on my iSkin. As I felt it starting to glow and shimmer, I watched his reaction. He didn't move or say anything for a while, he just sat there in mute disbelief, staring open-mouthed at the shifting colours and shapes of my skin. Without saying anything, I showed him my hands, and then I lifted up   25
my shirt and showed him my chest, letting him see that my iSkin was everywhere.

'Shit, man,' he whispered eventually. 'How the fuck do you *do* that?'

'It's a long story,' I said.   30

'You see this, Tweet?' he said to the black guy without taking his eyes off me.

'Fucking right.'

---

1 wince: change your facial expression because of pain   **2** tech: technical

'Shit,' said Hashim. 'He's a fucking *freak*[1], man.'

I couldn't bear to look at Lucy. I hadn't looked at her since admitting to Ellman that I was iBoy. And now ... well, Hashim was right. I *was* a freak. And who in their right mind wants anything to do with
5 a freak?

I turned off my iSkin.

Ellman said, 'You can turn it on and off, just like that?'

'Yeah.'

'Fuck ...' He looked at me. 'So how does it work?'

10 'I don't know ...'

I could hear O'Neil crashing around in my room now, emptying drawers, throwing stuff around ...

I said to Ellman, 'He's not going to find anything.'

'No? What about the Taser?'

15 I sighed. 'There's no Taser.'

'And the phone stuff, the computer stuff ... whatever it is you've been using to track and hack and all that shit?'

I tapped my head. 'It's all in here.'

He shook his head. 'I don't get it.'

20 I looked at him. 'If I tell you everything, absolutely everything, will you let me check on my gran? I just want to make sure that she's OK, you know? Make her comfortable.'

Ellman thought about it for a moment, then nodded. 'OK.'

So I started telling him everything. How the iPhone that Davey
25 Carr had thrown from Lucy's window had cracked open my skull and left bits of itself inside my brain, and how those bits had somehow become part of me, giving me all the powers of an iPhone and more ... but as I told Ellman all this, I wasn't looking at him or thinking of him ... I was just staring at the floor, thinking of Lucy. I was
30 telling my story for her. I still couldn't physically look at her, but I was looking at her in my heart.

When I'd finished explaining everything, I finally looked up at Ellman. His icy-blue eyes were fixed on mine, his face emotionless.

---

1 freak (derog.): weird person

'That's it?' he said.

'Yeah. I mean, I know you probably don't believe it, but –'

'Show me.'

'What?'

'Show me what you can do.'   5

'What about my gran? Can I go and check on her now?'

'No.'

'But you said –'

'I was lying.' He smiled. 'Now, show me what you can do, or I'll go
and get your gran and rip her fucking head off.'   10

I stared at him for a moment, hating him, despising him, wanting to *hurt* him more than anything else in the world, but I knew he
wasn't bluffing[1]. I knew he had it in him to kill Gram without even
thinking about it. So I just nodded at him, and I watched as he felt
his phone vibrate.   15

'Answer it,' I said.

He took his BlackBerry out of his pocket and opened the text I'd
just sent him.

It read: *your dead.*

He looked at me, grinning. 'I'm impressed.'   20

'I sent you some pictures too,' I said.

He opened up the photographs. One of them showed him hitting
Gram with the phone, another one was of Hashim and Lucy ... others showed O'Neil and the guy called Tweet.

Ellman studied them all for a while, then looked at me. 'And this   25
is all in your head, yeah?'

I nodded.

He said, 'You got WiFi?'

'I've got everything.'

'So you could be calling anyone right now?'   30

'I could be, but I'm not.'

'Good. Because you know what'll happen if I hear a siren, or if
anyone comes anywhere near this flat, don't you?'

---

1 bluff: say you will do sth. you aren't really going to do

I nodded. 'I'm not going to call anyone.'

He leaned towards me. 'It won't only be your bitch who gets it –'

'She's not my *bitch*,' I said coldly.

'She'll just be the first,' he continued, ignoring me. 'Any trouble
5 from you, anything at all, and I'm going to do the bitch first, then her
family, then your old woman, *and* I'm going to make you watch me
doing it ... and then I'll fucking do you.' He smiled. 'All right?'

'Yeah.'

'OK, good.' He lit a cigarette. 'Now what about all this electric
10 stuff I've heard about? Yoyo says you zapped him or something. Is
that right?'

'Yeah.'

'Show me how you do it.'

I looked at him. 'Who do you want me to zap? I can do it to you,
15 if you want.'

He grinned at me. 'Come here, Tweet.'

Tweet came over and stood in front of me. He was huge – big,
strong, solid – and as he stood there staring down impassively[1] at
me, there was no trace of fear in his eyes. He wasn't frightened of
20 pain.

Ellman said to me, 'Can you do it without putting him in hospital?'

I nodded, looking up at Tweet. 'I can hurt him as much or as little
as you want.'

25 Ellman smiled. 'Do it.'

I hesitated for a moment, considering my options. I knew that I
could take out Ellman and Tweet with a big burst of power, but that
still left Hashim and O'Neil. O'Neil was still searching my room – I
could hear him crashing around – so it was possible I could get to
30 him before he realized that anything was wrong.

But Hashim ...?

I glanced over and saw him watching me. His hand was so tightly
taped to the gun, and the gun so tightly taped to Lucy's head, that

---

1 impassively: showing no emotion or expression

even if I *could* have zapped him from here – and he was right over the other side of the room, so I was pretty sure that I couldn't – it only needed the slightest twitch[1] of his finger for the pistol to go off. And I guessed that being electrocuted would more than likely make his finger twitch.   5

I glanced at Lucy.

Unbelievably, she winked at me. God, it made me feel so good.

'What are you fucking waiting for?' Ellman said.

I looked at him, looked up at Tweet, then reached out and touched Tweet's knee. Like I said, he was a really *huge* guy. So, just   10
to make sure that he felt it, I gave him a zap that was somewhere between not-too-bad and pretty-bad. And he felt it, all right. He yelped – in a surprisingly high-pitched[2], almost girly[3], kind of way – and as his knee flashed blue and his leg jerked out from under him, he toppled over[4] and crashed to the floor.   15

'*Shit,* man!' he hissed, clutching at his knee. '*Jesus!*'

'Y'all right?' Ellman said to him.

'Yeah …' he sighed, rubbing his whole leg. '*Fuck*, that hurts.'

O'Neil came bursting[5] into the front room then, alerted by the sound of Tweet falling over. 'What's going on?' he said, looking at   20
Tweet. 'What's happening?'

'Nothing,' Ellman said. 'Everything's cool.' He looked over at O'Neil. 'You didn't find anything, did you?'

Still staring at Tweet, O'Neil shook his head. 'Not yet … but I haven't checked the other rooms yet.'   25

'Don't bother,' Ellman told him. 'It's all sorted[6].'

'What do you mean?'

Ellman ignored him, turning back to me. 'Do you have to actu-ally touch people to do that? I mean, can you do it from a distance?'

I hesitated for a moment, instinctively holding back. Ellman said,   30
'Don't fucking *think* about it, just answer me.'

---

1 twitch: *Zucken*   **2** high-pitched: very high (of a sound)   **3** girly: like a girl
4 topple over: fall   **5** burst into sth.: enter sth. suddenly   **6** sorted (infml.):
(here) clear; organized

I sighed, realizing that there was no point in lying. If I told Ellman that I *could* zap from a distance, he'd want me to prove it. And I wouldn't be able to. And if I told him that I wasn't going to prove it, he'd hurt Lucy. So I had no choice but to tell him the truth.

5 'I can zap stuff from about a metre away,' I said. 'No more.'

He nodded, watching as Tweet got to his feet.

'OK?' he asked him.

Tweet glared at me. 'Yeah ... yeah, I'm all right.'

Ellman grinned at him. 'You don't *look* all right.'

10 'I'm fine,' Tweet growled.

Ellman turned to me. 'Yo said he tried to stab you, but you did something to his knife.'

I nodded. 'It's the electricity ... it gives me some kind of force field.'

15 'Yeah? So if Tweet wanted to smack you in the head for what you've just done to him, what'd happen?'

'He'd get hurt even more.'

Ellman smiled. 'You bulletproof too?'

'I don't know,' I shrugged. 'No one's tried to shoot me yet.'

20 Ellman looked at me for a moment or two, his eyes seeming to gaze right through me, and then O'Neil called out, 'She's waking up,' and we both looked over at him. He was leaning round the doorway, peering down the hallway.

'The old woman,' he said, turning back to Ellman.

25 'She's coming round.'

'Tie her up,' Ellman said. 'Get her out the way.'

As O'Neil nodded and headed off down the hallway, I had to force myself not to say anything, not to do anything ... not to give in to the murder in my heart.

30 I looked at Ellman. He was just sitting there now, smoking a cigarette, staring at nothing, his face a mask of concentration ...

I glanced over at Lucy. Blood from the cut on her face had dripped onto her nightgown, and her face was pale and frightened, but as she looked back at me in the silence, I could see a hidden strength

35 in her eyes, some kind of faith ... a belief that, despite everything

that had happened – and everything that *was* happening and could possibly happen – we'd both get out of this in the end.

She truly believed it.

I smiled at her, trying to show her that I shared her belief.

Even though I didn't.

'It's a shame,' Ellman said.

I looked at him. 'What?'

He sighed. 'You and me … we could really have been something together. With your powers and my experience … I mean, fuck Crow Town, we could have had anywhere we wanted. We could have made fucking *millions* …' He looked disdainfully[1] at me. 'But you could never do it, could you? You're too fucking weak. Too fucking *righteous*[2].' He shook his head. 'No, I couldn't work with that. It'd drive me mad.' He sighed. 'Like I said, it's a shame … but business is business.' He smiled at me. 'That's all it is, you know … all this … the old woman, the bitch over there … you … it's all just business.'

I didn't even bother looking at him.

He sniffed. 'Yeah, well … we'd best get on with it.' He stood up and called out, 'Yo? You finished in there?'

O'Neil called back from Gram's room, 'Yeah, just a minute …'

'What you doing?'

'Nothing, just looking around …'

'Leave it. We're going.'

'There's some nice stuff in here. Laptops, jewellery –'

'I said fucking *leave* it!' Ellman barked. Then he turned to Tweet. 'Call Gunner, make sure we're clear, then check the corridor.'

Tweet pulled a phone from his pocket, hit a button, and went out into the hallway. I listened in to the call and tracked it to another mobile in the square down below, somewhere near the entrance to the tower.

Yeah?

We're coming out. Everything all right?

Yeah, it's quiet.

---

1 disdainfully: without respect   **2** righteous [ˈraɪtʃəs]: *rechtschaffen; anständig*

'Get up,' Ellman said to me.

I got up.

Tweet came back in. 'It's all clear.'

Ellman nodded. 'You go first. Hash, you follow him.' He turned
5 to O'Neil, who was standing in the doorway. 'You follow Hash, OK?'

O'Neil nodded.

Ellman said to me, 'You follow Yo. Understand?'

'Yeah.'

'I'll be right behind you. Hash?'

10 'Yeah?' Hashim said.

'How's it going with that gun?'

'My fucking hand hurts.'

Ellman said to me, 'You hear that? His hand hurts. It's been taped
to the gun for about an hour now, so his finger's probably getting a
15 bit numb[1]. It won't take much for him to pull the trigger. And it'll be
your fault if he does. You got that?'

'Yeah, I've got it.'

'All right, let's go.'

---

1 numb [nʌm]: unable to feel

10110

Here are comedy and tragedy ... Here is melodrama ... Here are unvarnished[1] *emotions. Here also is a primitive democracy that cuts through all the conventional social and racial discriminations. The gang, in short, is life ...*

Frederic Thrasher[2]
The Gang *(1927)*

It was 03:15:52 when we left the flat and walked down the corridor to the lift. There was no one around. The tower felt cold and empty. An early-morning silence pervaded[3] the air, adding to the sense of emptiness, and the sound of our footsteps echoed dully in the stillness. As we approached the lift – which had been jammed open[4] with an iron bar[5] – I wondered if this was going to be my final journey ...

My final time in this corridor.

My final time in the lift.

My final time in the concrete splendour[6] of good old Compton House.

I smiled to myself, thinking – well, it could have been a lot worse, couldn't it? Of course, it could have been a whole lot better too ...

As we got into the lift and the doors closed, I glanced at Lucy. The picnic we'd had just a few hours earlier seemed to belong to a different world now, a world that existed a thousand years ago. And while, at the time, it had felt like the beginning of something between me and Lucy, it was now starting to feel like it was all there was ever going to be: the beginning, the middle, the end. But even so, if this *was* to be my final journey – our final journey – that brief

---

1 unvarnished (fml.): plain   **2** Frederic Thrasher: (1892–1962) American sociologist who studied gangs, crime and juvenile delinquency   **3** pervade: (here) fill
4 jam sth. open: (here) force sth. open   **5** iron bar: long, thin piece of iron
6 splendour: beautiful atmosphere

time we'd shared on the roof together would still be the best time of my life.

Yeah, I thought, smiling at Lucy, it could have been a whole lot worse.

5 'What are you smiling about?' Hashim sneered at me.

I looked at him. 'Not much. Just thinking how lucky I am, that's all.'

'Lucky?' he said, shaking his head. 'You fucking freak.'

As the lift reached the ground floor, I said to Ellman,

10 'What have you done with Lucy's mum and her brother?'

He didn't say anything, he didn't even bother looking at me. He just waited, his eyes taking in everything, as Tweet checked out the ground floor, making sure there was no one around. Then, after a signal from Tweet, Ellman gave Hashim the nod[1], and Hashim moved

15 out of the lift with Lucy. O'Neil followed them. Ellman looked at me, jerking his head, and I followed O'Neil, with Ellman close behind me.

Outside the tower, two black Range Rovers with tinted windows[2] were waiting by the doors.

20 Now that I was sure we were leaving the tower, I sent the text that I'd already written in my head to the local police and ambulance services. The text read: *URGENT!!! PLEASE HELP!!! MS CONNIE HARVEY, AGED 54, HAS BEEN ATTACKED AND HAS SUFFERED A SERIOUS HEAD INJURY. SHE NEEDS IMMEDIATE MEDICAL*

25 *ATTENTION. SHE HAS BEEN TIED UP AND LEFT IN HER ROOM BY UNKNOWN ASSAILANTS[3] AT FLAT 4, 23RD FLOOR, COMPTON HOUSE, CROW LANE ESTATE, CROW LANE, LONDON SE15 6CG. MRS MICHELLE WALKER AND HER SON BEN MAY ALSO NEED ASSISTANCE AT FLAT 6 ON 30TH FLOOR. THIS IS NOT A HOAX[4].*

30 *PLEASE HURRY.*

---

1 give sb. the nod: give sb. permission to do sth.   **2** tinted windows: black windows that you can't see into   **3** assailant [ə'seɪlənt]: attacker   **4** hoax [həʊks]: joke; trick

The two Range Rovers both had their engines running. While Tweet and Hashim and Lucy headed for the one in front, Ellman told me to follow O'Neil to the other one. I watched over my shoulder as Hashim and Lucy got awkwardly[1] into the back of the first one, with Tweet getting into the front passenger's seat, then Ellman opened the back door of our Range Rover and told me to get in.

I got in.

He got in beside me.

O'Neil sat in the front passenger seat.

The guy in the driver's seat had his hood up, and all I could see of his face in the rear-view mirror was a pair of dark glasses and a raggedy twist of beard on his chin. From his phone records, I knew that he was Gunner.

'All right?' he grunted at Ellman.

Ellman ignored him, watching the car in front pull away. Then he just said, 'Go.'

*

We turned right out of Compton and headed south along Crow Lane, both cars cruising along at a steady 40mph – not fast enough to get stopped, not too slow to attract attention. Ellman lit a cigarette and leaned back in his seat, looking totally relaxed and at ease. I gazed out through the window for a while, watching the estate pass by – the kids' playground, the low-rises, the towers ... Fitzroy House, Gladstone, Heath. There were a few people around – some gang kids hanging around the towers, one or two passing cars – but they might as well have been on another planet for all the good they were to me. I didn't need telling again that Hashim would shoot Lucy if I tried anything. So I gave up thinking about it.

'Where are we going?' I asked Ellman as we passed Heath House and carried on heading south.

'You'll find out when we get there,' Ellman said.

---

1 awkwardly: (here) with difficulty

I looked at him. 'How did you know it was me?'

'Eh?'

'iBoy ... how did you know it was me?'

He shrugged. 'Does it matter?'

5 'Not really ...' I grinned at him. 'But if this was a James Bond[1] movie, this would be the perfect moment for the mad super-villain[2] to show Bond how clever he is by unnecessarily explaining everything to him.'

Ellman smiled. 'Yeah, just before he tries to kill the fucker.'

10 'And Bond escapes.'

He looked at me. 'Real life ain't the movies.'

'True.'

He smiled. 'I mean, you think I'm going to hang you from a rope over a pool of fucking sharks[3] or something?'

15 'Probably not.'

He laughed. 'And you're not exactly James fucking Bond, are you?'

'I suppose not ... what about you?'

'What about me?'

I smiled at him. 'Are you the mad super-villain?'

20 'Yeah, fucking right. I'm Hell-Man ... I'm the Devil –'

'And I'm iBoy.'

He looked at me, genuinely amused.

I said, 'So, how did you find out?'

He laughed. 'It was the kid, the bitch's brother ... what's his
25 name?'

'Ben?'

'Yeah. He told Troy and Jermaine that when you were trying to throw Yo out the window, and his sister was watching, he heard her whispering something to herself.' Ellman shook his head. 'The little
30 shit thought she said *eBay*, but then Yo here remembered one of his crew[4] calling you *iBoy* a couple of weeks ago ... you know, like he was just fucking around with you at the time. So then we started think-

---

1 James Bond: fictional British secret agent 007 in films and books, first written by Ian Fleming in 1954   **2** villain: criminal   **3** shark: *Hai*   **4** crew: team; group

ing about it, looking into it, you know ... and here we are.' He looked
at me. 'Satisfied?'

'Yeah.'

'You ready to be strung up[1] over the sharks now?'

'No problem.'   5

He grinned at me for a moment, then he turned away and spent
some time looking out of the car window, checking all around, making sure that everything was OK.

'You see anything?' he said to Gunner.

'No, it's cool,' Gunner said.   10

'OK, take the right by the bridge and head back north. Yo, call
Marek and let him know.'

As O'Neil called the car in front and passed on the directions to
the driver (who I guessed was Marek), Ellman leaned back in his
seat again and carried on smoking his cigarette.   15

I gazed out of the window for a while, trying to work out where
we were going, but all I could tell was that we seemed to be going
round in circles. I tuned in to the GPS signal inside my head, logged
on to Google Map, and let my iBrain do its stuff.

'So, anyway,' Ellman said casually, turning back to me. 'You're   20
Georgie Harvey's boy, yeah?'

I didn't say anything, I just stared at him, wondering how the hell
he knew my mum's name.

He smiled. 'I don't suppose you remember her much, do you?
You must have been about ... what, six months old when she died?'   25
He looked at me, smoking his cigarette, waiting for me to say something. When I didn't, he took another drag[2] on his cigarette, flipped
it out the window, and went on. 'Georgie was really something, you
know. Did anyone ever tell you that? She was one hot piece of ass.
Feisty[3] too.' He grinned at me. 'Shit, man, that bitch could fight.'   30

I was so confused, so utterly stunned by what he was saying, I
could barely breathe, let alone speak.

---

1 string sb. up: hang sb.   **2** drag: (here) breath   **3** feisty: energetic; lively

'What's the matter?' Ellman said, grinning at me. 'Didn't you know about me and your mummy?'

I heard O'Neil sniggering[1], but I didn't take my eyes off Ellman. I *couldn't* take my eyes off him. 'You knew my mum?' I whispered.

5 'Yeah,' he said, leering[2], 'I *knew* her ... in fact, I was the first guy that Georgie ever *knew*. Of course, there were plenty more after me –'

'You're lying,' I said.

He looked at me. 'You think so?'

10 I nodded. 'You never knew my mum.'

He laughed again. 'I'm just telling you the truth, that's all.'

'The truth?' I said, sneering at him. 'What do you know about the truth?'

He stopped laughing suddenly and stared at me, his eyes dead
15 cold. 'I'll tell you what I know,' he said icily. 'Your mother was a fucked-up little whore who'd do anything for a line of coke[3], I know that. And I know how much effort it took me to break that bitch down and get her out on the streets where she belonged ... and then what does she do? After everything I've fucking done for her? She
20 gets herself knocked up[4] and says she wants out ... she wants out of the game ... she wants to get *clean,* for fuck's sake ...'

Ellman paused for a moment, his eyes drifting away from me, and all I could do was sit there, totally numbed, unable to digest what he was telling me ... or, at least, what I *thought* he was telling
25 me. It was simply too painful to believe.

'Yeah, well,' Ellman said, his voice quite casual again. 'She got what she deserved.'

'What?'

'She knew what'd happen if she left me. I mean, no one leaves me.
30 No one. And she knew that. She knew what I had to do.'

'What ...?' I said, my voice barely audible. 'What did you have to do?'

---

1 snigger: *kichern*   **2** leer: smile unpleasantly   **3** line of coke: small amount of cocaine spread out in a thin line   **4** knocked up (infml.): pregnant

Ellman looked surprised, as if the answer was obvious.

'I had to kill her.'

'Kill her?'

He shrugged. 'What else could I do?'

I shook my head in disbelief. 'My mum died in a road accident –' 5

'It wasn't an accident.'

I stared at him. 'Are you seriously trying to tell me that you were the driver of the car that ran over my mum?' He looked at me for a moment, his face deadly serious … and then, all of a sudden, his face broke into a smile and he started laughing. 'I had you going for a 10 while there, didn't I?' he said. 'I really had you going …'

'I don't understand –'

'I didn't *kill* her,' he said, still laughing. 'I was just fucking with you, that's all.'

'You *didn't* kill my mum?' 15

He shook his head, grinning. 'Like you said, what do I know about the truth?'

O'Neil and Gunner were both laughing too now, snorting away at enjoying Ellman's excellent joke, and as the car filled with the sound of their stupid braying[1] voices, I just looked out of the window and 20 tried to think about things. Was Ellman lying or not? Had he really known my mother? Had anything he'd told me about her been anywhere *near* the truth?

I couldn't think about it. It was too hard.

I blanked out[2] my emotions for a while and concentrated instead 25 on trying to coordinate the cyber-map inside my head with what I could see through the car window. It didn't take me long to work out that we were on the west side of the towers now, heading back north towards the industrial estate …

I looked at Ellman. He'd stopped laughing now and was just sit- 30 ting there, smoking another cigarette, gazing indifferently[3] at me.

'Why do you do it?' I said to him.

---

1 braying: like the sound of a donkey   **2** blank out sth.: deliberately forget sth. unpleasant   **3** indifferently: not caring

'Do what?'

'All this ... fucking people up, hurting people, raping, killing ... I mean, why do you *do* it?'

He shrugged. 'I told you before, it's just business.'

5 I stared at him. 'Business? How the hell is raping and killing people business?'

He sighed. 'You don't understand –'

'No, I don't.'

'It's all about power,' he said. 'Everything ... the whole fucking 10 world, it's all about power. If you've got it, you survive. If you haven't, you don't. Simple as that. Power is the law. It rules the fucking world. You understand? And down here ...' He looked out of the window, indicating the passing streets, the towers in the distance, the world of Crow Town. 'The only law down here, the only means of acquiring 15 and establishing and maintaining your power, is violence.' He stared hard at me. 'Rape, murder, whatever ... it's not personal. I don't do it for fun. I mean, I'm not saying that I *don't* enjoy it, because I do, but that's not *why* I do it. I do it because it shows everyone else who I am, what I can do ... it shows the world what I am.'

20 'And that's it?' I said. 'You kill and rape and brutalize people just to show the world what you are? That's your *reason*?'

He shrugged. 'It's as good a reason as any.'

I stared at him. 'But you must know it's *wrong* –'

'Wrong?' he laughed. 'What the fuck's *wrong* got to do with any-25 thing?' He looked at me. 'D'you think it's *wrong* for a dog to kill a cat?'

'That's totally different.'

'Why?'

'Dogs are animals – they don't know any better.'

'What, and you think *I* do? You think any of us do? Fuck, man ... 30 we're all fucking animals – none of us know any better.'

As we sat there staring at each other – a wimp and a devil, iBoy and Hell-Man, together in the back seat of a black Range Rover – I wondered for a moment if perhaps, in a twisted kind of way, he was right. Maybe neither of us *did* know any better. Maybe we *were* just 35 animals. And maybe ...

I stopped thinking about it then. The car was beginning to slow down. I looked out of the window and saw that the Range Rover in front of us had turned right and was heading slowly up an unlit lane[1]. We followed it. The lane was uneven[2], pitted[3] with cracks and pot-holes[4], and as the car lumped and rolled its way upwards, the twin beams of the headlights illuminated the ghosted remains of the old industrial estate: rusted[5] skips, vacant[6] factories, empty industrial units, abandoned warehouses ...

The car in front was turning right again, this time into a square of wasteground that had probably once been a car park ... a car park for the employees who'd probably once worked in the dilapidated[7] warehouse on the far side of the wasteground.

'Follow them round the back,' Ellman told Gunner.

We followed the car in front as it rumbled across the wasteground, over to the warehouse, round the back ... and that's where we stopped.

I looked over at the other car, trying to catch a glimpse of Lucy, but it was too dark to see anything.

'Don't worry,' Ellman said to me. 'You'll see her in a minute.'

I looked at him. 'What are you going to do with her?'

'The same thing I did to your mother.'

'What?'

He smiled coldly. 'You should have seen the look on her face when I ran that bitch over.'

'But you said –'

'Yeah, I know. I said I was only joking about Georgie ... but I wasn't.' He grinned at me. 'Or maybe I was ... but I guess you'll never know now, will you?'

He moved so incredibly quickly then, hammering his head into mine with such stunning speed and power, that I didn't have time to feel confused. I didn't have time to feel anything. The only thing I

---

1 unlit lane: dark path or alley   **2** uneven: (here) not flat   **3** pitted: with small marks or holes in the surface   **4** pot-hole: *Schlagloch*   **5** rusted: *verrostet*
6 vacant: empty   **7** dilapidated: old and falling apart

was vaguely aware of was a sudden shuddering impact, a momentary flash of blinding pain ...

And then nothing.

10111

The universe we observe has precisely the properties[1] we should expect if there is, at bottom, no design, no purpose, no evil, no good, nothing but blind pitiless[2] indifference[3].

Richard Dawkins[4]
River Out of Eden: A Darwinian View of Life *(1995)*

The next thing I knew, I was opening my eyes and staring across the interior of the warehouse at Lucy. My head was throbbing[5], my 5 vision was blurred, my mouth was soured[6] with the taste of blood ... and, after I'd struggled uselessly for a few moments, I realized that I could barely move. I was securely bound to an iron girder[7] by tightly wound lengths[8] of wire. My hands, my feet, even my neck ... everything was so firmly tied that the only thing I could move was my 10 head.

But none of that mattered.

All that mattered was Lucy.

She was about twenty metres away from me, on the other side of the warehouse. She was on her knees, and Ellman was standing 15 in front of her with a long silver knife in his hand. Her mouth was still taped up, but the gun had been removed from her head, and Hashim wasn't with her any more. Instead, he was standing right beside me. And now that he'd realized I was conscious again, he raised the pistol and levelled[9] it at my head. 20

As Ellman sensed Hashim's movement and glanced over at me, the blade of his knife caught the pale yellow light of an electric lantern hanging from the wall, and just for a moment the reflected flash of light seemed to illuminate the whole warehouse. It was a

---

1 property (fml.): (here) quality; characteristic   **2** pitiless: mean; cruel   **3** indifference: lack of interest or sympathy   **4** Richard Dawkins: (born 1942) British evolutionary biologist, author of several popular science books   **5** throb: (here) experience regular bursts of pain   **6** soured: tasting sharp and sour   **7** girder: *Eisenträger*   **8** length: (here) long thin rope   **9** level at sth.: point at sth.

fairly big place, with rust-ridden[1] sheet-metal[2] walls, a crumbling concrete floor, and dozens of frayed[3] electric cables dangling[4] from the ceiling. There wasn't much else to see: the blackened remains of old machinery, some cracked wooden crates[5], empty gas canisters,
5 a couple of dilapidated chairs …

'What do you think?' Ellman called out to me. 'Do you like it?'

I didn't answer him, I was too busy checking out where the others were. Hashim, as I said, was right beside me; O'Neil was behind Ellman and Lucy, leaning on a windowsill; Tweet was sitting in one
10 of the old chairs, calmly smoking a joint; and the two drivers, Gunner and Marek, were standing over to my left by a pair of wooden doors.

Six of them.

One of me.

15 And I didn't even have any iPowers.

'What's the matter, kid?' Ellman said. 'You not talking to me any more?'

I looked up to see him crossing the warehouse towards me.

He grinned at me. 'How's your head? I haven't broken anything
20 in there, have I? You know, smashed a few circuits or something?' He stopped a few metres away from me. 'Or can't you tell without a signal?' He reached into his pocket, brought out his BlackBerry, and studied the screen. 'Nope,' he said, shaking his head. 'Still no bars[6].' He looked at me, smiling. 'How about you? You got any?'

25 I said nothing.

He put his phone back in his pocket. 'I'm guessing,' he said, 'that without a signal, you're fucked.' He looked at me. 'Am I right?'

Again, I said nothing.

---

1 rust-ridden: *voller Rost*   **2** sheet-metal: *Metallplatten*   **3** frayed: *ausgefranst*
4 dangle: hang or swing freely   **5** crate: wooden or plastic containers for transporting goods   **6** bars: (here) *Balkenanzeige für Netzwerkverbindung*

He carried on smiling at me. 'No signal. No WiFi. No phone, no power.' He nodded his head, miming[1] the headbutt[2] he'd given me. 'No force field either.' He glanced at Hashim. 'What d'you say, Hash?'

Hashim grinned. 'Yeah, I'd say he's completely fucked.'

Ellman stepped closer, staring into my eyes. 'Of course, you *could* be bluffing, couldn't you? You could be *pretending* to be powerless, lulling us all into a false sense of security[3], and then, when we least expect it – *zap!* He clapped his hands together. 'You fry us all.' He grinned at me again. 'But the only problem with that is that you can't fry us all, can you? I mean, right now, you could probably blast me and Hash, but the others are too far away. So even if you *did* take out the two of us, there'd still be Tweet over there, and Gunner and Marek, and don't forget Yoyo ... you see what I'm saying? You blast me and Hash, you're still going to be tied to this girder, and Yoyo's still going to get to play with your girly.'

I looked over at Lucy. She was still kneeling there, her head bowed down, her eyes empty and still, shocked into nothing ...

I couldn't let anything happen to her.

Not again.

I had to do something.

'What do you reckon, Hash?' I heard Ellman say. 'You think he's bluffing?'

'Like you said, it don't make no odds[4],' Hashim said. 'They're both going to get fucked anyway.' He started laughing then, a curiously childish sound, which for some reason really irritated me. I ran my tongue round the inside of my mouth, turned my head, and spat a gob[5] of blood into his face.

'Fuck!' he yelled, jerking away.

Ellman laughed as Hashim wiped the bloody spit from his face. I glanced over at Lucy again and saw that she hadn't moved. She was still just kneeling there, dead to the world.

---

1 mime sth.: act sth. **2** headbutt (n): hit with your head **3** lull sb. into a false sense of security: make sb. think they're safe when they're not **4** it don't make no odds: it doesn't make any difference **5** gob: (here) mass of liquid

'*Luce!*' I called out. '*Luce!*'

She raised her head and slowly looked over at me.

'It's going to be all right!' I called out to her. 'Don't worry, every-thing's going to be –'

5   A crack of pain ripped into my face as Hashim hit me with the barrel of the gun. I tried not to cry out, but I couldn't help it. The pain was so raw, so ugly, it felt like my face had been torn apart. I turned my head towards Hashim, watching through tear-stung[1] eyes as he raised the gun again, his eyes blazing with anger, and I braced
10 myself for another blow ...

But then I heard Ellman's voice, 'That's enough.'

I saw Hashim hesitate, desperate to hurt me, but not quite des-perate enough to disobey Ellman. Still glaring at me, he lowered the gun and stepped back.

15 'Not now, OK?' Ellman said to him. 'I want him conscious for now ... I want him to know what's happening. All right?'

Hashim nodded.

'Afterwards,' Ellman said. 'You can do what you like ...' He turned to me. 'You know what's going to happen now, don't you? I mean,
20 you know what I'm going to do.' I didn't say anything, I just stared at him. But I wasn't actually looking at him. My eyes were open, but in my mind they were closed. I was digging deep inside myself now ... deep into my iBrain, my iSenses, my iPowers ... looking for some-thing ... anything ... searching, searching, searching ...

25 There was still no signal, no reception, but I had to find some-thing ... I *had* to. I *had* to be iBoy to stand any chance of saving Lucy.

Ellman had started taunting[2] me about my mother again now – '... and I'll tell you something else about me and little Georgie, and this'll *really* give you something to think about ...' – but I wasn't lis-
30 tening to him. I couldn't listen. I was iBoy, and we weren't there. We were deep down inside ourselves, reaching out, stretching ... stretching ... stretching up into the sky ...

---

1 tear-stung: itching and burning pain from tears   **2** taunt (v): tease; insult

'... and I bet *she* thought about it too ... I mean, we did it a lot, me and Georgie, even when she was working the streets, she still wanted me all the time ... they always do ...'

... and we knew it was there somewhere, we knew the signal was there ... maybe half a kilometre away, maybe less ... a few hundred 5 metres ... just round the corner ... it was there, they were there. The radio waves from the nearest base station, the frequencies ... the cycles ... the pathways were there ... and the stray[1] static electricity all around us, we both knew that that was there too ... and if we could somehow focus it back to our signal receptors ... 10

We closed our wide-open eyes and concentrated.

'... so, anyway,' Ellman continued, 'the thing is, when Georgie got knocked up back then, there's a pretty good chance it was me ... and if it was me ... well, fucking hell ...' He laughed. 'Do you see what I'm saying?' 15

... and now we were feeling something ... a boost[2], a rise, something in the air, something out there that was lifting us up ... out of our head ... taking our reach and pulling it up through the roof, into the night sky, up over the old buildings and factories ... and then ...

'I could be your fucking *father*.' 20

Then we had it.

'Hey! Are you listening to me?'

A connection. A solid connection.

'Say something, fucker! Fucking say something!'

We had a *connection*. 25

I opened my still-open eyes and saw Ellman's face, twisted with rage, staring into mine.

'If you were my father,' I said to him. 'I'd kill myself.'

Without saying a word, he raised the long silver knife in his hand, gently placed the needle-sharp tip[3] against my forehead, and slowly 30 drew the blade down my skin, deliberately not cutting too deeply, still wanting to keep me wide awake ...

---

1 stray: (here) separated; disconnected   **2** boost: (here) increase in power
3 tip: (here) sharp end

And I could feel the pain, I could feel warm blood running down my face.

But it didn't change anything. We were still connected.

'Fucking superhero,' Ellman sneered, taking the knife away and
5 examining the bloodied tip. 'Looks like you bleed the same as every other fucker I've ever cut.' He looked at me. 'Now let's see how you beg[1].'

I could feel the power surging inside me as he turned away and began walking over to Lucy ... but what could I do with it? If I zapped
10 Ellman and Hashim now, it wouldn't make any difference. I'd still be tied up. And the wire that was binding me to the girder was wound so tightly, and there was simply so much of it, that my chances of blasting[2] it away or melting it with a burst of electricity were pretty slim[3]. And even if I *could* zap my way out of the wire, taking out
15 Ellman and Hashim at the same time ... well, O'Neil and the others would still be there. And although there was a chance, just a very slight chance, that once Ellman and Hashim were out of the picture, Gunner and Marek and Tweet might decide to cut their losses and run ... there was no way that O'Neil was going to back down[4].

20 He'd get to Lucy before I could get to him.

And I couldn't let that happen.

I couldn't let *him* get anywhere near *her*.

I was, as Hashim had so eloquently put it, completely fucked.

And so, with a wretched[5] heart, I just stood there and watched as
25 Howard Ellman strode through the dusty light towards Lucy.

---

1 beg: ask for help   **2** blast sth. away: demolish sth. by explosion   **3** slim: (here) unlikely   **4** back down (v): admit defeat   **5** wretched ['retʃɪd]: miserable; pathetic

11000

Knowledge is power.

Francis Bacon[1]
Meditationes Sacrae. De Haeresibus *(1597)*

I'm still not sure if knowledge really *is* power, but as Ellman stood
in front of Lucy with the knife in his hand, looking down at her with
absolutely nothing in his eyes – no malevolence[2], no desire, no emotion at all ... well, at that moment, knowledge was all I had.   5

My iBrain *knew* things.

Facts, news, information ...

And I knew that I had to do something with it, because Ellman
was leaning towards Lucy now, tearing the tape from her mouth,
and I could see that she was crying ...   10

And I was too.

And crying wasn't going to help.

'Tom ...?' I heard Lucy sob.

Her voice was faint, weak with fear, and her face was pale and
greyed with shock, but when our eyes met, I could see that she still   15
had that hidden strength in her eyes ... and that, incredibly, she was
trying to smile at me.

I smiled back.

And Ellman slapped her across the face.

'Don't fucking look at *him*,' he told her, his voice quite calm.   20
'Look at me. You *hear* me? You keep your fucking eyes on me.'

She stared up at him, her eyes cold with hatred.

Ellman casually raised the knife in his hand, holding it close to
her face. 'You stay on your knees, you keep your eyes on me ... and
I might not cut you. Understand?' Lucy said nothing, just carried   25

---

1 Francis Bacon: (1561–1626) English philosopher and statesman. His essay "De
Hæresibus" [Of Heresies] appeared in "Essaies. Religious Meditations. Places of
Perswasion and Disswasion", 1597. (Original lat.; Nam et ipsa scientia potestas
est = Knowledge is power)   **2** malevolence: evil; wickedness

on staring at him, and I could tell by the look in her eyes that she
had no intention of giving up without a fight ... and that meant that
I had to act now, *right* now, before she got herself killed. I had to
look deep inside myself and use *everything* I had – my iSenses, my
5 iKnowledge, my iPowers, my self ... I had to focus it all, all at once,
all in a timeless moment, on my one and only hope.

I closed my eyes.

The iKnowledge was already there – If a lithium battery is overcharged[1], lithium metal will plate[2] (adhere[3]) to the anode, and oxy-
10 gen will be generated at the cathode. This is highly flammable and
a fire hazard[4] – and the iNews was already there – A man has died
after his mobile phone exploded, severing[5] a major artery in his
neck ... local reports said that this was the ninth recorded cellphone
explosion since 2002 – and I'd already scanned the warehouse and
15 checked the location of all six mobile phones. Ellman's was still in
the inside pocket of his suit jacket, Hashim's was in the back pocket
of his jeans, O'Neil's was in the front pocket of his track pants,
Tweet's was tucked[6] into his belt, Gunner's was in his T-shirt pocket,
and Marek's was in the front pocket of his jeans.
20   I opened my eyes.
     Ellman was standing closer to Lucy now. Lucy was still on her
knees, still staring at him, and O'Neil had got out of the chair and
was standing nearby, his eyes alight[7] with sick excitement. Smiling
coldly, Ellman edged the knife towards the top of Lucy's nightgown.
25 Lucy made a sudden lunge[8] for the knife, but Ellman was ready,
whipping[9] his knife hand away from her and slapping her across the
face with his other hand, all in one rapid movement. As Lucy cried
out and fell back to her knees, I yelled across at her.

---

1 overcharged: receiving too much electrical power   **2** plate sth. (v): cover sth.
with a thin layer of another metal   **3** adhere: (here) stick   **4** hazard: danger; risk
5 sever sth. ['sevə]: cut sth.   **6** tuck sth. into sth.: place sth. firmly into sth.
7 alight: lit up   **8** make a lunge for sth. [lʌndʒ]: jump suddenly to grab sth.
9 whip sth. away: move sth. quickly away

'*Lucy!* Don't look at me … don't *look*. Don't do *any*thing, OK? *Don't*
fight him. Don't move. Just wait … trust me. Please, just trust –'

Hashim clubbed[1] the butt[2] of the pistol into my head, shutting
me up. The impact dazed me for a moment, but I didn't seem to
feel any pain, and when I looked over at Lucy again, I saw that she   5
wasn't moving. She was just kneeling there, not looking at anything,
as Ellman moved the knife towards her again.

I closed my eyes.

We were reaching out now – iBoy and me – we were reaching
out into cyberspace, reaching out along the myriad[3] pathways, from   10
base station to base station … from cell to cell … from mobile to
mobile to mobile … all around the world … we were connecting …
connecting to a thousand phones, a million phones, a billion phones
… and somehow we were accessing them all, connecting to them
all, instructing them all to ring the six numbers in this warehouse.   15

I opened my eyes.

Half a second had passed. Ellman's knife had pierced[4] Lucy's
nightgown, and now he was slowly pulling the knife upwards, slic-
ing[5] through the thin white cloth … and Lucy was staying perfectly
still.   20

I quickly closed my eyes again and went back inside myself, trying to ignore the pounding beat of my heart. We had all the phone
calls ready now – a million … a billion incoming calls – and we were
holding them all back, keeping them waiting in their hordes[6], and at
the same time we were focusing our electric power, concentrating   25
it, directing it, sending it through the radio waves inside the warehouse into the batteries of the six mobile phones. We were charging
them, overcharging them, overloading them with every ounce[7] of
power we had …

And when I opened my eyes again, I knew straight away that   30
something was happening. In the yellowed light of the lantern, I

---

1 club sth.: hit sth.   **2** butt: handle of a gun   **3** myriad: countless; many
4 pierce sth.: make a hole in sth.   **5** slice through sth.: cut easily through sth.
6 in hordes: *in Scharen*   **7** ounce: Unze (= 28,3 Gramm)

could see that Ellman had sliced open the front of Lucy's nightgown, and O'Neil was looking on with eager eyes, and now Ellman was holding the knife to Lucy's neck, guiding her head towards him ... and then, suddenly, he froze. And behind him, I saw O'Neil looking
5 puzzled for a moment, and then he glanced down at his pocket, and he put his hand on the outside of his pocket, and quickly jerked it away.

His phone was getting hot.

And so were the phones of all the others. They were all looking
10 slightly agitated, frowning at the sudden heat in their pockets ... and now, I knew, I had to close my eyes for the last time and finish it. I had to close my eyes and rejoin iBoy, and together we had to give all the phones a final huge surge of power, and at the same time release all the waiting calls ... and then all we could do was hope.

15 Hope that the phones exploded.

And that when Hashim's went off, the explosion didn't take us with it.

We paused for a moment, making one more final adjustment, and then we opened our eyes and let it all go.

20 The four explosions went off almost simultaneously – *BAM!BAM!-BAM!BAM!* – and an instant later, I felt something slamming into me. I thought for a moment that I *had* been hit by Hashim's explosion, but there was very little pain, and when I heard a groan[1] of agony[2] and I looked down at my feet and saw Hashim lying on the
25 ground, with the back of his trousers blown away and half of his backside missing, I realized that the blast had simply blown him off his feet and he'd smashed into me on the way down.

He was a mess. There was blood everywhere. Bits of blackened flesh were scattered on the ground, and I could see the tip of a bro-
30 ken bone showing through the scorched[3] and bloody crater[4] in his backside.

---

1 groan (n): (here) long deep sound of pain   **2** agony: extreme pain
3 scorched: burnt   **4** crater: *Krater; Höhle*

But I didn't have time to dwell[1] on it.

I quickly looked up and scanned the warehouse, making sure that Tweet and Gunner and Marek were out of action, and once I'd seen that they were all either seriously wounded or – in Gunner's case – possibly dead, I turned my attention to Ellman, O'Neil, and 5 Lucy.

Lucy was still on her knees, gazing around at the carnage[2] with a look of utter disbelief on her face, and Ellman and O'Neil were just standing there, either side of Lucy, both of them too shocked to move. But I knew that their shock wouldn't last for ever, especially 10 Ellman's, so I had to act quickly.

'*Lucy!*' I called out sharply. '*LUCE!*'

As she snapped out of her daze and looked over at me, I saw Ellman's eyes turn towards me too.

'*Move,* Lucy!' I yelled. 'Get *away* from him! *NOW!*' Ellman rap- 15 idly came to his senses and turned back to Lucy, trying to grab her before she moved, but he wasn't quick enough. Lucy hadn't even bothered to get up off her knees, she'd just thrown herself to one side and rolled across the ground, and now she was scrambling to her feet and stumbling across the warehouse towards me. 20

'Get her!' Ellman barked at O'Neil.

O'Neil hesitated for a moment, and then he set off after her. And I suppose that was the moment when I could have called out to them, when I could have warned them off. I could have told O'Neil to stop running and stay where he was, and then I could have 25 reminded them both of what I'd just done to the others, and asked them to think about why I'd not done it to them ... and eventually they would have realized that the only reason I hadn't made their phones explode was that they'd been too close to Lucy at the time ...

That's what I *could* have done. 30

But I didn't.

---

1 dwell on sth.: think about sth. for a long time   **2** carnage [ˈkɑːnɪdʒ]: bloodshed; massacre

I just closed my eyes for an instant, doing what I had to do, and then I opened my eyes again and watched as the front of O'Neil's track pants exploded – *BAM!* – and his legs kind of twisted and buckled[1] as he ran, collapsing beneath him in a burst of blood, and
5 he hit the ground hard, screaming and moaning and clutching at his groin just as Lucy stumbled to the ground at my feet – out of breath, sobbing hard, her knees all cut up and bloody. We looked at each other for a moment, smiling through our pain, and then I raised my eyes and stared over at Ellman. He hadn't moved. He was just stand-
10 ing there, gazing curiously at O'Neil ... and I think he knew then that it was all over, that his time had come.

And he was right.

I waited for him to look at me, and when he did – slowly fixing me with those empty blue eyes – I met his gaze for a second or two
15 ...

And then I watched, with no emotion at all, as his chest exploded.

---

1 buckle: (here) start to collapse

11001

... my mind is all in bits.

Goethe[1]

Fragments again.
Snapshots.
Disconnected moments.

... Lucy getting to her feet – her knees all scratched and bloodied, [5]
her face cut and bruised, her nightgown cut open ... both of us sobbing our eyes out ...

... Lucy's fumbling[2] hands, and her desperate silence, as she tries to untie me from the girder – pulling and twisting and tearing at the wire, cursing every now and then as the metal slices into her fingers [10]
...

Shit.
Fuck it.
Bastard bloody thing ...

... Lucy and me, standing there in the pale yellow light, holding each [15]
other, hanging on to each other ... our bodies shaking, our tears pouring out, neither of us able or willing to talk ...

... and the carnage all around us. Bodies, blood, bits of flesh ... we can't think about it, can't look at it, can't care about it. Dead or alive, we can't afford to care about them. [20]
We just have to go.
Get out of there.
Leave them.

1 Goethe: Johann Wolfgang von Goethe (1749–1832) German poet. The quote is from Faust I. , Gretchen singing *"... mein armer Sinn ist mir zerstückt."* **2** fumble: use your hands awkwardly

Go ...

... walking home in the early hours of the morning, both of us shivering with cold and shock, Lucy wearing my jacket over her mutilated[1] nightgown ... hobbling[2] awkwardly in my socks and trainers ...

5 Are you OK?

Yeah ... no.

Holding hands, holding each other, helping each other.

All right?

Yeah ...

10 We can't talk about it – what happened, what's *going* to happen, what I've done, what it means – it's all too much for now. Too complex, too confusing ... too many unanswerable questions.

We can't do it.

Not now ...

15 ... Crow Lane, Compton House, flashing blue lights in the darkness ... the police are all over the place. I barely have time to say goodbye to Lucy before we're both taken away for questioning.

---

1 mutilate sth.: (here) destroy sth.   **2** hobble: walk with difficulty

11010

To love is not to look at one another: it is to look, together, in the same direction.

Antoine de Saint-Exupéry[1]
Terre des Hommes *(1939)*

Questions. That's pretty much all there was over the next two days: questions from the police, questions from doctors, questions from Gram ... what happened? how did it happen? who? why? where? when?

What could I say?

I don't know ...

Can't remember ...

I'm not sure ...

It was never-ending. Question after question, hour after hour, day after day ... and it wasn't until the Thursday evening that I finally managed to get a bit of time on my own. I knew that I wouldn't have long – Gram had just nipped out to the shops, and the police were coming back later to talk to me again – so I didn't waste any time, I just grabbed my jacket, left the flat, and headed up to the roof.

And now, here I was again – sitting alone on the edge of the world, watching the sun go down. It was another mild night, the air clear and still, and the sky was layered[2] with an evening redness that glowed with the promise of long hot summer days to come. But as I sat there on the roof, gazing out at the horizon, I couldn't imagine *any* days to come. Tomorrow, next Wednesday, next month, next year ... there was nothing there for me, nothing at all. There was nothing beyond the horizon.

Not for me.

My mind was still all in bits.

I closed my eyes and looked inside myself.

---

1 Antoine de Saint-Exupéry: (1900–1944) French writer and pilot   **2** layer sth.: (here) cover sth.

I could see a past, the last few days, yesterday ... I could see Gram
sitting next to me on the settee in the front room, her greying hair
shaved to her scalp around the stitched-up wound on her head, and
I could hear myself telling her most of what Ellman had said about
my mother, her daughter, and I could see the tears in Gram's eyes
when I asked her if any of it was true.

'Georgie wasn't a bad girl,' she'd told me, smiling sadly. 'But she
was always a bit wild, a bit rebellious ... not that I minded that, of
course ... but when she was about seventeen she started taking
things a bit too far, you know ... mixing with the wrong kind of people, getting into drugs ...' Gram shook her head at the memory. 'She
lost her way, Tommy. And you know what it's like when you lose
your way around here ...'

'Did she know Ellman?'

Gram nodded. 'He was the *man,* you know ... everyone wanted
to know Howard Ellman. He had the drugs, the money, the cars, the
girls ...' She sighed. 'Georgie thought he was *exciting.* I tried telling
her what he was really like, but she just wouldn't listen ...'

'Was she ...?' I asked hesitantly. 'I mean, were they ...?'

'Sleeping together?' She nodded again. 'Georgie was out of her
head most of the time – she didn't know what she was doing ...'

'Ellman called her a whore,' I said quietly.

Gram looked at me, her eyes moist with tears. 'Your mum made
a lot of mistakes, Tommy. Like I said, she lost her way ... but in the
end she found herself again. When she found out that she was pregnant, she pulled herself together, got off the drugs, got away from
Ellman ... and that took a hell of a lot of guts[1], a lot of courage.' Gram
paused, putting her hand on my shoulder. 'She was your mother,
Tommy. If she was still alive now, she'd love you as much as I do, and
you'd love her.'

I could see us holding each other then, both of us crying our eyes
out, and I could hear Gram saying sorry to me, over and over again,
for not telling me the truth about Mum before, and I could hear her

1 take a lot of guts (infml.): be hard to achieve

trying to explain that she hadn't kept the truth from me because she was *ashamed* of Mum or anything, but simply because she couldn't see what good it would have done for me to know all the ugly details of her life.

And I understood that.   5

Because, in exactly the same way, I couldn't see what good it would do for Gram to know all the ugly details of what Ellman had said about Mum. She didn't need to know that Ellman might have killed her, or that he might ... just might ... be my father ...

She didn't need that pain.   10

So I kept it to myself.

Inside myself ...

I could see the present too. I could see two dead bodies lying in the mortuary: Gunner, with half of his chest blown away, and Eugene O'Neil. The blast from O'Neil's phone had severed his femoral artery[1]   15 and he'd bled to death on the warehouse floor.

I could see Hashim and Marek still in their hospital beds, both of them seriously injured and scarred for life, but at least they were probably both going to have a life.

Tweet's injuries were so severe that it would be a miracle if he   20 survived.

And Howard Ellman ...?

I couldn't see him.

After undergoing emergency surgery to his chest, heart, and lungs, Ellman had been moved to the intensive care department of   25 a private hospital in West London. That same night, although still in an 'extremely critical' condition, and despite the police guard outside his door, he'd somehow managed to escape from the hospital and disappear without trace. The police had no idea how he'd got away, or where he was, and neither did I. But the prevailing medical   30

---

1 femoral artery: *Oberschenkelarterie*

opinion was that without expert care – and probably even *with* it –
he'd be dead within the next twenty-four hours.

I opened my eyes for a moment, remembering my complete lack
of feeling as I'd watched Ellman's chest explode ... and I wondered
now if I still felt (or *didn't* feel) the same. About Ellman, O'Neil, the
others ... dead or alive ...

Did I care about them?

Did I feel any remorse, any guilt, any shame?

The answer, whether I liked it or not, was no.

And I *didn't* like it.

I didn't like what it made me.

I closed my eyes again, looking for the presence of Lucy ... and
I knew she'd be there. I could always see Lucy in my mind – her
sunset eyes, her lips, her smile, her drowning tears[1] – but my mind
wasn't reality. My mind wasn't the truth. And the truth was that I
just couldn't see how I could ever be with Lucy again. Why on earth
would she ever want to be with me? I'd almost got her raped and
killed. I'd put her through the very same hell that she'd already been
through once. I'd failed to protect her. I'd lied to her, tricked her,
betrayed her ... and all for what? For revenge? To make me feel better? To make me feel like a *hero?*

Shit ...

I wasn't a hero.

I was never a hero. I was nothing.

No good to anyone. I was a freak.

A mutant.

A murderer.

I was losing my mind ...

And, even worse, my heart had grown cold.

I'd lost myself.

No matter what I did, I could never be Tom Harvey again. Even
if I told everyone everything – Gram, the police, Mr Kirby – I could
never rid myself of iBoy. He was with me for ever now. He was me,

1 drowning tears: (here) overflowing mass of tears

and I was him. And eventually – *inevitably* – the rest of the world would find out about us … and when that happened, our life really would become a freak show.

And I wasn't sure I could live with that.

And despite everything that my rational mind kept telling me, ₅ I just couldn't stop thinking about the unthinkable possibility – no matter how unlikely it was – that Ellman *hadn't* been lying … that he really was my father. And every time I thought about that, I remembered what I'd said to him in the warehouse: *If you were my father, I'd kill myself.* ₁₀

I opened my eyes again and gazed down over the edge of the roof. Thirty floors up … it was a long way down. And as I looked down through the darkness, I began to picture myself down there on the day that it happened, all those weeks ago … walking home from school, feeling pretty much the same as I always felt … kind of OK, ₁₅ but not great … alone, but not lonely … thinking about Lucy, wondering what she wanted to see me about … then hearing a shout from above and looking up and seeing the iPhone hurtling down through the bright blue sky towards me …

And now, as I gazed down from the roof, remembering the past, ₂₀ something strange happened. My perspective suddenly changed, and instead of picturing myself as me, looking up at the iPhone, I was picturing myself as the iPhone, tumbling down through the sky towards the other me, the me that was down there … only the sky wasn't blue now, it was black. It was night-time. And it wasn't all ₂₅ those weeks ago … it was now.

Right now.

And I was falling … down, down, down … down through the silent darkness … hurtling down into oblivion[1] …

And I could see something on the ground down below. A light. ₃₀ There was a light down there.

---

1 oblivion [əˈblɪvɪən]: nothingness

Just outside the entrance to the tower, thirty floors below, some-one was riding a bike across the square. And as I leaned further for-ward and peered over the edge of the roof, I could see the front light of the bike moving slowly over the ground, directly beneath me …
5 and then, all at once, I was seeing myself falling again, only this time I wasn't the iPhone, I was myself … I was Tom Harvey, I was iBoy … I was both of us … and we were falling from the roof, dropping like a stone … down, down, down … heading straight for the light of the unknown cyclist … and we knew that we were going to land on him,
10 or her … we were going to land head first on them, and our iSkull was going to crack open their skull, and their brain was going to be lacerated by broken iSkull fragments and pieces of us …

And as I leaned even further forward, almost toppling off the edge now, I heard myself laughing. At least, I assumed it was me,
15 because I was the only one there … and it sounded vaguely like me … and I could feel my throat moving, my vocal cords vibrating …

Yes, it was definitely me. I was laughing …

I didn't know why.

And, for some reason, that made me feel incredibly sad, and all at
20 once I wasn't laughing any more, I was crying … sobbing uncontrol-lably … the tears streaming out of me like the tears of a frightened child.

I didn't want to die …

But I didn't want to live …
25 I just didn't *know* …

'Tom …?'

The voice came from behind me.

I waited a moment, trying to steady myself, wiping the tears from my eyes, and then I slowly turned round and looked up … and
30 there she was, gazing down at me with a worried frown.

'Hey, Luce,' I said.

'Are you all right?' she asked softly. 'You don't look so great.'

I sniffed, wiped my eyes again, and smiled at her. 'I'm fine … I was just, you know … just thinking about stuff …'

'Yeah, I know,' she said, sitting down next to me. 'It's all been a bit much, hasn't it?'

'Yeah, you could say that.'

'I just did.'

I looked at her.   5

She smiled at me. 'You've got snot all over your face ... come here.' She pulled a tissue from her pocket, licked it, and started cleaning all the snot and tears from my face. I winced a little as she wiped around the knife cut on my forehead. 'Sorry,' she said, shaking her head. 'God, you're a mess.'   10

'You don't look too great yourself,' I said, glancing at the cuts and bruises on her face.

'Thanks a lot.'

'You're welcome.'

'There,' she said, giving my face a final wipe, 'that's better.'   15

'Thanks.'

She nodded, putting the tissue away, and for a few seconds she was quiet. Then, without looking at me, and with her voice perfectly calm, she said, 'You weren't thinking of jumping off the roof, were you?'   20

'What?'

'Because if you were ...' She looked at me, her eyes suddenly bright with anger. 'Listen to me, Tom Harvey. I know you've been through a lot recently ... I mean, we both have. And I know you're probably feeling really confused right now about all this iBoy stuff,   25 all the shit you've got in your head and all the shit you've had to deal with ...' She paused then, moving her face to within an inch of mine, and her voice became slow and deliberate. 'But if I *ever* catch you even *thinking* about killing yourself ... well, believe me, I'll make sure it's the last thing you ever do.'   30

We stared at each other for a while then, and as Lucy's eyes drilled[1] into mine with an intensity that was almost physically pain-

---

1 drill into sth.: (here) look very intensely at sth.

ful, I honestly didn't know if I had intended to jump or not. I didn't know if I could have jumped or not.

I just didn't know ...

All I knew – and all that mattered – was that I hadn't jumped,
5 and that Lucy was here, sitting beside me.

I looked at her, smiling. 'The last thing I ever do?'

She shook her head. 'It's not a joke, Tom ... I'm serious.'

'I know ... but you're kind of implying that if you ever catch me thinking of killing myself, you'll kill me, which sort of defeats the
10 object[1], doesn't it?'

She couldn't help grinning. 'Yeah, all right, Mr Super Brain ... so I got my words mixed up a bit –'

'A *bit?*'

She looked at me, still smiling, but there was genuine concern
15 behind her smile ... and that really meant a lot to me. In fact, it meant everything.

'I'm sorry, Luce,' I said quietly, looking back at her.

'It's all right, I'm always getting my words mixed up –'

'No ... I mean about everything.' There were tears in my eyes
20 again now. 'I'm just so, *so* sorry ...'

'Shhh ...' she said gently, putting a fingertip to my lips. 'You don't have to be sorry ... you don't have to be anything. Just be with me, OK?' She took her finger away, leaned in close, and kissed me. 'All right?' she whispered. 'Just be with me.'

25 I nodded, still crying.

Lucy smiled. 'Let's get comfortable.'

As she slowly leaned back and lay down on the roof, looking straight up at the sky, I didn't move for a moment. I just sat there, staring out at the dying horizon, wondering if perhaps there was
30 something out there for me after all, a future beyond the horizon ...

And then Lucy tapped my backside with her foot and said, 'Hey, Super Brain, it's getting lonely down here.'

---

1 defeat the object: do something that has the opposite effect of what you wanted

And I leaned back and lay down beside her, and she took my hand in hers, and we just lay there together in a dream of silence, gazing up at the stars.

ADDITIONAL TEXTS

Pigeon English

Pigeon English *by Steven Kelman, tells the story of eleven-year-old
Ghanaian immigrant Harrison Opoku, who has just arrived in a tough
London estate with his mother and sister. His first-person narrative high-
lights the problems of urban gangs, immigration and poverty. The novel
was partially inspired by the murder of ten-year-old Damilola Taylor in* 5
Peckham, London in 2000.

Jordan showed me his knife. I didn't even see where it came from. I
never suspected it in a million years. It has a green handle[1] the same
as the knives from Mamma's block[2]. It's like her tomatoes knife. It
even looks too deadly for tomatoes.   10
   Jordan: 'This is my war knife. No one f—s[3] with me, man. I'm telling you, when the war starts I'm gonna be ready for them.'
   He was looking at the knife proper[4] hard like it was his favourite
thing. His eyes were all big. He showed me how to carry it so nobody
can see. You just put it down your leg. You have to hold the handle   15
or it will just fall through your trousers onto the floor. It works best
if your trousers are elastic at the top. Otherwise you can just use
your pocket.
   Jordan: 'It's well[5] sharp, look.'
   He scratched the knife on the wall. He wrote cock[6] with it like it 20
was a pen, you could see the letters loud and clear.
   Jordan: 'You should get one, you need it. I'll get one for you, my
mum's got loads.'
   Me: 'No thanks. I don't really need one.'
   Jordan: 'Course you do, everyone needs one. Try and get one the   25
same as mine, then we can be war brothers, innit. What's the matter, don't you wanna be brothers?'

---

1 handle: part of the knife that you hold   **2** block: (here) piece of wood or plastic
in which you keep kitchen knives   **3** fuck with sb.: (here) annoy sb.   **4** proper
(sl): very   **5** well (sl): very   **6** cock (sl): penis

He held the knife near my face. He twisted the blade around in the air like he was trying to open a lock with it. I felt like the lock. Everything went slow until he put the knife down again.

Jordan: 'Rarse[1], you should've seen your face, man! You were shit-
5   ting yourself!'

Me: 'No I wasn't! You're not even funny!'

Everybody says there's a war but I haven't seen it yet. There's a hell of wars going on all the time:

Wars
10 Kids vs Teachers
Northwell Manor High vs Leabridge High
Dell Farm Crew vs Lewsey Hill Crew
Emos[2] vs Sunshine
Turkey vs Russia
15 Arsenal vs Chelsea
Black vs White
Police vs Kids
God vs Allah
Chicken Joe's vs KFC[3]
20 Cats vs Dogs
Aliens vs Predators

I haven't seen any of them. You'd know if there was a war because all the windows would be broken and the helicopters would have guns on them. The helicopters don't even have guns, just torchlights[4]. I
25 don't even think there's a war. I haven't seen it.

© *Stephen Kelman, 2011,*
printed with permission of Bloomsbury Publishing, London

---

1 rarse (sl): wow   **2** emo (sl): person who is very emotional, wears dark clothes and listens to sad music   **3** KFC: Kentucky Fried Chicken   **4** torchlight: *Taschenlampe*

Don't demonise gangsters – they're human too

In the summer of 2011, a protest in Tottenham following the death of
Mark Duggan (a man who was shot dead by police) began a series of
riots that went on for three days. In cities all over the UK, buildings
were destroyed, shops were looted and five people died. The riots mainly
involved young people in urban areas (particularly in poorer parts of 5
London). Ever since, these youths have been the topic of debate over
the increasing gap between society and so-called "gangster" culture.

The fallout from the Mark Duggan inquest[1] once again raised the
issue of gangs. Many people ask: why would anyone want to get
involved in an activity that may lead to prison, or the graveyard? 10
Surprisingly, that's a question gang members often ask themselves.

Over the years I've spent a lot of time in young offender insti-
tutions and prisons facilitating[2] a programme that helps offenders
improve their writing and focuses on their long-term futures. Typi-
cal things I've been told include, "I carry a knife because everyone 15
else carries a knife" or "That's how it is on the streets." These atti-
tudes are easy to condemn – until you remember how difficult it
is for anyone to opt out[3] of the social environment in which they
live. Not many of us are brave enough to face being sneered at or
cold-shouldered[4] by our peers for standing out against the crowd. 20
For boys trying to become men in poor areas, that challenge is even
harder.

And when it comes to finding responses on this issue, demonis-
ing individuals and communities isn't the answer. I wasn't happy to
be pulled over for a stop and search[5] while going to participate in 25
a programme for the BBC. Nor was I completely convinced when it
was explained that I might be a gang-banger's girlfriend, carrying his

---

1 inquest: official investigation to find out why a person died   **2** facilitate sth.:
(here) manage sth.   **3** opt out of sth.: say you don't want to do sth.   **4** cold-
shoulder sb.: ignore sb.   **5** stop and search: action taken by the police on the
street to stop people they believe are criminals and check they aren't carrying
weapons, drugs or other illegal things

weapons. I'm in my 40s. A suit-wearing, middle-management relative of mine, who's never been in trouble with the law, was even less impressed when he reported a crime recently and ended up being arrested for it. And remember, we both come from that notorious
5 "hard-working families" demographic.

Meanwhile, it seems some sections of the media are just as much into postcode wars[1] as any gang. Mark Duggan came from Tottenham? That's all they need to know. They scoffed at the notion he might have been a much-loved family man. Dehumanising people,
10 while at the same time asking them to show common humanity, isn't going to work.

We need to think carefully about how we relate to young people from these backgrounds. I've seen plenty of evidence that Malcolm Muggeridge was right when he said that prisons have produced
15 more great art than any Arts Council or Ministry of Culture. One young man I met, who began by saying he "didn't write", ended up winning awards for his poetry. He may have been unusual, but I've seen many others discover skills and talents they didn't know they had.

20 But why did they have to go to prison to find these gifts? And why doesn't a rich society like ours seem to have any use for them? When one youngster couldn't read out the work he'd written about his life because he was in tears and had to ask another to read it for him, you realise that making assumptions and bandying[2] around
25 cliches about "evil" is a waste of time. "Evil" has a context like everything else.

No one likes crime, especially its victims; it messes everything up. No one likes hearing what they think are excuses being made for it either. But the truth is that all crime has a backdrop[3]. And in
30 the case of gangs, part of that backdrop is poor communities that

---

1 postcode war: fight between gangs from different areas with different postcodes *(Postleitzahl)*   **2** bandy sth. around: (here) say sth. without thinking   **3** backdrop: (here) context

have been on a downward curve[1] for decades and are now being expected to pick up the tab[2] for the mistakes of the rich. It's perfectly legitimate to demand that individuals from estates take responsibility for what they do. But there are others in our society who should also accept some responsibility. And they're far more powerful than ⁵ any "gangsta[3]".

by Dreda Say Mitchell

http://www.theguardian.com/commentisfree/2014/jan/13/
dont-demonise-gangsters-theyre-human-too

---

1 downward curve: (here) process of getting worse   **2** pick up the tab for sth.:
take responsibility for sth.   **3** gangsta (sl): gangster

Acknowledgements

The editor and publishers gratefully acknowledge permission to repro-
duce copyright material in this book. Every effort has been made to
trace and contact copyright holders, but in a few cases this has proved
impossible. The editor and publishers apologize for these unwilling cases
of copyright transgression and would like to hear from any copyright
holders not acknowledged.

Guardian online article by Rose George, copyright © Rose George, 2004, reprinted by
permission of the author; excerpt by Arthur Koestley from The Ghost in the Machine
(copyright © Arthur Koestler, 1975) is reproduced by permission of PFD (www.
pfd.co.uk) on behalf of The Estate of Arthur Koestler; 'Broken' Words & Music by
Randy James Bradbury, Fletcher Dragge, Jim Lindberg & Byron McMackin, copyright
© Songs Of Universal, Inc. on behalf of Westbeach Music (75%). All Rights Reserved.
International Copyright Secured. Used by permission of Music Sales Limited; Supersizing the Mind, copyright © Andy Clark, reprinted by permission of OUP; 'Electricity
is Human Thinking', copyright © H. Bernard Wechsler, reprinted by permission of the
author; One Blood by John Heale, copyright © John Heale, reprinted by permission
of Simon & Schuster; algorithm definition quoted from article entitled ALGORITHM,
http://en.wikipedia.org/wiki/Algorithm, made available for use under the terms of
http://creative-commons.org/licenses/by-sa/3.0/; Taser definition quoted from
article entitled TASER, http://en.wikipedia.org/wiki/Taser, made available for use
under the terms of http://creative-commons.org/licenses/by-sa/3.0/; the extract
from 'since feeling is first' is reprinted from COMPLETE POEMS 1904–1962, by
E. E. Cummings, edited by George J. Firmage, by permission of W.W. Norton &
Company. Copyright © 1991 by the trustees for the E. E. Cummings Trust and George
James Firmage; The Gang by Frederic Thrasher, copyright © Frederic Thrasher 1927,
reprinted by permission of Chicago University Press; The River of Eden copyright
© 1996 Richard Dawkins. Reprinted by permission of Basic Books, a member of the
Perseus Books Group; Terre des Hommes by Antoine de Saint-Exupery, copyright
© Antoine de Saint-Exupéry 1939, reprinted by permission of Penguin Books.

The Author

Best known for his novels *Lucas* (winner of the North East Book Award 2004), *Martyn Pig* (winner of the Branford Boase Award 2003) and *iBoy* (winner of the Angus Award 2012), Kevin Brooks grew up in Exeter, England and studied Psychology and Philosophy at Birmingham, Aston University in 1980 and Cultural Studies in London in 1983. He has had a variety of jobs including: musician, gasoline station attendant, crematorium handyman, civil service clerk, hot dog vendor at the London Zoo, post office clerk, and railway ticket office clerk.

© culture-images/Lebrecht